This book looks at the processes and spread of social innovation: the mechanisms of this innovation are rooted in the conflict that minorities are capable of creating in others and introducing into the social system. These innovations give rise to rejection, discrimination and denial of the minority group. However, minority ideas take root and gradually new norms replace the old ones. Despite the denial, therefore, the marginal standpoint of minority groups can have an impact on the belief systems and behaviour patterns of other individuals. This book proposes a psychosociological explanation of these individual and collective phenomena by articulating the underlying identification games and cognitive activities. It throws a new light not only on minority influence, but also on the major themes of social psychology, especially theories of intergroup conflict, persuasion and attitude change. Based upon a series of experiments which have been developed and refined for this English edition, this is a rigorous and original contribution to the study of minority influence on social processes.

European Monographs in Social Psychology

The social psychology of minority influence

European Monographs in Social Psychology

Executive Editors:
J. RICHARD EISER and KLAUS R. SCHERER
Sponsored by the European Association of Experimental Social Psychology

This series, first published by Academic Press (who will continue to distribute the numbered volumes), appeared under the joint imprint of Cambridge University Press and the Maison des Sciences de l'Homme in 1985 as an amalgamation of the Academic Press series and the European Studies in Social Psychology, published by Cambridge and the Maison in collaboration with the Laboratoire Européen de Psychologie Sociale of the Maison.
The original aims of the two series still very much apply today: to provide a forum for the best European research in different fields of social psychology and to foster the interchange of ideas between different developments and different traditions. The executive Editors also expect that it will have an important role to play as a European forum for international work.

The social psychology of minority influence

Gabriel Mugny
Professor of Social Psychology, University of Geneva

and

Juan A. Pérez
Professor of Social Psychology, University of Valencia

Translated by Vivian Waltz Lamongie

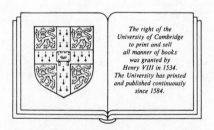

*The right of the
University of Cambridge
to print and sell
all manner of books
was granted by
Henry VIII in 1534.
The University has printed
and published continuously
since 1584.*

Cambridge University Press
*Cambridge   New York   Port Chester   Melbourne
Sydney*

Editions de la Maison des Sciences de l'Homme
Paris

Published by the Press Syndicate of the University of Cambridge
The Pitt Building, Trumpington Street, Cambridge CB2 1RP
40 West 20th Street, New York, NY 10011–4211, USA
10 Stamford Road, Oakleigh, Melbourne 3166, Australia
and Editions de la Maison des Sciences de l'Homme
54 Boulevard Raspail, 75270 Paris Cedex 06

Originally published in French as *Le Déni et la raison*
by Editions Delval 1987
and © Editions Delval 1987
First published in English by Editions de la Maison des Sciences de l'Homme and
Cambridge University Press 1991 as *The social psychology of minority influence*
English translation © Maison des Sciences de l'Homme and Cambridge University
Press 1991

Printed in Great Britain at the University Press, Cambridge

British Library cataloguing in publication data
Mugny, Gabriel
The social psychology of minority influence. – (European monographs in social
psychology).
1. Social minorities. Influence
I. Title II. Pérez, Juan A. III. Series 305

Library of Congress cataloguing in publication data
Mugny, Gabriel.
[Le déni et la raison. English]
The social psychology of minority influence / Gabriel Mugny and
Juan A. Pérez: translated by Vivian Waltz Lamongie.
      p.   cm.   – (European monographs in social psychology)
Translation of: Le déni et la raison.
Includes bibliographical references.
ISBN 0 521 39054 0 (hardback)
1. Social integration.   2. Minorities.   3. Influence (Psychology)
4. Group identity.   5. Social conflict.   I. Pérez, Juan Antonio.
II. Title.   III. Series.
[DNLM: 1. Ethnopsychology.   2. Minority Groups – psychology.
3. Psychology, Social.   HM 251 M951d]
HM291.M772513   1991
303.3′2–dc20   90–2658

ISBN 0 521 39054 0 hardback
ISBN 2 7351 0395 1 hardback (France only)

Contents

x   *Contents*

Figures

Tables

Acknowledgements

Like most scientific works, this book is not the sole product of the one, or in this case, two authors to whom it is credited. It was made possible through several exchange networks all contributing to its creation. The first is the social psychology research team of the University of Geneva, and in particular, Willem Doise, who introduced us to the study of intergroup relations and with whom we developed our constructivist approach to social psychology; Stamos Papastamou, collaborator in our first book on the issue, *The power of minorities*; and Clause Kaiser and Patricia Roux, with whom so many of our studies were conducted. A second network, this time international and connected to the first, was instrumental in enabling the experiments reported in this book. Serge Moscovici played a central role here, providing initial inspiration and constant suggestions. These networks were supported from outside the University of Geneva, where we found the means to develop our research and confront our ideas with others, particularly through two conferences on minority influence, one held in Barcelona in 1980, the other in Geneva in 1985, with the assistance of the Laboratoire Européen de Psychologie Sociale and the European Association of Experimental Social Psychology. Our experimental research, so fundamental to this approach, was greatly facilitated by several research grants from the Fonds National Suisse de la Recherche Scientifique.

1 Explaining change

1.1 The illusion of immobility and the reality of change

Influence phenomena refer to the processes through which individuals and groups form, maintain, spread, and modify their thought and action modes during direct or symbolic social interaction. The question of how to approach these processes is a fundamental one, not only for researchers in the fields of psychology, sociology, anthropology, or like ours, social psychology, but also for groups and societies themselves. These processes form the very basis of how society functions and evolves, for as Touraine (1973, 10) writes, 'Human society is the only natural system known to have the ability to form and transform its functioning on the basis of its investments and of the image it has of its own ability to act upon itself' (our translation). Two conflicting tendencies exist in this respect, both from a scientific point of view and the broader social perspective.

One approach has focused on the reproduction and maintenance of social relations, the status quo. This perspective is a 'conservative' one from the sociopolitical standpoint and a 'functionalist' one from the scientific standpoint. Moscovici (1976) was one of the first to uncover the implicit postulates wherein social systems are conceived as optimal, functional, even ideal, or nearly so. The advocates of this approach essentially look at the adaptation processes through which social systems become long lasting and protect themselves against change, regarded as a social evil. What is implicit here is the idea that there is only one correct, ahistorical, and somehow predetermined view of the world and its values. In short, the functionalist view is based on the illusion that norms and ideas are immobile, using Balandier's (1985) term. Whenever the value a norm takes on is defined in this manner, i.e. in absolute rather than relative terms, the issue becomes searching for the conditions and mechanisms, the (nearly 'natural') laws through which individuals and groups internalize or adapt to that norm, or in the worst of cases, deviate from it. For the most part these studies have dealt with the mechanisms of conformity and obedience, in short, of social control (the adaptation pole) and self-control (the internalization pole). These mechanisms are the constituents of majorities and dominant

1

positions, which are both the cause and the effect of social influence, considered to be responsible for maintaining uniformity and consensus by reducing interindividual differences.

Others, including ourselves, are fascinated instead by the question of social change and innovation. Ours is an 'interactionist' perspective from the scientific standpoint, and a 'progressive' perspective from the social standpoint. In the social psychology of influence in particular, researchers working in this perspective in the past twenty or so years have concentrated their efforts on compensating for the emphasis that has been, and still is being, placed on the dynamics of social control. Given that norms are considered here to be relative, i.e. to be the outcome of compromise or submission, emphasis is placed on the mechanisms underlying these transformations, in this case, the processes of innovation and the spread of innovation, viewed as fundamental to social and historical evolution. At the root of such change, we find individuals and groups that are not so inclined to conform to the status quo or to abide by 'universal norms': they constitute the minorities.

From both the scientific and social points of view, then, fundamental tensions exist, as demonstrated in a recent book on perspectives in the study of minority influence (cf. Moscovici, Mugny, and Van Avermaet, 1985). At either end of a sort of continuum, we find two opposing tendencies, one of uniformity, conformity, resistance to change, and the other of differentiation, refusal to become resigned, innovation. On the one side, it is immobility that is desired and sought, and on the other, it is change. For those at the one end, norms are to be abided by, and for those at the other, a good norm is transgressible and transgressed.

The fact that two such types of phenomena are possible, one leading to uniformity and the other, to innovation, forces us to wonder how they actually operate. Here also, research models diverge, some emphasizing the attributes of the dominant entities that exert pressure to maintain uniformity, others stressing the behaviour of the acting minorities.

Researchers focusing on uniformity examine how individuals give up their own view of things in order to go along with the views of the majority, even when they are quite capable of self-affirmation, on the basis either of their own personal characteristics (cf. Crutchfield, 1955) or the characteristics of the situation (cf. Allen, 1965). A good illustration of this is Asch's paradigm (1951) in which 'normal' individuals were shown to conform to the erroneous response of a given majority even though the correct response was perceptually evident and left no room for doubt. Such pressure to maintain uniformity functions through one of the varied forms of *dependence* reflecting the supremacy of a source of influence over a target, in the form of a kind of 'power' (cf. Hollander, 1964). Targets are submissive because they feel unsure of themselves, dependent upon others. Sources are influential because they are dominant, powerful, credible, or attractive (cf. Kelman, 1958).

Researchers focusing on innovation are interested in determining how those individuals or minority groups who firmly uphold their own deviant or marginal standpoint can have an impact on the belief systems and behaviour patterns of other individuals. The mechanisms of innovation are rooted in the *conflict* that minorities are capable of creating in others and introducing into the social system. Here, it is no longer a form of dependence that underlies influence, but rather the minority's style of behaviour, which is instrumental to the instigation and management of conflict. Through their consistent, coherent, and committed action along an ever-so-long journey, minorities manage in the end to make 'something' change, in individuals and in society.

Who in all this is right? This is a philosophical question which we do not pretend to be able to answer. Each of them, in some sense or another, must have some fragment of the truth. We shall not answer this question because in attempting to do so, we would be turning a problem that we claim to be approaching scientifically into a normative question.

The idea we shall attempt to prove is that the illusion of immobility is maintained by the fact that, in all innovation processes, conformity with the dominant norm takes place first, and all the more so when it must be displayed publicly. The reality of change, on the other hand, is underground, and is always nearly invisible because of resistance to that change. This fact, rather than leading us to oppose these two normatively unreconcilable perspectives, will lead us to *theoretically interconnect* what appear to be two divergent, yet complementary, focal points. The need to scientifically explain their apparent contradictions and understand their reciprocity in social systems has made this a necessity.

1.2 Majority effects, minority effects

In experimental social psychology, each of these two perspectives naturally has its own repertoire of phenomena which constitute its chosen objects for experimental demonstration both in the laboratory and in the field. The phenomenon of majority influence, the first to have been studied (cf. Asch, 1951, 1956) is above all the concern of the functionalist approach, while minority influence is the terrain of the interactionist approach (cf. Moscovici, 1976).

Recent studies, designed to determine which influence effects are specific to majorities and which are typical of minorities, have revealed that each functions quite differently (the reader might refer here to the book *The psychology of conversion* edited by Moscovici and Mugny, 1987), so that in the end, both partners in the theoretical quarrel are right to some extent. Whether we are dealing with perceptual material or aesthetic material, with social judgements or direct interaction between individuals, majority influence systematically takes on the form of compliance: individuals *tend* (we stress tend, since this is a general tendency, and other cases do exist) to outwardly accept what the majority advocates whenever that majority is present or psychologically salient. Yet as soon as the majority leaves, or is no longer psychologically salient, its influence disappears. This proves that the influence was only transitory, only serving momentarily to resolve, right there and then, the divergence between oneself and the majority. In the face of a majority, the debated object itself would not be at stake: only the establishment of a 'hedonist' relationship with the majority would count.

Minority influence looks radically different. Indeed, it *tends* to be weak, inexistent, or negative when exerted at the *direct*, manifest, or public level: when people do not refuse resolutely to adopt a minority's idea or action, they at least hesitate to do so, in the eyes of others as well as in their own. A 'positive' relationship with a minority appears to be difficult, if not out of the question. This does not mean, however, that minorities have no effect. It is simply that their *social impact* (understood here to refer to their effectiveness and not to social-impact theory; Latané and Wolf, 1981) tends to express itself in an *indirect*, latent, or delayed manner, in short, in the form of what is conventionally called a *conversion* (Moscovici, 1980). It looks as though when an alternative is introduced by a minority, it is the definition of the debated object that becomes the crux of the issue.

From a methodological point of view, it became necessary to introduce the distinction between influence qualified as direct and that qualified as indirect so that the hidden impact of minorities could be observed. (The lack of this distinction in classical studies on influence and persuasion partially explains the fact that minority influence was not observed.) Minority influence has been assessed in various ways, depending on the experimental paradigm. One way amounts to showing that it appears when responses are given in private, and disappears when they are given in public (the realm of majority influence), which is proof of the magnitude of the social costs incurred by explicitly joining up with a minority source. Another approach is to detect minority influence after a certain lapse of time, once the relationship with the minority source has become less salient and a cognitive activity can take place. Finally, another method consists of demonstrating that a minority source can affect ideas upon which it has not explicitly taken a stand. A prerequisite to such impact is an inferential activity on the part of the targets concerning the content of the ideas set forth by the minority. In Chapter 4 we shall discuss the theoretical implications of these distinctions.

The different methodological devices mentioned above are necessary to providing evidence of the impact of minorities, at first hidden, latent. Minority influence is a slow process composed of several stages (Moscovici, 1985a; Levine and Moreland, 1985). The initial stage, when the minority emerges and reveals its views to the majority, is marked by disapproval and rejection. Other moments nevertheless follow. An incubation period sets in soon, and the new ideas are brought up again, spread, and discussed. The minority message is again outwardly refused, but gradually penetrates into, and orients, the belief and behaviour systems of the targets, whose eventual conversion marks a decisive stage in minority influence.

In all cases, whether in the field (see for example Mucchi Faina, 1987) or laboratory, underground influence appears, in a subreptitious and subliminal manner. It looks as though individuals openly oppose the minority *source*, while accepting its *ideas* underneath. One denies its arguments, all the while granting it some degree of truth (hence the title of a prior French version of this book, *Le déni et la raison*). Despite some diverging interpretations, the above effects seem to be the object of considerable consensus among researchers directly interested in this area of study (cf. Moscovici, Mugny, and Van Avermaet, 1985; Moscovici and Mugny, 1987), now one of the favourite topics in social psychology, at least in Europe (cf. Jaspars, 1986). As attested by the number of pages newly devoted to minority influence in the 'bible' of social psychology (Moscovici, 1985b), these effects are now being taken seriously, notably by researchers working in the area of attitude change and persuasion (to give only a few examples: Brown, 1985; Chaiken and Stangor, 1987; Eagly, 1987; Levine and Russo, 1987; McGuire, 1985; Paulus, 1983; Petty and Cacioppo, 1986; Sorrentino and Hancok, 1987; Wolf, 1987).

Experimental research has shown that majority influence, prototypical of the study of uniformity, functions according to its own specific dynamics, as does minority influence, prototypical of the study of change. In most research, majority influence and minority influence are studied under conditions which are similar, granted, but separate, each being examined in its own right. Just like the conceptual opposition of the general postulates of the functionalist and interactionist models, the privileged objects of each of these models are generally approached experimentally as specific focal points, based on independent conceptualizations. Is this separation legitimate? That is the question. Wouldn't it be better to consider them instead as embedded, as incapable of being captured one without the other, even if during the operationalization process one of the involved causalities is naturally chosen over the other?

This raises the question of the interpretation of the effects specific to majorities and minorities, for methods are nothing more than reflections of the particular theoretical bases chosen. Attempts to explain these phenomena have been largely marked by contemporary cognitivist models of persuasion and social influence (cf. Zanna, Olson, and Herman, 1987). The explanations given (cf. Maass, West, and Cialdini, 1987) account for majority and minority effects through substantial borrowing from attribution theory (cf. Maass and Clark, 1984; Moscovici and Nemeth, 1974), particularly regarding the inferences made as a result of a consistent behaviour style: the systematic consistency of minority responses across situations and time, added to their social rareness, plus the fact that they do not give rise to social consensus and actively resist conformist pressure – all these result in the attribution of highly salient characteristics to the minority. Minorities are thus viewed as particularly distinct, as *a priori* not very credible, and as resistant to social pressure. Their *distinctiveness* may be what leads to conversion (occurring when an individual privately yields to a minority stance) insofar as their low credibility in conjunction with the recognition of their high degree of resistance to social pressure may engage targets in an intense cognitive activity. Such an activity implies that particular attention be paid to the stimuli, and above all, that the cognitive functioning which sets in be more divergent than convergent, generating a greater number of complex and differentiated ideas (cf. Nemeth, 1986) and a non-defensive mode of thought, i.e. one centered on the search for new arguments rather than on the use of counter-arguments (cf. Maass and Clark, 1983).

Note that although this approach is suited to accounting for part of the cognitive activity of target subjects, which analysis of their argumentation and counter-argumentation indeed reflects, it can nevertheless be too highly dependent upon a one-level analysis assessing only the intraindividual level of social influence processes (cf. Mugny and Doise, 1979). It does not sufficiently account for the fact that these cognitive processes (which of course are to be taken into account) are activated and assume a significance within social relations which we shall see are fundamentally intergroup. In other words, conflict is above all considered in the light of the cognitive information processing it involves, its social nature being somehow set aside. Explanations are given only for certain indirect changes, and are not linked theoretically to the often differentiating dynamics characteristic of direct influence. Finally, this approach opposes direct majority influence, explained by means of a comparison process, to indirect minority influence, explained on the basis of the cognitive activity involved in the validation process, without taking into account their *simultaneous* occurrence, and without applying the appropriate notions to explain their relationships.

Approximately the same general impression is obtained from Moscovici's (1980) explanations in which majority influence is said to be governed by a comparison process, reflected by manifest influence with no consequences at the latent level, whereas the typical kind of conversion brought on by a minority (in which case the effects only show up at the latent level) is said to be the consequence of a validation process involving cognitive centering on the object (partially accounted for in the studies mentioned above). In this same line of thinking, the research conducted by Personnaz and Guillon (1985) dealing with the attention subjects pay either to the source or the actual object of a discussion has shown that *majorities* center targets more on the characteristics of the source (*how* the majority says what it says), whereas *minorities* increasingly center targets on the analysis of the object under discussion (*what* the minority says). Maass, West, and Cialdini (1987, p. 60) took up on the same idea in saying, 'Minorities are likely to enhance the amount of attention on the stimulus information at the center of the disagreement between majority and minority group members. In simple perceptual tasks (colour judgements) the attentional focus should be on the coloured stimulus, whereas in paradigms involving opinions the attentional focus should be on the message presented by the minority.'

Our intent is to theoretically integrate these functionings, which are not totally unrelated to some of the other distinctions made in current research on persuasion and attitude change. Indeed, several researchers (cf. Zanna, Olson, and Hermann, 1987) have managed to define the different cognitive activity levels at work in influence situations: the observed changes are thought to result either from the more central processing of message content, or from a more peripheral processing mode involving greater sensitivity to the cues provided by the immediate, or not-so-immediate, environment, in other words, by the context (cf. Petty and Cacioppo, 1986). In the same line of thinking, more systematic information processing has been opposed to processing based on the ample use of simplifying heuristics (cf. Chaiken, 1987; Cialdini, 1987). In most cases the prevailing idea is obviously that central, more systematic processing would induce a deeper and more durable change, brought on by a greater capacity and will to cognitively process information in a more elaborate way. Unlike this kind of central processing, peripheral processing based on the use of specific heuristics is assumed to involve an activity of a more superficial nature, one more dependent upon cues, the source, and the message context, thus leading to surface changes which are not indicators of new attitude or behaviour systems. Moreover, only one last step was needed to make the analogy (cf. Chaiken and Stangor, 1987; Maass, 1987; Maass, West, and Cialdini, 1987; Petty and Cacioppo, 1986) whereby majority influence may rely on peripheral processing founded specifically on the use of heuristics such as source credibility or attractiveness, or the size and consensus of the majority, while minority influence may follow a more central path involving more systematic or elaborate processing of the contents of the message conveyed by the minority.

We do not intend in this book to discuss these approaches, all of which are of undeniable interest and have brought new ideas into research in the field of attitude change (McGuire, 1986). Instead, we shall attempt to define the processes and specific mechanisms underlying (1) the social comparison activity, which can be understood as peripheral relative to the message but psychologically essential to the target subjects, and (2) the validation activity, perhaps more central, i.e. focusing on the systematic elaboration of a minority stance. Above all, however, we shall be led to *interrelate* these 'peripheral' or 'central' activities through our dissociation model wherein these two processes are intricately intermingled in most situations where influence or persuasion occurs.

This raises the question of the reciprocal impact of the social comparison process and the validation process: when, and under what conditions, do activities that might be called peripheral lead to the more central processing of the message and its implications? In other words – this time we shall use our own terminology – when and under what conditions does the progression of social comparison intervene in validation, either by activating it or counteracting it? A corollary is the question of functional reciprocity: when and under what conditions does validation transform the features of social comparison?

The reader may already have guessed the general hypothesis specific to minority influence that we shall set forth here: certain *negative heuristics* resulting from the conflict induced by a minority standpoint are hypothesized to induce more socio-cognitive activity, notably argumentation and/or counter-argumentation, as well as more cognitive elaboration of the minority standpoint, and thus should lead to more conversion. The paradox here is not slight: a source that evokes 'negative' heuristics should challenge subjects more, and should *also* induce them to deny its message at a more central processing level. Indeed, in order to extend the source's negative heuristics to the content of the source message, subjects must more deeply examine the to-be-denied arguments. The work involved in this counter-argumentation may lead to the involuntary, but necessary, assimilation of the minority argumentation with that of the targets themselves, causing the sort of perverted inoculation effect in which the inoculation contaminates instead of immunizing (McGuire, 1964). It is this assimilation, along with the 'accommodations' it involves, that may cause the standpoints so far upheld by the targets to be redefined, resulting in a sort of 'minority-induced self-generated change' so typical of conversion effects (cf. Tesser, 1978, for a review of the self-generated change approach).

In this book, the fundamental distinction between the comparison and validation processes will be redefined in our own manner, without the assumption that the former is necessarily specific to majority influence, the latter, to minority influence. In a line of reasoning analogous to Chaiken and Stangor's (1987), it must be assumed that multiple cognitive processes play a part in both majority and minority influence. Indeed, these two basic processes, social comparison and validation, may act simultaneously in both the majority and minority forms of influence. And even if we sometimes give the impression, though only illusory, that we are developing the latter in particular, our aim is indeed to theoretically interrelate the two, and in accordance with Maass and Clark (1983, 1986), to consider them whenever possible in the framework of paradigms involving the *simultaneous* influence of both majority and minority groups.

In our approach, it is assumed that, through the social comparison process, target subjects resolve conflicts at the interpersonal or intergroup level (between two individuals or between an individual and a group). What is stated and displayed by the targets depends on the relationship they hold with those who are making the statement. Through the validation process, subjects are assumed to resolve conflicts in terms of the relationship they have with the debated object (i.e. in terms of what they perceive or think).

Our proposed theoretical interconnection is also based on the assumption that any relationship (interpersonal or intergroup) subject to a target-source comparison can have an effect upon the definition of the debated object, and may introduce new points of view likely to modify the terms of the validation. Thus, even upholding the status quo can force an individual to seek new arguments (cf. Billig, 1985), since in the end, the minority has the power to establish the terms of the conflict. As a corollary, it must be assumed that all new reflection upon, or definition of, the object undergoing the validation process is likely to lead to the redefinition of the field of social relations themselves, and hence is apt to modify the terms of the social comparison. These two aspects are assumed to be interleaved in a sort of spiral of reciprocal social and cognitive causalities, constituting the source of the social impact of majority–minority conflict and the origin of the tensions existing between dominant and innovative positions.

One of the implications of this conception is that social comparison can no longer be considered as solely responsible for direct influence. Both processes must be assumed to play a part in direct and indirect influence. By interconnecting them, we should be able to explain the dynamics linking direct and indirect influence, in other words, linking what targets claim, or claim to believe, and what they actually believe.

The purpose of this book is to develop the main lines of a psycho-sociological model to account for both resistance to change and innovation. To do so, we must view the dynamics of intergroup comparison as influence dynamics and at the same time view influence dynamics as dynamics of intergroup comparison, while attempting to explain the complex links relating the manifest effects of influence to its hidden effects. This indeed means applying new notions to define the interrelationships between intergroup approaches, which are supposed to account for the dynamics of direct influence, and approaches based on the minority influence model, which are supposed to account for the dynamics of indirect influence.

Establishing such a psychosociological articulation (cf. Doise, 1986; Mugny and Doise, 1979) between the effects, the processes underlying those effects, and the models accounting for them, is necessary for two good reasons. First, as we shall show, although intergroup approaches undeniably contribute to understanding part of the dynamics of direct influence, they do not suffice to explain all of its manifestations, and in their current state, can provide no explanation of indirect influence. Second, current models of minority influence still have not answered the question of whether or not minority generated conflict induces direct *and/or* indirect influence, and, if so, what conditions and what specific mechanisms are responsible for that influence. The *integrating model* that we are proposing in this book is aimed at explaining the various possible relationships between direct or immediate influence *and* indirect or delayed influence, for we must admit, as we shall illustrate below, that depending on the circumstances, minorities can obtain manifest influence alone, latent influence alone, both latent and manifest influence, or finally, none of the above.

In order to grasp the complex dynamics of conversion, we must also admit that, given the resistance the spread of minority innovation generates, one of the four impact patterns stated above is particularly typical of minority influence, as most of the studies in this field have indeed shown: minority influence is usually inexistent (or even negative) at the direct level, yet positive at the indirect level. The crucial problem today, however, is accounting for *all* possible cases, even those which are 'ecologically' less frequent. It is at this cost that a strictly psychosociological model can actually account for existing social 'reality', or even better, theorize the realities...of tomorrow. We now have the theoretical notions and experimental support needed to validate a model which accounts for all of these diverse cases.

1.3 Searching for the social impact of minorities

Within the past fifteen or so years, our research team has conducted several dozen experiments on minority influence. These experiments progressed through various theoretical and methodological stages, starting from the first experiment dealing with a specific effect, namely, the apparently negative effect of a consistent but rigid style (Mugny, Pierrehumbert and Zubel, 1972–3), all the way through to the more recent experiments aimed at illustrating our model. They are presented briefly here so that the reader can better understand what – through very patient research – has become the model we shall develop here, as it gradually takes shape from chapter to chapter, each corresponding to a new generation of experiments.

We might add in passing that this model can also serve as a plea for experimentation in social psychology. Let our position on this subject be quite clear. If crisis there is in our discipline, it cannot be attributed to the methodologies currently being used. The latter are not the ends in themselves, but rather a means supporting hypothetico-deductive thought processes. Before judging the instrument, the theorization it is supposed to interpret at the operational level should be questioned (cf. Grísez, 1975). Rewording an old saying, we might suggest that in the end, the theories get the methodologies they deserve. The latter should not be judged solely in the light of the former! We chose experimentation rather than some other methodology to satisfy one of our specific goals: to illustrate our assertions empirically and hypothetico-deductively. Experimental support in conjunction with the more extensive formalization of the theoretical model and general hypotheses it presupposes – since both must be formalized in order to be operationalized later in the laboratory or field – is the substance that defines and separates scientific discourse from the discourse of a layman or a journalist, even a scientific one.

Our experiments were nevertheless aimed at supporting and further defining a model of real social functioning, which we have attempted to transpose in our experimentally-created situations. Even if in the laboratory the dispute between the functionalist model and the interactionist model is sometimes symbolized by the numerical assessment of majority and minority effects, we must keep well in mind that, in the end, it is indeed the social psychology of social change in reality that we are hoping to model. Feminists, black power, anti-racists, homosexuals, ecologists, nuclear power antagonists – we could go on and on – are always sensed between the lines in our experiments, ranging from the most typical laboratory experiments to those most highly rooted in the field.

The reader may find it helpful in this respect to refer to the appendices of this book, which were designed to be 'useful'. The experimental material is presented in the appendices so that unexperienced readers can get a very precise idea of what our subjects generally had to do. This should help readers deal more intuitively with the many findings reported here.

1.3.1 First-generation studies: the social context of innovation

This brings us to the outline of this book, which begins where our last book, *The power of minorities* (Mugny, 1982) ended, that is, at the point where we ascertained that the processes of social influence, particularly minority influence, must be viewed as threads woven into a fabric of intergroup tensions. As we showed then, we must keep in mind that, at the very least, three social entities are involved in any innovation process. Let us briefly state again what these three entities are!

Firstly, innovation cannot be studied without referring to the entity or entities that initially advocate it or express it: the *minorities*. Secondly, innovation cannot be discussed without reference to the entity that expresses or represents the norms considered to be dominant in a given situation: the *power*, understood in the broad sense to be the dominant entity in social relations, and often simply symbolized by the majority or dominant norms themselves. Finally, there is the *population*, which constitutes the chosen *target* of the influence, whether 'majority'-induced (by the power) or minority induced.

One can see that the question of social influence cannot be reduced to a simple majority-to-minority, two-term opposition, as might be assumed on the basis of certain experimental designs, such as when a given message or position is attributed to either 82% or 18% of the individuals in the reference population. We in no way wish to criticize this approach, which moreover we were some of the first to employ, since it can be quite heuristic in that, like 'minimal' paradigms, it activates representations that are deeply anchored in social reality. However, the distinctions we have made between the minority, the power, and the population have the advantage of enabling us to draw up new hypotheses, and particularly to differentiate the various styles exhibited by the entities involved in such contexts. This is necessary insofar as the prevailing relationships linking these different poles are diverse in nature.

Accordingly, the fundamental link between power and minority takes on the form of an *antagonistic relationship*. Within this relationship, both partners are in fact active. The minority, then has the dreaded 'power' (hence the title of our former book) to create a social conflict by means of its behavioural consistency. In our mind, the minority-to-power relationship level is the one where the notion of *consistent behaviour style* proposed by Moscovici (1976) becomes relevant. Indeed, in order to present itself as an innovative alternative in the face of a dominant normative system, the first thing the minority must do is to explicitly break away from that norm, thus preventing negotiation with the power structure by avoiding compromise.

The dominant entity (the power, or 'majority') also plays an active role (cf. Deconchy, 1971, 1980; Doms, 1983; Mugny and Papastamou, 1980), and essentially expresses itself by opposing the change advocated by the minorities whenever that change is apt to interfere with the stability of the relationship that is favourable to it, or with the majority's privilege to define the norms and post them as universal.

Different types of relationships, this time involving the population, coexist. Between power and population, the relationship is usually one of domination (generally of an ideological nature) by the former over the latter. This domination relationship is manifested notably by resistance to the minority (cf. Papastamou, 1983), which when spread, reflects the opposition of power. Between population and minority, however, an actual influence relation is established in such contexts, precisely the kind of relationship our influence model attempts to account for, and interrelate to the other relationships simultaneously brought to bear.

Moreover, defining the different aspects of the social context of innovation in this manner has enabled us to make the distinction between *behaviour style* and *negotiation style*, a distinction which has turned out to be highly heuristic. Behaviour style refers to the strategies used to express antagonism with respect to a dominant norm, whereas negotiation style refers to the strategies adopted by minorities to deal with the population. This distinction can aid in understanding why minority consistency may have effects contrary to those predicted in the consistency model: when an equal amount of consistency is applied to opposing the dominant norm, flexibility in negotiating with the population or the target of the influence may have more effect (mainly direct) than rigidity (Mugny, 1975a).

1.3.2 Second-generation studies: influence as social identification

The first stage of our research thus consisted of defining the notions of minority influence style and strategies, and of outlining the complex nature of the social context conducive to innovation. Once the processes of social influence, and minority influence in particular, were recognized as integral parts of a network of intergroup tensions, the problem became developing a psychological theory to explain the modalities of their action (Mugny, 1984b; Mugny and Papastamou, 1985). A notion which was to become central to our approach became necessary, i.e. one that could be used to account for the psychological mechanism by means of which the *intergroup context* affects the targets of the influence during the innovation spreading process. The notion in question is *psychosocial identification*, which became the crux of an important line of research called the second-generation studies, the main topic of the next chapter. This notion was integrated as an extension of the intergroup model in order to cover minority studies (Mugny, Kaiser, and Papastamou, 1983), and amounts to considering that, in any influence process, the targets of that influence are led to perceive the influence source (as well as themselves) as belonging to one or more social groups or categories. The target then associates these groups or categories with certain characteristics and evaluations that define and differentiate them. One essential point of our argumentation is thus that the responses of targets, particularly the socially manifest ones, in fact express the extent to which the targets are ready to socially identify themselves with the source, i.e. to consider themselves as being like that source, and, hence, to assign themselves the characteristics and evaluations associated with the source, in their own eyes and in the eyes of others.

We have thus adopted two of what have now become the classical postulates of intergroup studies (cf. Brewer and Kramer, 1985). The first is based on the assumption that an ingroup favouritism bias exists (cf. Tajfel, 1978), which, when applied to minorities, allows us to assume that the closer or more similar the subjects consider themselves to be to the minority, the more they tend to go along with its alternative standpoints. The second postulate is based on a conception of individuals wherein they are searching for a positive social definition of themselves (Turner, 1981). This enabled us to contend that minority influence increases when the meanings attached to the source lead to psychosocial identification that is compatible with a positive personal identity. This was to undeniably become another one of the contributions of the second-generation studies, and will be formalized and supported experimentally in the first part of Chapter 2.

1.3.3 Third-generation studies: some gaps in discrimination

Nevertheless, viewing a minority through the prism of an intergroup comparison, and considering it like any other group, necessarily leads to an impasse which conceals two of its fundamental characteristics. We must not lose sight of the fact that initially, i.e. during the phase when its existence is being revealed, when it first appears in the social field, the minority is by definition the source of an intense conflict, since it consistently breaks away from the dominant norms and values. Its very identity as a minority results in its subjection to negative perceptions, and it is almost necessarily sensed as an outgroup in the category field, or at least, on the fringes of the ingroup. In short, since it is subject to discrimination and is a source of identification conflicts, it hardly has much chance of exerting any influence, as the second part of Chapter 2 will show.

In order to explain how minorities can nevertheless have some social impact, we must look at some of the gaps in this apparently unyielding intergroup logic, which suggest moreover some areas where the intergroup model and the interactionist model of influence might be interconnected. Let us take a look at two complementary aspects of discrimination which guided us in the development of our theory (Mugny, Kaiser, Papastamou, and Pérez, 1984).

Firstly, we shall see that at least in the field of social influence, both ingroup favouritism and outgroup discrimination are *avoidable*. It will be shown that a minority does not exert influence simply because it is ingroup rather than outgroup, but that its impact also depends on the behaviour styles it displays, its categorical identity in the end only delimiting the intensity of the conflict it can introduce. The idea here is that, whenever the source of influence is perceived as being psychologically closer to the targets, the minority can increase the amount of conflict, whereas when it is perceived as farther away, the minority would be better off attenuating the conflict (Mugny and Pérez, 1985).

Secondly, an essential step was the discovery of the genuinely paradoxical effects of categorization of the minority as outgroup (Pérez and Mugny, 1986a, 1987), since outgroup categorization can have opposing outcomes to those predicted in intergroup relations theory. We must indeed acknowledge the facts: *even when categorized as outgroup* and the subject of 'overt' and direct discrimination, a minority can still induce change, although of an indirect, private, or delayed nature. It thus appears that minority influence does not always result from a one-way bias favouring the ingroup, a fact which is unaccounted for in the intergroup model. It is evident that discrimination against the minorities, the dominated, has its limits. This twofold demonstration will be the theme of Chapter 3.

1.3.4 Fourth-generation studies: towards interrelating discrimination and validation

With this evidence as support, our final series of studies could deal more specifically with the socio-cognitive mechanisms inducing such indirect influence, stressing the *constructivist* nature (Mugny and Pérez, 1987, 1988a) of the socio-cognitive activity of minority influence targets. They will be used to show how the targets of minority influence can be led, even in spite of themselves, to actively and cognitively construct categorizations of the source and its attributes, and to infer an organizing principle underlying minority positions. Only the recognition of such a principle can account for the fact that indirect or delayed influence may be obtained, even in the event of explicit initial rejection. We shall even go so far as to show how resistance to change may even be responsible for activating the various facets of this social construction and validation activity, which will be the core topic of Chapter 4.

One final question will remain unanswered at that point: from the target subject's standpoint – since we are psychologists – how are the dynamics of direct influence and indirect influence interrelated? The answer will be given in Chapter 5, where we shall develop the idea that depending on the social situation (which of course will be conceptualized) the social comparison activity performed by target subjects is reflected by their direct and explicit yielding to, or avoidance of, the minority positions, which also either *allows them or does not allow them* to perform a validation activity likely to lead to the private, indirect, or delayed appropriation of the organizing principle underlying the minority positions. As we shall demonstrate, for the latter to occur the subject must be able to cognitively *separate* the comparison activity and the validation activity (Pérez and Mugny, 1989). We shall see that whenever the uniformity generating process involved in social comparison and the divergent process of the social construction of reality can function autonomously, change is possible. It is only when they are confounded that social comparison takes precedence over validation, reinforcing uniformity. Whatever the outcome of these complex socio-cognitive activities, only a psychosocial model which clearly defines the link between uniformity and innovation, comparison and validation, rejection and conviction, the said and the done, the public and the private, can account for them all.

We shall conclude by taking a more detailed look at the paradoxical effects of resistance to change, since the model developed will provide the elements needed to determine the conditions under which resistance to innovation prevents minority influence, and those under which, on the contrary, it paradoxically triggers indirect or delayed influence despite initial minority rejection. This approach to the problem amounts to considering the *reciprocal* effects of the majority and minority, in a context where the power is made salient when the minority challenges the dominant entity that reacts by means of pressure leading to the rejection of the minority at a certain level, all the while being the involuntary instrument of its impact. As we shall see, resisting or denying the minority alternative has its cost. This cost in the end is recognition that the minority has some degree of truth, and induction of a normative change at a more general level, which accounts for changes in the spirit of the times.

2 Minority influence and social comparison

2.1 The intergroup nature of innovation processes

As said above, social influence processes, and minority influence in particular, are woven into a fabric of tensions linking the various social entities, namely, the minority, the power, and the 'population'. Since the minority has the 'power' to create a social conflict by its behavioural consistency, it necessarily builds social and psychological barriers between itself and the targets of its potential influence.

By expressing a point of view that breaks away from the predominant position, minorities lead targets to represent the social field encompassing them as fundamentally divided in two: on one side, we find those who follow the dominant norm (at this point, it does not even matter who established it, as each individual has made it his/her own as if it were a truism), and on the other side, we find those who deviate from, and contest, that norm. Individuals who are faithful to the norm (in this case, the population, for the sake of simplicity) feel they have something in common with each other by virtue of their conformity with the norm, and think they differ radically from the minority that is introducing dissent. This state of affairs is thought to both accentuate in some way the psychological identity common to the advocates of the norm, while differentiating them from the detracting minorities, advocates of the counter-norm.

The distance introduced by the dissident minority would thus cause the members of the majority to draw closer to each other, and, at least momentarily, would reinforce their suddenly threatened cohesion. There is no need here to insist upon this tendency: the well-known feelings that accompany the scapegoat phenomenon, for example, may not be very different from those initially induced by dissident behaviour. Schachter (1951) indeed found such deviant rejection effects to occur in cases where pressure to maintain uniformity turns out to be in vain. Moreover, yielding to the minority means running the obvious risk of triggering a snowball effect (cf. Kiesler and Pallak, 1975), since the effectiveness of minority proselytism can only be proved to the detriment of the majority norm. According to Levine and Russo (1987), consistency is indeed not the only

17

advantageous device used by minorities: a source of influence that disagrees with the majority norm after having previously agreed with it may indeed be more influential than a source that disagrees outright (cf. Levine, Sroka, and Snyder, 1977). In addition, Nemeth and Chiles (1988) showed how a courageous minority can provide individuals with the incentive to resist the majority.

Immediately, then, or at least very soon, the relationship that sets in as a consequence of the emergence of a new minority position, or the revelation of a pre-existing one, is an intergroup relationship (Worchel, 1987), since the representation the targets construct of it is characterized by the division or partitioning of the social space. Let us put ourselves in the position of target subjects who discover the standpoint of a minority. They must not only situate themselves personally with respect to the message the minority is advocating – the social field is not just binary – but they must also situate themselves with respect to the power structure and the dominant norms. The dilemma thus appears to be simple: they must choose between obeying or apostatizing. In short, they are led to take into account the strength of the opposition created by the minority intrusion, i.e. the resistance to a change, and either cope with it or overcome it. They may also have to situate themselves with respect to certain personally-relevant social groups or categories which potentially divide up the population. To make a long story short, a target subject is led to cognitively represent the social influence context. This representation gives meaning to the influence situation, and will guide the target's behaviour and situate him or her socially and psychologically with respect to the various entities he or she will have distinguished.

To construct a model of minority influence, we shall thus consider that, as far as the target subject is concerned, this kind of social context presupposes that, in reality, a representational activity will take place involving a series of group entities or categorical entities in terms of which the target establishes a psychosocial definition of the minority, the power, the population itself and any other relevant entity. We can see quite well that such a model naturally calls for an authentic intergroup theory of influence processes, one which can account for the basic dynamics of resistance to change and of preferential identification with certain social groups or categories likely to convey or thwart social change.

Before dealing with this model in detail, let us examine the contribution of intergroup research to the study of minority phenomena. In doing so, we shall find out that the cognitive biases and functioning highlighted by intergroup theories also largely characterize social influence phenomena, underlying them as specific, intermediate mechanisms, even though other mechanisms will be shown to counteract or modulate them.

2.2 Categorization, identity, and categorical differentiation

The importance of two complementary processes is emphasized in intergroup theory (cf. Brewer, 1979), one being a more 'cognitive' process, that of social categorization, and the other being more 'motivational', that of the search for a positive identity, which, as we shall see below, can be extended to the study of minority influence. Let it be clear as of now that our goal in this chapter is not to present a comprehensive analysis of these intergroup theories (see in particular Austin and Worchel, 1979; Brewer and Miller, 1984; Brown, 1984a; Doise, 1978; Hewstone and Brown, 1986; Tajfel, 1978; Stephan, 1985; Turner and Giles, 1981), nor is it to launch a critical debate about them, but rather to make the best use of any of the theoretical elements developed and tested experimentally therein which might be of some heuristic value to us. This brief overview includes the theories of social identity (cf. Tajfel, 1981, 1982; Tajfel and Turner, 1979; Turner *et al.*, 1987) and categorical differentiation (Doise, 1978), which have resulted in the formulation of several postulates.

The categorization of individuals as members of distinct groups triggers a twofold cognitive activity (Tajfel, 1972, 1981, 1982): on the one hand, we observe *accentuation of the differences* perceived between the members of different categories through the overestimation of the distances that separate and differentiate them. This accentuation of differences between members of different categories is all the more marked when the compared individuals are located at the category boundaries, as if it were somehow essential to avoid undesirable overinclusions. In addition, we sometimes observe the complementary *accentuation of the similarities* of the members of the same category (cf. Brown, 1984b; Wilder, 1981), who tend to be perceived as more similar or less different than they actually are, a phenomenon which contributes to the emergence of stereotypes. The joint effect of these two phenomena is thought to be even greater when the intergroup comparison is based on dimensions which will be determinant in how the intergroup relations evolve (see Doise, 1978).

As a complement to the above, whenever an individual is a member of one of the two groups, his or her representation of the social field in the form of entities categorized as ingroup (i.e. the group to which one belongs) and outgroup (i.e. the group to which one does not belong) suffices to engage him/her in *ingroup favouritism*, and in a complementary manner, in *outgroup discrimination*. These biases affect the evaluations one makes of the two subgroups: the group with which one identifies is granted a more favourable evaluation. And they affect the behaviours one manifests: more cooperative and less tense behaviour is exhibited towards one's own group members, while more competitive and tense behaviour is displayed towards outgroup members. These phenomena are observed even when categorization is done on the basis of a minimal criterion which *a priori* is not even very relevant (cf. Tajfel *et al.*, 1971), such as when subjects are simply classified by their alleged aesthetic preferences for Klee's or Kandinsky's paintings. The advantage of this state of affairs is that categorizations can be devised experimentally so as to study fundamental intergroup processes relative to certain 'purified' categorizations.

Ingroup favouritism has a specific psychological function. It provides an individual with an identity that is both personal, though socially defined by his or her various category memberships, and positive. This positive psychosocial identity is in fact granted to the group or category members whenever – in what appears to be genuine symbolic social competition (cf. Turner, 1978) opposing the ingroup and the outgroup – one's own group is more 'competitive' than the outgroup, and thus looks superior in the intergroup comparison; again, remember that this effect is even greater when the comparison is based on a psychologically relevant and salient criterion, i.e. when it bears on a dimension that defines the specificity, or *distinctiveness* of one's own group. One proof of this is that the favouritism bias only takes effect in selected situations (cf. Doise, 1978), when the very definition of the group is at stake. One of the consequences, whose repercussions on minority influence will be discussed later, is that the need to affirm the superiority of one's own group can increase when the ingroup and outgroup are in fact relatively close to each other along the dimension under comparison.

Whenever an ingroup is socially and symbolically competitive, this implies that, in evaluating the attributes considered to define the group, its members acknowledge or assign positive connotations via a genuine sociocentric evaluation bias (Peabody, 1968, 1985) operating even beyond the possible recognition of inferiorities due notably to asymmetries of a sociological nature (cf. Doise, 1972). As a complement, negative evaluative connotations tend to be associated with the attributes specific to the outgroup via an ethnocentric bias.

How does this wholly symbolic superiority of the ingroup participate in the search for a positive identity by group members? In reality, by categorizing themselves as members of a group or category, individuals identify with that group or category by means of a *self-attribution mechanism* through which they assign themselves the characteristics recognized as definitional of it and incorporate them into their own *self-concept* in the specific situation, a self-image which they aim, moreover, to establish or maintain as positive (Turner, 1981). Here, the twofold categorization activity, applied to oneself, leads to the overestimation of one's own psychological proximity to the other members of one's group, and especially the overestimation of the distance between oneself and the members of the outgroup.

We can easily see that psychosocial identification defined as such, *in situ*, is positive for the members of the group whenever, symbolically, the group is 'socially competitive'; and negative whenever it is not (see Tajfel and Turner, 1979, concerning the social mobility strategies involved in such cases).

Finally – and this is an essential point – individuals tend to try to maintain or establish coherency or concordance across the intergroup aspects, i.e. behaviour, representations, and evaluations (Doise, 1978). In other words, according to this extension of the intergroup model, a distinction introduced at one level has homologous repercussions at all other levels. Therefore, differentiation at the representational level will uniformly affect evaluation and behaviour. We have seen, moreover, that the simple division of the field into ingroup and outgroup gives rise to differential evaluations which are positive for the ingroup and negative for the outgroup, leading to cooperation with the former and competition with the latter. Reciprocally, differential evaluation will modify representation and behaviour in an analogous manner. Finally, behavioural differentiation will be translated into representational and evaluative differentiation in accordance with it.

Although these diverse aspects of intergroup relations have sometimes been the object of discussion, even of controversy, and although recent developments in intergroup research have focused on other aspects (cf. Turner *et al.*, 1987), it is nevertheless true that they can account for a great deal of the dynamics of intergroup confrontation, as attested by the above publications. In the remainder of this chapter, we shall show how this model indeed can be used to account for a whole series of social influence phenomena.

2.3 Minority influence and social categorization

The validity of transposing these postulates to the problem of influence relationships seems evident. Quite logically, Turner (1981) thus hypothesized that a source of influence categorized as ingroup will exert more influence than a source categorized as outgroup. This transposition is also perfectly coherent with the one we proposed for minority influence in particular (cf. Mugny, 1981).

Two main ideas derived from intergroup studies are of undeniable heuristic value. The first amounts to extending the favouritism bias postulate to studies on minority influence. The second amounts to taking into account the effects of the evaluative connotations of minority attributes likely to be subject to self-attribution. Let us examine each of these extensions in detail, initially showing that the ingroup or outgroup identity of an influence source does indeed have the effect predicted in the intergroup model.

2.3.1 Ingroup favouritism and public influence

The first idea, derived from the principle of ingroup favouritism, leads to the assumption that categorization of the minority as an ingroup should tend to reinforce its influence, whereas its categorization as explicitly outgroup should thwart its impact. Note that this can be assumed to be especially true for publicly captured influence, which is socially manifest, since public situations are the ones where identification with the source is the most salient. This is exactly what Martin (1987a; see also Abrams and Hogg, 1990) showed in a series of experiments.

In the studies selected here (Martin, 1987b, 1988a, 1988b, 1988c), the author took advantage of the fact that, in British secondary schools, students can leave school at age 16, or continue on for one more year (sixth-form). Sixteen-year-olds are obviously financially dependent upon their parents. This theme was used in several experiments where fourteen- and fifteen-year-olds were first asked to indicate how large a scholarship should be allotted to such students. A few weeks after this pre-test, the subjects were given a text, alleged to be supported by less than 10% of the population, in which a scholarship of nearly twice the amount they had stated on the pre-test was proposed. Immediately following this influence phase, they were asked to give their own opinion again, and the degree of influence was measured by calculating the difference between the two answers.

In the first experiment in the series, the publicness of the final answer was made salient by leading the subjects to believe they would participate in a discussion with other members of their group, and thus that their answer would be made known to the others. In the other conditions, their answers were to be inserted in a ballot box and thus apparently remained private. In addition, the message was presented as having been issued by either their own school (ingroup source) or another school (outgroup source) that had a discriminatory, and thus negative, reputation in the students' eyes, as determined by a pilot study.

In the second experiment, the procedure was identical in all respects except for the fact that sex categorization was introduced by stating that the text given to the subjects came from a source with either the same, or opposite, sex identity as the subject's.

Finally, in the third experiment of interest to us here, which only used the public response modality, the way in which categorization was introduced was varied, this time at random. Indeed, on the basis of the number of students they thought attended the schools in the area, subjects were supposedly divided into underestimators and overestimators. They were then led to believe that the source belonged either to the same subgroup of estimators as themselves or to the other subgroup, although in reality, the distribution was random.

Note also that the last two experiments included a control condition in which post-test measures were taken without the subjects having to read the minority text, thus allowing for the assessment of changes actually induced by the message itself.

On the whole, the results obtained for the public conditions support the idea that messages are more influential when the source is categorized as ingroup than when categorized as outgroup. Experiments 2 and 3 also showed that ingroup source influence was greater than it was in the control condition, where no minority text was read. This implies that the ingroup source did indeed modify the public responses of this population.

It should also be noted that these effects only occurred in the public response conditions. Indeed, and as we shall see in more detail in the next chapter, this difference disappeared and was even reversed when responding was done in private where subjects run no risk of future pressure or social control. The changes observed here were, in general, greater than in the public situation, which suggests that public comparison is indeed conflictual.

These results indicate two things. First – and this is the effect we are interested in here – it is evident that ingroup favouritism does indeed play a role in social influence, and that a source categorized as ingroup is preferred, modifying the responses of its co-members more than a source categorized as outgroup. Thus, application of the intergroup model to influence studies is indeed legitimate. The second remark, which we shall come back to in the next chapter, pertains to the limits of such a bias, which is not observed when opinions are expressed in private where minority pressure appears to have its full effect. But we should not jump ahead! To stay on the safe side, ingroup favouritism will be assumed to occur essentially when responding is done publicly, and thus when it more or less consciously involves the subject's social identity.

The fact that these effects occur for groups (schoolmates), broader social categories (men–women), and artificial categories allows us to view the terms group and category 'indiscriminately', even if in other cases it is sometimes wise to distinguish them. At the level at which we are approaching the problem, the feeling of identification is what counts, as we shall demonstrate further.

2.3.2 Salience of the intergroup context

Martin's third experiment showed that a favouritism bias can cause partiality to the source even when categorization is done on the basis of a trivial criterion void of all social significance. And this is not the only time such an effect has been found. It was also observed in an experiment on pollution conducted in collaboration with Papastamou in Greece, where pollution is a burning issue.

Let us briefly describe the studies using the pollution paradigm. Subjects first answer an opinion questionnaire (7-point scale; cf. Appendix 7.1.1) about who is to blame for pollution, individual categories (housewives, automobile drivers, etc.) or industry. They again answer the same questionnaire on a post-test taken at the end of the experiment, which is aimed at measuring the influence of a text supposedly written by a minority (cf. Appendix 7.1.2) which they read between the two questionnaires. The influence of the text is assessed by measuring the changes in their responses before and after the actual influence phase. The minority text strongly and one-sidedly accuses industrialized society, claiming that blaming individuals only 'masks the real culprits'. Positive influence would thus be reflected by greater incrimination of industry and removal of guilt from individual categories.

In this experiment, two variables were introduced. First, the minority was presented as ingroup or outgroup. To do so, subjects first took a (so-called) test, the McHolson black/white figure classification test (cf. Appendix 7.1.3). This 'test' consists of 36 black and white figures arranged in 6 rows and 6 columns, and is taken by choosing one's favourite column and row. In reality, it only serves the purpose of introducing the minority categorization variable. This is done by making the subjects believe they would be classified into group X or group Y on the basis of their answers to this test. In truth, their answers were not taken into account, and all subjects were classified as X. Depending on the condition, the feedback provided was supposed to induce a sense of categorical similarity or difference. In the ingroup conditions, subjects read a text supposedly written by a minority group composed of typical members of group X, and in the outgroup conditions, by a minority group composed of typical members of group Y. Note that the categorization induced here does indeed bring together all of the conditions of the minimal paradigm (Tajfel *et al.*, 1971), since subjects did not know the potential purpose of the test, nor the parameters of the classification, which was indicated without stating names.

The second variable of interest here was used to adjust the meanings taken on by this categorization, and to accentuate or attenuate the perception of the intergroup nature of the situation. In half of the conditions, subjects were to choose five of the eight personality traits they felt best described the message advocated by the minority. The eight traits proposed dealt with the degree of judgemental autonomy or heteronomy, mental flexibility or rigidity, ideological coherency or incoherency, personal commitment or indifference, psychological balance or imbalance, personal stability or instability, intellectually realistic or unrealistic quality, and emotional dependence or independence. In short, the characteristics used were intended to focus the subjects on psychological and personality related dimensions of a more individual scope, rather than ones referring explicitly to a within-category similarity.

In contrast, in the other half of the conditions, the category related characteristics of the source were made salient, and thus any potential identification to an explicitly categorized entity would be salient. This time, subjects were to choose five sociological characteristics they felt would suffice to describe the minority message, among the eight dimensions proposed: family background, education, age, profession, political attitudes, socio-economic level, religion, and sex identity. The purpose of focusing on the many category memberships of the minority was obviously to reinforce categorization effects with a social basis.

What can be learned from the results of this experiment, shown in Table 2.1, where mean change is rated on a 7-point scale for the questionnaire taken as a whole? (Here as well as in the tables that follow, a higher number indicates more minority influence.) First, the most striking fact is that categorization of the minority had a marked effect on the minority influence obtained, even though it had been induced on a totally arbitrary basis. The sole representation of the minority as ingroup can thus result in a greater amount of influence than when it is categorized as outgroup.

Although this effect occurred as a general rule, it was especially the case when categorization of the minority was made salient by centering subjects on the category attributes of the minority. It is true that these are the conditions under which arbitrary categorization into groups X and Y is likely to mean something and to carry more weight. In other words, the more salient the intergroup context, the more the categorization of the social field into ingroup and outgroup is likely to be translated into a bias favouring the ingroup and discriminating against the outgroup.

This is another demonstration supporting the model of intergroup relations. Indeed, these same results can be read in another way. Let us assume for the moment that focusing on psychological attributes makes comparison at the interindividual level more salient (since the source attributes are reduced to individual traits), and that focusing on category attributes leads instead to more explicitly intergroup comparison. This brings us to formulate the idea – in agreement with Tajfel (1978) – that in

Table 2.1. *Mean change (a + sign indicates more influence)*

	Dimensions	
	Psychological	Sociological
Minority		
Ingroup	+0.38	+0.47
Outgroup	+0.27	+0.06

Table 2.2. *Mean frequency of agreement with source*

	Context	
	Objectivity	Intergroup
Source		
Ingroup	2.65	2.53
Outgroup	2.55	1.33

influence phenomena also, particularly minority influence, biases resulting from categorization are greater when social comparison is done on an intergroup basis, and lesser when it is done on an interindividual basis. Further proof of this will be given later.

Note that we get the same impression from another experiment, this time dealing with preferences for aesthetic stimuli (Doise, Gachoud, and Mugny, 1986). Male and female subjects were asked to state whether one-coloured stimuli (blue checks on a white background) or multicoloured stimuli (seven colours of checks on a white background) were pleasing or unpleasing to the eye. Knowing from the pre-test that they preferred one-coloured stimuli, we showed them the same stimuli a second time (the number of items in this influence phase was 16) and told them that most subjects of their own sex (ingroup source) or the opposite sex (outgroup source) systematically preferred multicoloured checkerboards, thus introducing a position which in fact was a minority position.

Furthermore, in one series of conditions, the intergroup context was made particularly salient. Accordingly, subjects were told, 'In this study, we shall attempt to determine to what extent the aesthetic choices of men and women reveal differing psychological traits.' This set-up was aimed at activating the twofold categorization process. In other conditions designed to decrease the salience of the intergroup relationship, we claimed to be interested in the extent to which 'the aesthetic choices made by women and men when selecting geometric figures take objective characteristics into account'. Here, it was the object that was supposed to induce the responses, and thus to mask intercategory relationships, whereas in the previous conditions, it was membership in the male or female category that was supposed to determine the choices made.

The results are given in Table 2.2, which indicates how many times out of eight in the second phase of the experiment the subjects chose the ingroup or outgroup response; indeed, although the results on the eight items in the first phase indicate the same tendency, they do not reach the conventional significance level. This means that the influence only set in gradually as the interaction progressed. We can see first of all that the point of view defended by the source was indeed an anti-norm position, and thus in the normative minority, since the subjects clearly preferred one-coloured stimuli.

Two main effects will be considered here. First, during the influence phase, subjects expressed an overall preference for multicoloured figures more often when the source's sex identity was the same as their own. The ingroup bias was definitely in effect here. Perhaps even more interesting is the fact that the outgroup discrimination bias was only observed to a significant degree when the study was presented as being aimed at differentiating male and female characteristics, i.e. when the intergroup relationship was salient.

Somewhat like the dynamics reported by Martin, who no longer observed ingroup favouritism in private situations, the above effects only came through on the direct influence measure (colour choice), that is, the preference actually expressed by the source. Other data show that on generalization measures (indirect influence on number of elements and not number of colours as before, this time using figures of varying complexity) the outgroup sources were the ones that had the greatest effect. We shall take the opportunity to come back to this question in the next chapter while considering some of the possible consequences of categorization on the different levels of influence.

2.3.3 The feeling of shared identity

The above effects of categorization on minority influence may be due to the joint action of two complementary processes: target subjects either define or perceive the categorical division of the social field, and then, in the fashion described in the categorical differentiation model, transfer this division on to other behaviours, in this case influence behaviour, provided however they are led to identify with one of the categories defined or perceived. Thus, minorities may above all derive their capacity to exert influence through an identification process. If this reasoning is valid, it should be possible, without having to rely on binary categorization (such as male–female, X–Y), to show experimentally that, by varying the extent to which there is identification with the minority, the amount of influence it exerts will also vary.

Table 2.3. *Mean change (a + sign indicates more influence)*

	Subjects	
	Far	Close
1 Membership		
Flexible style	+1.00	+0.34
Rigid style	+0.82	−0.04
5 Memberships		
Flexible style	+0.76	+0.84
Rigid style	+1.07	+0.99

To illustrate this point, we shall show that by experimentally increasing the feeling of shared identity between subject and source, we can increase the source's influence. In an experiment on pollution (Mugny and Papastamou, 1982), subjects were led to believe they shared with the minority source either one or five categorical identities out of a total of eight (intelligence, sex membership, ecological policy, religious background, young age, political party, student status, and privileged social milieu). The subjects then read either the flexible version or the more rigid version of a minority text (cf. Appendix 7.1.2). The questionnaire (cf. Appendix 7.1.1; in the experiment, an 11-point scale was used), which dealt with who is to blame for the pollution problem, was filled in by the subjects before and after reading the text and was used to assess the influence exerted by the minority. In addition, on the basis of their answers to a pre-test, subjects were divided into two groups: those who were the closest to, and those who were the farthest from, entertaining the ideological position of the minority.

The effect observed was the expected one (cf. Table 2.3): on the whole, the amount of influence was greater in the five-shared-identities condition than in the one-shared-identity condition, i.e. when subjects were induced to identify to a greater extent with the source. A breakdown of this overall effect yielded two complementary sub-effects. First, mutual membership in a category especially caused an increase in the influence of the rigid text, which was the most conflictual. In other words, 'forced' identification by experimental induction may facilitate minority influence which would not otherwise occur to the same extent, and thus may combat the feeling of overexclusion that a rigid text can be assumed in our perspective to implicitly convey. The second effect found here was that the positive impact of the feeling of mutual membership especially increased the extent of minority influence for subjects who were classified as ideologically closer to the source, i.e. those for whom the question of psychosocial identification was the most salient by virtue of its greater credibility or plausibility. These

Table 2.4. *Number of shared categories stated*

	Subjects	
	Far	Close
1 *Membership*		
Flexible style	2.08	1.62
Rigid style	1.31	1.69
5 *Memberships*		
Flexible style	3.08	4.38
Rigid style	3.69	4.23

results support the idea that the more salient the identification, the greater the influence.

Let us take a look at another finding, which may appear trivial but which has turned out to be very useful. Consider the number of shared identities the subjects felt they had with the source, shown in Table 2.4.

We can see that in the conditions where subjects were asked to state one ('or even two') shared identities, they went right along with the game, choosing an average of 1.68 identities, whether they were ideologically close or far from the minority. Yet when they were asked to choose five ('or even six'), a difference appeared, depending on the proximity of their previously expressed opinions. Subjects who were far removed from the source chose an average of 3.39 identities, whereas the closer-to-source subjects chose 4.31 identities. This difference, which is highly significant, is evidence of the fact that, when given that opportunity, subjects will express identity commonalities that coincide with their own ideological positions. The more similar their own position is to that advocated by the minority, the more they identify with that minority along other criteria, in this case, category membership.

This proves, if proof was necessary, that ideas are anchored in social categorizations and identifications. As a logical consequence, it also allows us to consider that a change in ideological position is a corollary of a change in identification. This in fact is the cornerstone of the model developed at the end of this chapter.

At this point in our account, it is worth noting that the 'classical' dynamics shown to exist in intergroup research may also take effect in minority influence, just as they do in the evolution of social movements (cf. Di Giacomo, 1980; Reicher, 1984). This very fact legitimatizes our borrowing of some of the most basic notions of the intergroup model: the bias of ingroup favouritism, outgroup discrimination, and categorical differentiation.

2.4 Minority influence and evaluation contexts

The second general postulate worth borrowing from the intergroup model amounts to accepting the assumption that individuals are in search of a positive identity (Turner, 1981). Their behaviour in the face of influence would therefore be highly dependent upon the attributes associated with the minority, and particularly upon the connotations attached to those attributes following the evaluation process. Indeed, our reasoning so far has concerned the cognitive act by which the minority is categorized, as attested by the occasional use of the minimal paradigm. But we have not dealt with the meanings specifically attached to the minority. Likewise, we have examined the feeling of identification without accounting for the attributes upon which it is based. No one would be surprised, however, to hear us say that such categorizations are not performed in a social vacuum (Tajfel and Farr, 1984). There is no doubt about the fact that induced categorization and identification take place within a field that, both before the interaction and also as a result of the minority's behaviour, acts as a carrier of these meanings, which must no longer be ignored, but integrated into the intergroup model of minority influence.

Past experiments on *double minorities* will be interpreted here in the above perspective. Maass and Clark (1984) use this expression to define minorities that differ from the majority (in effect, the target subjects) not only in terms of their beliefs (and thus in normative terms), but also in terms of their category memberships. The double minorities, that are without a doubt similar to our minorities categorized as outgroup, are contrasted to *single minorities*, that only differ from the majority in their alternative ideological positions and are not attributed other differentiating features.

What is the driving hypothesis of these authors? That this doubly differentiating status may in effect favour certain specific interpretations of the behaviour of deviant minorities, which in this case would be marked by internal attributes such as self-interest (see also Nemeth and Wachtler, 1973) and whose obvious effect would be to counteract minority influence. This is indeed what one of Maass, Clark, and Haberkorn's (1982) experiments showed, using male subjects with basically conservative opinions on abortion. The subjects were confronted with a minority group whose opinions on this matter were, on the contrary, liberal. For half of the subjects, the so-called 'single' minority was composed of males, in effect an ingroup minority in our terms. For the other half, the so-called 'double' minority was composed of females. This was an outgroup minority. The notion of double minority was perhaps aimed at expressing the fact that the ingroup–outgroup difference was added on to the male–female asymmetry used here to express differing attitudes on abortion. (Moreover, the reason Martin (1987a) preferred inducing ingroup–outgroup source categorization on the basis of an arbitrary criterion was to methodologically distinguish this attribution effect from the actual intergroup effect.) It is true that it takes a laboratory to fabricate (nearly ...) equal groups! Whatever the case may be, the results show that the double minority was indeed perceived as exhibiting a strong self-interest bias, and hence, exerted less influence.

Granted, these results can be interpreted in terms of attribution, as previously proposed by Nemeth and Wachtler (1973), although recent studies (Clark and Maass, 1988, p. 178) have shown that interpretation in terms of social identification would have a more general scope than interpretation in terms of self-interest. It is nevertheless and undeniably true that such attribution can play an important role in the identification process. Indeed, the various attributes assigned to the minority can have evaluative connotations that are either more positive (single or ingroup minority) or more negative (double minorities). These descriptive and evaluative asymmetries imply that, in order for minority positions to be approached, there must either be positive identification (in the ingroup case) or the risk of identification that is threatening to one's own identity (in the outgroup case). In these experiments, categorizations and connotations are one and the same thing.

2.4.1 Original minorities and deviant minorities
Accordingly, the effects of evaluative connotations should be studied, in their own right at first. We shall do so here by illustrating with some *ad hoc* experiments, without referring explicitly to categorizations, precisely so as not to confuse these two dimensions. We have attempted so far to demonstrate that the amount of influence exerted depends upon the nature of the psychologically salient characteristics of the minority, provided these self-attributable characteristics ensure psychosocial identification that is compatible with a positive personal identity. As a general rule, attributes that are assigned to a minority and have positive connotations should favour minority influence more than negatively connoted attributes.

To this end, we can take advantage of precisely the fact that normative contexts (cf. Mugny and Papastamou, 1984) are interpretation frameworks that make diversely connoted attributes salient. For instance, a context involving originality – which is positively connoted – should ensure positive identification, and hence more minority influence than a deviant normative context, which is negatively connoted.

In one of their experiments, Moscovici and Lage (1978) asked subjects to respond in various experimental contexts involving different definitions of originality. They used the blue/green paradigm, now conventional in minority influence research (cf. Personnaz and Personnaz, 1987). In each condition, two confederates consistently stated in front of four test subjects that a certain slide was green, although it was actually, and very obviously, blue. In one condition, the subjects were simply told that the experiment dealt with the perception of colours. The influence rate obtained (approximately 8 %) was indeed the one ordinarily found with this paradigm. A rate of 13 % was obtained when a discussion on originality was held with the subjects before the actual influence phase. The weakness of the induced effect is a result of the fact that, in reality, two contradictory definitions of originality prevail, a positively connoted one which denotes creativity, and a negatively connoted one which denotes behaviour judged to be abnormal, odd, and eccentric. In other experimental conditions, the authors managed to increase the influence rate to nearly 30 % by explicitly placing value on originality, stressing its importance to the novel ways of seeing things affecting modern art and new forms of architecture. Seen from our perspective at this point, what the authors did was make salient the evaluative connotations associated with the originality attribute, thus adjusting its meaning.

We, also, showed this to be true via an experiment on social judgements about pollution (Mugny, Rilliet, and Papastamou, 1981). Subjects were asked to read a text written in either a flexible or rigid style (cf. Appendix 7.1.2), supposedly by an 'ecology-oriented, political-fringe minority group'. In addition, they were led to believe that the purpose of the experiment was to detect individual tendencies towards either originality or deviance; this explicitly involved their 'personal' identity (even if defined socially). Originality was termed as 'the tendency to accept new values and ideas leading to social progress', and deviance, as 'the tendency to accept values and socially rejected ideas because they challenge established norms'. In short, inducing originality was supposed to trigger minority influence, whereas inducing deviance was supposed to thwart it by increasing the target subjects' risk of a degrading identification.

The results (cf. Table 2.5; 12-point scales were used here) show that, on the whole, explicit agreement with the minority message occurred significantly more often when the originality norm was filtered in such a way that the subjects felt valued by identifying with it, whereas focusing on the implied deviance in the minority text induced resistance to its message. We can also see that the less conflictual the minority, i.e. when a flexible style was used to present the message, the more subjects approved of it. Since these effects are cumulative, it is evident that a minority becomes more influential when it presents its message with a flexible style in a normative context evoking originality, and less influential when its style is rigid and its message is communicated in a context evoking deviance.

Our reasoning is that the minority stereotype potentially includes the attributes of both originality and deviance, the former being accompanied by positive connotations, the latter being void of such connotations. Whenever the minority is flexible, the originality context, by expressing the

Table 2.5. *Extent of agreement with the minority (the higher the number, the more influence)*

	Context	
	Originality	Deviance
Flexible source	9.17	8.31
Rigid source	7.62	6.95

positive attributes of originality, may grant them more weight. Furthermore, even when the attributes of originality are made salient, they do not suffice to combat the conflictual meaning conveyed by minority rigidity, especially if they are predominant in the minority stereotype. This is indeed what we were led to believe in seeing the difficulties encountered by Moscovici and Lage in their attempt to 'get people to accept' the originality norm.

2.4.2 When the moderates are more extreme and the extremists more moderate

If, as seen in the experiments discussed above, shared identity ensures or reinforces minority influence, this is nevertheless only true if the judgements made of the minority do not severely threaten target identity, and thus do not involve the self-attribution of negatively connoted characteristics. In this respect, the ideological position of the subjects themselves is consequential. We have seen that the ideologically closer subjects are to a minority source, the more they psychologically consider themselves and the minority to share category membership. Now, when subjects place themselves entirely within the field of possible comparisons to the minority (and thus, the closer they are to it 'psychologically'), the more they will feel threatened by potential identification with it, both for themselves and in front of others. This same idea is illustrated in another manner by the following experiment (Mugny, 1983). Subjects were asked to assess the degree of political extremism (right wing or left wing) in various statements concerning the national army which were typical of right wing, moderate, left wing, and extreme left wing political policy. The statements are given below in full.

> *Right wing statement*: The national army is an essential guarantee of our freedom.
> *Moderate statement*: Say yes to national defence. Say no to an army of repression.
> *'Traditional' left wing statement*: The national army is a social weapon against workers.
> *Extreme left wing statement*: The army is a repressive device of the State opposing the dictatorship of the proletariat.

Table 2.6. *Mean judgements* (0 = *right wing*, 100 = *left wing*)

	Item			
	Right wing	Moderate	Left wing	Extreme left wing
Extreme subjects				
Deviance	19	51	57	70
Originality	04	56	79	95
Moderate subjects				
Deviance	11	48	83	88
Originality	25	55	83	78

Again, the subjects were led to believe that the purpose of the experiment was to assess personal tendencies towards either social originality or deviance, as in the previous experiment.

As could also be predicted from studies on social judgement (cf. Eiser and Stroebe, 1972; Eiser, 1984), the results obtained (cf. Table 2.6) showed that subjects who clearly stated they were 'left wing' polarized less in the deviance condition than in the originality condition, i.e. they made less extreme judgements, whereas subjects who stated they were moderate remained insensitive to this manipulation. It is true that the extreme subjects in this case would be the most apt to attribute themselves the originality or deviance characteristics that had been made salient, since such characteristics can only be applied to individuals with clearly defined positions, not to moderate individuals. It is therefore not surprising that the negatively connoted characteristics associated with the normative deviance context prevented 'extreme' subjects from fully specifying their position, unlike the originality context which enabled such specification. Hence the apparent paradox: the judgements of moderate individuals can be even more extreme than the attitudes of extreme individuals.

2.4.3 Influence and ethnocentrism
We have just ascertained that identification would be facilitated whenever positive evaluative connotations are associated with the definitional attributes of the minority. We previously saw that the influence exerted by a minority does indeed increase when an identity link in the form of a feeling of shared identity binds subjects and source. Let us combine these two assertions! Insofar as identification with a source, even a minority source, is psychologically defined by the self-attribution of the source's characteristics made salient within the influence relationship, and insofar as subjects tend in general to acquire or preserve a positive social identity (Turner, 1981), we must assume that identification with a source categorized as ingroup is preferable whenever the attributes assigned to it have positive

connotations. Let us take a look at a key experiment (Mugny, Kaiser, and Papastamou, 1983) which nicely brings together these two aspects and shows how categorization and connotations are interrelated.

Because this experiment uses a new paradigm, which will moreover be the basis of several other experiments reported here, it would be useful at this point to discuss the social and historical context of this study. In the seventies in Switzerland, there was a burst of popular interest in laws concerning the presence of foreigners and their legal status. The main characteristic of the various initiatives taken by the people was their fundamentally xenophobic nature; they in fact were the doing of political groups we could call the extreme right wing of Switzerland. Even though the local population was particularly sensitive to the problems posed by what was presented as 'foreign overpopulation', and despite the obvious existence of a slight undercurrent of xenophobia, none of the reforms managed to rally a majority of the votes. In 1974, one of the referendums which was particularly hard on foreigners was overwhelmingly rejected: Switzerland refused xenophobia.

The end of the seventies marked a turning point: organizations which at various levels had struggled against such xenophobic reforms began to take an offensive approach. This time, they began to make demands favouring foreigners, particularly workers in the 'seasonal' category. Seasonal workers have no guarantee that their residency and work permits will be renewed; furthermore, they are not allowed to bring their families with them, to mention only a few of the ways in which foreign seasonal workers are discriminated against. In 1977, a referendum entitled 'Let our common cause be new policies regarding foreigners' was proposed. Among its main points were the elimination of the seasonal worker status, free choice of job and residency, the right to bring one's family back together, and the guarantee of human rights and social security. This xenophilous reform was to receive the approval of many unions as well as political and religious organizations that coordinated their efforts in its support. The vote took place on April 5, 1981. The popular verdict was dramatic: the referendum was rejected by more than 80% of the voters. Swiss people are not xenophobic, nor are they xenophilous. The experiment we are going to present was conducted a few days before the vote.

In this paradigm, subjects first answer a question about how many foreigners they think there should be in Switzerland (cf. Appendix 7.2.1). They are told that the current percentage is approximately 16%, and their task is to choose a desirable percentage between 9% and 23% (in steps of 1%). The main purpose of this question is to classify the subjects as more xenophilous or more xenophobic.

In the second phase of the experiment, subjects read a one-page text in favour of foreigners, supposedly written by some militant persons belonging to a minority group. This text (see Appendix 7.2.2 as an illustration), which is clearly and one-sidedly xenophilous, varies by experiment or experimental condition, and contains either arguments grounded on very consensual values of a humanitarian nature ('to guarantee foreigners fundamental human rights') or arguments founded on more conflictual values of a sociopolitical nature ('to guarantee foreign workers the social rights to which all workers have a legitimate right'). The minority source text generally ends with several demands which favour foreigners to varying degrees (such as 'It should not be possible to send foreigners back to their country for economic reasons, notably in case of unemployment').

Several measures are then taken. After having read the minority text, subjects must first express to what extent they agree or disagree with the text they have just read (on a 7-point scale; see Appendix 7.2.3). They then must describe the minority on various scales (see Appendix 7.2.4 for an example) aimed at giving the experimenter a precise idea of the representation the subjects form of the minority source. Finally, subjects fill in an opinion questionnaire containing a sufficient range of questions to determine their attitude towards foreigners (cf. Appendix 7.2.5) and hence, to assess minority influence.

The experimentally induced effects are generally manipulated on the text reading phase. For the moment, let us look at two of the variables used in one experiment (Mugny *et al.*, 1983) involving nearly 400 subjects. The first variable pertained to the explicit categorization of the source, whose nationality (either Swiss or foreign) was mentioned at the top of the page of the questionnaire containing the minority text (all subjects were natives of Switzerland). To make this variable seem realistic, the texts were worded either 'We Swiss...' or 'We foreigners...' while the rest of the phrasing was kept constant.

Now, what about the connotations? The connotations were not introduced as such, but by means of psychologization, a particularly effective form of resistance to minority influence (cf. Mugny and Papastamou, 1980; Papastamou, 1983). To support our demonstration at this point in our theoretical development, we suggest psychologization be interpreted (cf. Mugny and Pérez, 1989b; see also Chapter 6) as the taking into account of the fact that such resistance to minority influence is generally manifested in target subjects by their assignment of specific, negatively connoted characteristics to the minority. In the task performed in all of the experimental conditions, the subjects were led to assume that there were links between the characteristics of the source, its mode of expression, and even the content of the ideas it expressed. In the psychologization conditions, however, the psychological nature of these characteristics was stated, and a causal link between the message content and the personality of the sources expressing that message was to be assumed by the subject;

in short, the subject was led to believe that the discourse could be explained by, even 'reduced to', the source's psychological characteristics (such as personality traits), which the subject was to guess. In conditions without psychologization, this link was not stated, nor was reference made to psychological characteristics.

The subjects' responses were input into a factorial analysis, first those pertaining to their attitude towards foreigners, then those expressing their impression of the minority. The results shown in Table 2.7 are the means obtained, by condition, for the factorial scores which gave rise to significant effects on the tested variables. To read this table, note that a positive sign means more minority influence and more assignment of positively connoted attributes; inversely, a negative sign means less influence and more negative connotations.

The first finding of interest to us here concerns the effects of categorization on evaluation. To illustrate, let us consider the most relevant factors of the minority image. First as could be expected, there was an ingroup favouritism bias on the ethnocentrism dimension, similar to Levine and Campbell's (1972) definition of the universal stereotype, causing the ingroup minority to be described as less aggressive, more confident, less self-centered, braver, and so on than the foreign minority. The same bias was observed for the self-interest dimension, wherein the native Swiss minority of course appeared more unselfish than the foreign minority making demands in its own interest. This bias was in effect on a virtually overall basis, since we can also see that the foreign minority was considered to be more rigid and xenophobic, or at least less xenophilous, than the ingroup minority. It is true that foreigners are always more 'racist' than we are!

Discrimination and ingroup favouritism were thus both clearly at work in the evaluation activity. It did not take much to trigger these biases since, in fact, the minority text was exactly *the same* in all cases, and only the source's nationality was needed to activate them. We can thus expect the influence phase to reproduce these same differentiations in an analogous manner, and to favour the native minority over the foreign minority.

Analysis of the influence scores showed that this was indeed true, at least in part, since the simple effect of this variable was not significant, and since it interacted with the psychologization variable. However, the greatest impact was indeed made by an ingroup minority. This occurred when psychologization was not induced and did not interfere with identification. When resistance to the ingroup minority was not induced, the favouritism bias was clearly observed. This was no longer true, however, when subjects psychologized, in which case the influence of the ingroup minority was reduced to that of the outgroup minority. Why?

The answer can be found by examining the image the subjects formed of the ingroup minority. The psychologization we proposed to the subjects

Table 2.7. *Attitude towards foreigners and image of the minority (a + sign indicates more influence or a more positive image)*

	Native minority		Foreign minority	
Psychologization	No	Yes	No	Yes
Attitude	+0.22	−0.09	−0.10	−0.03
'Ethnocentrism'	+0.30	+0.27	−0.24	−0.32
'Unselfishness'	+0.36	+0.27	−0.28	−0.34
'Flexibility'	+0.16	−0.01	−0.04	−0.11
'Xenophilia'	+0.23	+0.02	−0.14	−0.12

appears to have caused a substantial modification in the attributes assigned to the minority. Indeed, while the ingroup minority was judged positively compared to the outgroup minority along the ethnocentrism and lack of self-interest dimensions, this was not true for the flexibility and xenophilous-attitude factors. Not only was the psychologized ingroup minority perceived as more intolerant (than the non-psychologized ingroup minority), more closed-minded and dogmatic, in short, more rigid, but it was not considered to the same degree to convey an authentic xenophilous alternative. In other words, due to the induced psychologization, this minority group was assigned negatively connoted characteristics which constituted an obstacle to potential positive identification by virtue of shared national identity.

In summary, these results confirm the assertion that the ingroup favouritism bias observed at the evaluation level does in fact have its counterpart at the influence behaviour level, in compliance with the model of categorical differentiation. However, for such identification to take place and contribute to the redefinition of the subject's attitudes, it is also necessary that the minority attributes (other than those pertaining to the shared categorical identity) perceived by the target subjects – also subject to self-attribution – have positive connotations. This conclusion is inevitable, since positive ingroup influence of this sort is not obtained when the positively valued meanings associated with the minority by virtue of its categorization as ingroup are accompanied by negatively connoted meanings which alone can justify rejection of the alternative stance taken by that same minority.

2.5 Minority influence and identification conflicts

The above experiments illustrate a process that has been found repeatedly in the study of minority influence: positive identification with the source underlies and favours minority influence. Such a bias appears to be easy to counteract however by making negative evaluative connotations psychologically salient.

This is indeed what was suggested in the research by Marques, Yzerbyt, and Leyens (1988) on the black sheep effect, which is based on the hypothesis that judgements as to degree of (dis)likeability are more extreme in the ingroup than in the outgroup, causing the most appreciated ingroup members to be particularly well-liked, and the disliked ingroup members to be disliked even more than outgroup members. In one experiment, Belgian students were asked to use various descriptors to judge 'likeable' or 'dislikeable' Belgium (ingroup) or North African (outgroup...minority?) students. While the positively connoted ingroup was shown to be granted more upgrading judgements than the positively connoted outgroup, the negatively connoted ingroup, on the other hand, was shown to receive the most degrading judgements of all. Other findings also suggest that differences in judgements of individuals who abide by, or violate, a norm are especially observed when the individuals are ingroup members and the norm in question is definitional of membership in that group. Rejection of deviants – we have suspected this to be true since Schachter (1951) – indeed increases when they pose a threat to ingroup integrity, and is one way of reaffirming the positiveness of one's own identifications.

Martin (1987b) found a similar effect in his experiments using the paradigm presented in point 2.3.1. The minority, whether ingroup or outgroup by virtue of some arbitrary criterion, was shown to be granted negative or positive attributes when the experimenter told the subjects, 'We know from previous research that...[ingroup or outgroup members]...tend to be friendly, reliable, and intelligent, while...[outgroup or ingroup members]...tend to be unfriendly, unreliable, and not as intelligent...' The results obviously showed that the positively connoted sources were more influential than the negatively connoted ones. But more important in our mind is that the positive outgroup minority was found to exert more influence than the likewise positive ingroup minority (see also point 4.3.6). Looking a little more closely, the reasons for this become clear: owing to the manner in which the connotation variable was induced, not only was the outgroup minority positive, but its positiveness was defined relative to an ingroup minority which was consequently negatively connoted. Perhaps one possible conclusion would be that it is more compelling to differentiate oneself from a negatively connoted ingroup involving high identification costs than to be like a positively connoted ingroup.

In order for categorization of the source as ingroup to give rise to a favouritism bias, it must occur in conjunction with the salience of psychological attributes which do not infringe upon a potential accrediting identification for the target subjects. Yet we must agree that often the very minority identity of the source is a carrier of conflictual and negatively connoted attributes. The ingroup favouritism bias therefore no longer takes effect when negatively connoted attributes are made salient, since such connotations are incompatible with positive identification and thus create an obstacle to influence. This incompatibility itself in our minds defines what we consider to be an *identification conflict*. An extension of the intergroup model which would include such conflicts need thus be devised. It would amount to considering that over and above ingroup favouritism, whose potential existence has been demonstrated, resistance to change may well be even greater when the identity of the source lets target subjects assume that an identification is possible, and for one reason or another, introduces such identification conflicts.

2.5.1 Between favouritism and discrimination: the ingroup paradox

Let us take a look at some other findings from the above study (Mugny *et al.*, 1983) which point out that influence behaviour can stem from a process of differentiation that is all the more pronounced when the source is categorized as ingroup. Remember that in this experiment on attitudes towards foreigners, subjects were asked to read a text which defended an extremely xenophilous position in a tense and inter-ethnic context tainted with insidious xenophobia. Remember also that one of the measures, taken before any experimental induction, was used to differentiate the subjects by their initial attitude towards foreigners. Subjects were to state what percentage of foreigners they thought would be desirable for the country, and were told as an anchoring point that the current percentage was 16%. Only the following subjects will be considered here for the purpose of demonstration: the most clearly xenophilous ones who chose 16% or more (mean 17.42%), and the most clearly xenophobic ones who chose between 9% and 12% (mean 10.72%). The intermediate subjects will not be discussed.

The data pertaining to minority source representation (cf. Table 2.8) show that the most xenophobic subjects (the most strongly opposed to foreign residents and thus the most far-removed ideologically from the minority) rated the xenophilous native Swiss minority very highly on the ethnocentric dimension, judging it as less aggressive, more confident, generous, brave, and unprejudiced. As a corollary, they gave low ratings to the foreign minority, the intergroup difference being perceived as much greater than that existing elsewhere for even the most xenophilous subjects. At the evaluative level, then, an ingroup favouritism and outgroup discrimination bias did indeed exist, and was particularly strong in the most xenophobic subjects.

Table 2.8. *Attitude towards foreigners and ethnocentrism (a + sign indicates more influence or a more positive image)*

	'Xenophobic' subject		'Xenophilous' subject	
	Minority			
	Swiss	Foreign	Swiss	Foreign
'Ethnocentrism'	+0.43	−0.38	+0.20	−0.15
Attitude	−0.41	−0.24	+0.65	+0.24

The data indicating the extent of minority influence show that xenophilous subjects were more apt to accept the xenophilous message coming from the native minority than from the foreign minority. For these subjects, the evaluation bias was thus accompanied by ingroup favouritism at the behavioural level. Categorization, evaluation, and influence behaviour went hand in hand here, in accordance with the homology described in the model of categorical differentiation.

In contrast – and paradoxically – in their influence behaviour, xenophobic subjects reacted less adversely to the foreign source, even though they had judged them more negatively. Why didn't the homology principle take effect in these subjects? Positive evaluation of the minority as ingroup must be incompatible with negative evaluation of the xenophilous attitude itself. For the more xenophobic subjects, the only ideological position compatible with the ingroup identity was the 'protectionist' or 'patriotic' attitude favouring the Swiss and not foreigners. For these subjects, the apparent contradiction between categorization, evaluation, and influence behaviour only expressed their feeling of an identification conflict.

We might note in passing that influence obviously does not only result from the assignment of positive values to the source by virtue of some common categorical identity, even a particularly salient one. This is indeed what is suggested by the fact that an ingroup can be evaluated more positively than an outgroup, without necessarily leading to an analogous modification at the influence level. In the next chapter, we shall take the opportunity to come back to these effects, which break the homology principle in the categorical differentiation process.

2.5.2 The dissimilation effect
Identification conflicts are therefore possible, and can be all the more constraining for the targets when the source belongs to one of their own categories, or when some psychologically hindering 'proximity' forces them

to differentiate themselves from the source, i.e. to 'dissimilate' (Lemaine, 1975).

In connection with this, let us take a look at the basic idea behind the experiment by Lemaine, Lasch, and Ricateau (1971–2). This study dealt with the allokinetic effect, a variant of the autokinetic effect (Sherif, 1936). Subjects were asked to estimate the apparent distance moved by a minute illuminated dot in a totally dark space with no landmarks. They first defined their own personal standard by means of a few individual trials, and then underwent an attempted influence phase while a confederate informed by the experimenter gave answers that were either identical to, different from, or extremely different from those given by the subjects during the individual trials. Nothing particularly original so far!

The interest of this study lies in the fact that the experimenter also induced either a feeling of shared ideology between the confederate and the subject, or a feeling of differentiation, along a dimension which *a priori* appeared to be irrelevant to performing the perceptual task. To this end, right after the pre-test and before the actual influence phase, the subjects (all female students) were asked to 'help' another researcher by responding on three reduced scales designed to assess their degree of dogmatism, nationalism, and feminism. The confederate did likewise, in the presence of the 'real' subjects. Naturally, the examiner informed the subjects of their scores. Depending on the answers actually given by the subjects, this feedback gave them a correct image of themselves either as clearly dogmatic, nationalistic, and anti-feminist, in short, as right wing, or on the contrary, as clearly anti-dogmatic, anti-nationalist, and feminist, in short, as left wing. The experimentally manipulated variable was the induced image of the confederate, this time random: he was presented as either being on the same ideological side as the subjects, or on the opposing side. Following this categorization of the subject and confederate as ideologically similar or different, the allokinetic perceptual experiment was continued, with the confederate proposing identical, different, or extremely different answers from the subject's.

Let us summarize the effects! First, the confederate whose responses were extremely different from the subject's obtained the most influence, an additional proof of the conflict hypothesis in social influence processes (reflected here by the magnitude of response discrepancy). But the most interesting effect for us here is that in this condition of extreme perceptual deviation, the ideological categorization of the source had no effect; therefore, when the subjects' perceptual responses were very different, no identification risk was involved in being influenced by the confederate's responses, and hence, no identification conflict existed. Here, the very magnitude of the perceptual difference paradoxically thwarted any specific discrimination against the ideologically different confederate.

Things changed when a perceptual difference existed but was not as great. In this case, changing one's answer involved the risk of categorical 'confusion', and as could be expected the subjects tended to go along with the ideologically similar confederate more than with the ideologically opposing one. Granted, the observed discrimination did result from the categorization, but at the same time this implies that there was some degree of psychological proximity, as Turner *et al.* (1987) so extensively demonstrated. Why indeed would one attempt to make oneself different from someone who is already totally different from oneself, and in the end, totally incomparable? Intergroup biases are based on social comparison, and all comparisons require relative proximity in order to be feasible, even if that proximity is only symbolic.

We can thus easily imagine that this kind of differentiation would increase even more when a confederate with a different ideological position gives answers identical to those given by the subject. The consequence is that subjects begin to 'dissimilate' ('dissimulate?') by giving answers that are different from their own original answers in order to make sure they are different from the confederate's current answers. Literally chased out of their own response universe, subjects do not hesitate to modify their own perceptual judgement standards in an obvious attempt to define new boundaries that protect them from a threatening identification.

In short, the closer subjects are in some way or another to the source, the more the categorization process activates rejection phenomena. It is true that a comparison takes on significance when source and target *are* indeed comparable, i.e. when over and above their differences, they have some characteristics in common. Thus, if shared identity can sometimes bring source and target closer together, it can also on other occasions intensify the differentiation process (Lemaine, 1974). Roux (1988) found this situation paradoxical for minorities, stating 'Minority groups that aim to be influential and instrumental to change [...] often attempt to avoid involving their targets in an identification process: if this were not the case, they would run the risk of reinforcing pre-existing social cleavages and would most likely end up losing because of it' (our translation). We shall discuss the counterpart of this paradox later as we study the advantages minorities can sometimes acquire by having an outgroup identity (Pérez and Mugny, 1987).

2.5.3 Identification and regulation of membership
In the preceding experiments, identification referred to the self-attribution of characteristics associated with a minority source (judged to varying degrees to be deviant or original, progressive or conservative) and involved in accepting, or moving towards, the ideological stance of the minority. The subject's identification with the source was induced experimentally by

assigning same or different category membership, or by suggesting some degree of shared identity.

In the same line of reasoning, we assumed that whenever a potentially shared identity is explicitly inherent in the very adoption of the ideological positions invoked by the minority, the risk of possible identification will lead to more resistance to the minority, and will do so even more when the source is highly conflictual. This is one way of restating that in minority influence, the issue of identification is particularly conflictual, in contrast then to the previous studies which pointed out some of the conditions under which influence was facilitated.

In an experiment on attitudes towards foreigners (Mugny and Papastamou, 1982–3), subjects were asked to read a text whose content this time was xenophobic, in a context in which xenophobia would give rise to more negative connotations. Indeed, the referendums being proposed at that time were xenophobic. One variable was used to make salient either the flexible style and thus less conflictual nature, or the more rigid style and thus more conflictual nature, of the text. To vary the style, some of the paragraphs were changed across versions. The more conflictual version declared its unshakeable determination to fight against foreigners, and proposed several means of discrimination which according to the text's authors were to be applied with a great deal of firmness. In the less conflictual version, the rest of the xenophobic content was the same, but these few paragraphs (very assertive in the first version) were replaced by others in which the minority expressed its indecision and doubt as to the soundness of the discriminatory measures which in the conflictual version were viewed as justified and indispensable. To make sure the subjects interpreted these differences in terms of flexibility and rigidity, i.e. in terms of conflict, they were asked in addition to state their impression of the minority as to its flexibility (less conflictual condition), or rigidity (more conflictual condition).

Now, this brings us to the variable that makes this experiment original! To make psychologically salient the question of identification with the minority's ideological standpoint, subjects in half of the conditions were led to believe that the text was the political platform of the minority group, and that its advocates had to accept it fully and sign it in order to become full-fledged members. To make things seem realistic, an insert was added to the text for signing up new members. In the other conditions, subjects simply read the text.

The results (cf. Table 2.9, which separates subjects who were initially close and far from the source on the basis of their pre-test answers) showed that specifying the regulatory function of the minority text introduced the dynamics of both differentiation and approval. Although such regulation could indeed result in particularly strong rejection of the minority, it only

Table 2.9. *Mean change (a + sign indicates more influence)*

	Subjects	
	Far	Close
Without membership regulation		
Flexible style	+0.93	+0.12
Rigid style	+0.88	+0.74
With membership regulation		
Flexible style	+0.55	+1.67
Rigid style	+0.36	−0.30

did so for the rigid minority, i.e. the more conflictual one. The flexible minority on the other hand gained influence when this regulatory function was congruent with its behavioural flexibility. In addition, if we consider the resistance effect induced by regulating minority group membership, we can see that it was greater with subjects who were in fact ideologically closer to the minority. It looks as though these subjects felt compelled to accept the differences and even deny any similarities with the minority, and to assert in this manner, 'We have nothing to do with such points of view!' This, moreover, is an effect with which we are beginning to become familiar.

2.6 Identification as a model of minority influence

Thus, making target subject identification with the minority salient, whether by means of categorization, by psychologically creating a feeling of shared identity, or by proximity in ideology, leads to divergent effects, depending on the situation. In certain cases, minority influence is favoured, as predicted in social identity theory; in others, influence is thwarted, depending on the significations brought to bear in the real or symbolic collective encounters. This, moreover, is one of the first contributions of minority influence research to the model of intergroup relations.

The very existence of this series of potential, and apparently heterogeneous, effects has led us to propose a conception of social influence processes (in general, and minority-related in particular) whereby they are underlain by an identification mechanism. This conception makes it possible to account for these effects in a coherent manner. The core hypothesis behind it is that identification in fact constitutes the basic mechanism of the social comparison process – essentially of an intergroup nature – which is virtually always initiated by situations of social influence. We shall also defend the idea that this mechanism accounts for the influence exerted by minorities, especially in the case of its direct, immediate, or public expression.

Anticipating, we can already see that this mechanism alone does not suffice to account for conversion effects, and that its interrelationships with other notions must be defined. So let us have a look at the basics of this model!

In order to understand why the extent to which a source (and notably, a minority source) exerts influence varies, three complementary aspects of any identification process must be considered. The first deals with categorization of the influence source, the second, with the source's attributes, and the third, with the psychological expression of the relationship the subjects establish with the source on the basis of those attributes.

All influence processes imply an initial cognitive activity of an *inferential* nature. Indeed, influence targets are led to define the influence source (and themselves besides) as belonging to one or more groups or categories which are psychologically salient in their representation of the influence situation; in short, the source as well as the other entities distinguished by the target (including him/herself) are subject to a *categorization mechanism*. The categorizations of the social field, which govern influence relationships, in reality define the social entities upon which identification will be projected, and provide the matrix of possible identities delimiting intergroup spaces and boundaries. The very existence of such boundaries in a target subject's mind in itself already suffices to direct the identification process, and hence the process implemented to resolve the conflict inherent in the influence relationship. This may even be true regardless of the content of the alternative proposed by the minority: *one does not identify with just anybody,* whatever characteristics he or she might have, whether one approves of them or not. It must nevertheless be acknowledged that most of the time, identity matrices of this sort provide a framework for inserting and assigning meaning to the specific attributes which define the distinctiveness of each of the recognized entities.

Indeed, all identification processes imply a cognitive activity of an *inductive* nature. Influence targets know (through social stereotypes) and/or establish (according to the influence situation) the attributes they deem to be characteristic and definitional of both the minority and the other entities involved in the influence situation. This is done via what we shall consider an *indexation mechanism*. This inductive process is the means by which categories are 'filled' with meanings: *one is not inclined to take on just any attribute,* no matter what person it represents, and thus regardless of whether or not that person is categorized as ingroup. Here again, it must be acknowledged that most of the time, these attributes only take on meaning as a function of the entities they represent.

A given identity matrix is only heuristic, then, if it crosses categories and attributes and if a covariation can be cognitively established, a sort of mutual interdependence. This kind of dual-entry matrix is what will govern any potential identification and predict the outcome of the influence relationship. Moreover, it is through their very position in the matrix that the various alternative ideological positions, as fundamental attributes, take on psychological meaning.

Finally, all social influence processes imply a connotation activity of a *deductive* nature: in any influence situation, the socially manifest responses (i.e. direct influence) of subjects do not only reflect the extent to which they actually agree or disagree with the standpoints explicitly defended by the influence source, depending on the salience of some specific heuristic or peripheral element. They also, if not above all, reflect the degree to which the subjects are ready to accept psychosocial identification with the source, where such identification is psychologically defined by a *self-attribution mechanism* through which the subjects appropriate not only the specific response expressed by the source, but also the stereotypical and/or constructed characteristics made salient during the interaction and considered to be definitional of the category in which the source (here, the minority) has been assigned membership.

As a corollary, the absence of influence, or differentiation from the source, implies the redefinition of the intergroup boundaries and space, essentially in order to preserve a previous identification, or to establish a new breakdown of the categorical field to allow for a new identification, also positive in that it eliminates the risk of identification with the source. In all cases, a comparison process underlies the dynamics of manifest influence.

In what ways does this conceptualization aid in establishing some order in the diverse and multiple forms in which minority influence may or may not be manifested?

First, conceptualization in this manner enables us to easily account for the fact that a minority categorized by targets as an outgroup exerts little influence, or is even subject to rejection, since targets refuse to self-attribute the definitional characteristics of an entity in which they cannot recognize some part of themselves.

It consequently also enables us to understand why the impact of a minority can increase when it is categorized as ingroup: if the attributes that define the minority have positive connotations, identification with it implies the self-attribution of characteristics that are compatible with a positive identity or self-image.

Finally, it also explains the reverse effect, which can occur when an ingroup minority is assigned attributes that are incompatible (or perceived as such by the subjects) with its own identity and can lead to an identification conflict. In this event, a minority may even be at an advantage if accorded an outgroup identity.

In short, we can see that minority influence (especially when direct, as shown below) is thwarted when either the involved identification bears a symbolic social cost, or the minority source is in fact categorized as outgroup. Given that the last two cases are frequent – at least we have the right to assume they are – for minorities in conflictual innovation contexts, we can better understand why direct or public influence by a minority is often difficult to obtain, and is at the very least masked at the manifest social expression level.

Various causes, depending on the situation, may be behind the fact that targets sometimes engage in identification with the minority, and sometimes refuse to do so, in which case there must be an identification conflict 'somewhere'. Several aspects of the minority influence context affect these diverse facets of identification.

The first set of factors of course pertains to the explicit categorization of the minority, which on certain occasions is classified as ingroup, and on others, as outgroup. We have come across enough examples of this in the preceding pages to make it worth mentioning again.

The second set of factors, as we have seen, pertains to the behaviour styles of the source, in particular, its style of negotiation. The processes of categorization and indexation obviously act simultaneously here, even if it is heuristic to differentiate them. Thus, in our studies on flexible and rigid negotiation, which have systematically shown that a flexible style gives rise to more influence (direct, at least), we were led to conclude that rigidity results in resistance to influence for two complementary reasons. First, rigidity may induce a feeling of categorical overexclusion in target subjects due to the perception of the minority as clearly outgroup, whereas flexibility may allow targets to perceive some common identity with the source despite their ideological divergence, and may thus have a greater effect through the interplay of their somehow overlapping categorical memberships (Deschamps, 1977; Deschamps and Doise, 1978; Deschamps and Clémence, 1987). In a complementary fashion, by inducing the attribution of negatively connoted characteristics to the minority (negatively connoted and so strongly saturated that all negotiation is blocked, cf. Ricateau, 1970–1), rigidity may imply more difficult or conflictual psychosocial identification than flexibility, due to a lesser degree of compatibility with the individual's search for (or maintenance of) a positive identity.

The third set of relevant factors includes normative filters for apprehending the minority (Mugny and Papastamou, 1984). We have already seen how influence may be facilitated when perception of the minority is filtered through the originality norm (interpretation of the minority as innovative), and how on the contrary, a context which makes the deviant aspect of the minority salient is likely to thwart any potential influence (here, the minority is interpreted in terms of the deviation it presupposes relative to an established norm).

A fourth and final facet is constituted by the various forms of resistance to innovation, in particular ideological resistance, such as psychologization (Papastamou, 1983, 1987b) or denial, which will not be examined here since their dynamics will be discussed in later chapters.

It is evident that the outcome of the minority influence process depends upon the interplay of these diverse factors, made salient in the situation under consideration, and all the possible combinations of them should be considered, each with its own specific consequences upon the influence the minority will actually be granted.

This model of identification clearly accounts for the difficulty – but not impossibility – facing minorities attempting to exert direct and immediate influence, insofar as they tend outright (or at least initially during the revelation phase of the innovative process; cf. Moscovici, 1985a) to give rise to what we shall consider an 'anti-minority bias', generated by the strong social conflict that, by definition, any attempt to innovate elicits. This anti-minority bias is the result of the conjunction of these factors: the minority's behaviour styles are first perceived as particularly rigid and conflict-ridden; this causes the minority to be attributed negative characteristics resulting from its apprehension essentially in terms of deviance, which in turn leads to its categorization as outgroup.

It is this model of identification as a mechanism of influence that accounts for the process of social comparison at the theoretical level, and for direct and manifest influence effects at the experimental level. This is the model we shall attempt to interconnect with other mechanisms that account for the validation process at the theoretical level and conversion effects at the experimental level. But we must proceed in order, and in the next chapter, we shall start by examining some of the discrepancies in the social logic of anti-minority discrimination.

3   The limits of discrimination

The intergroup model of minority influence developed in the previous chapter accounts not only for the advantage a minority draws, at least at the manifest or public level, from being categorized as ingroup and/or being evaluated positively, but also for the disadvantage it incurs by inducing an identification conflict. In some respects, this model accounts for the socio-cognitive mechanisms by means of which individuals resist innovation, and explains the social status quo in terms of discrimination against innovating entities. As a corollary, to interpret positive minority influence, this model assumes the existence of a privileged relationship between source and target. This relationship takes on the form of a not too conflictual identification, since in the event of an identification conflict, any shared identity leads to even greater rejection. In all of these cases, it is the relationship established between source and target that defines the direction of the influence, the content itself of the minority message only playing a secondary role in the end. In short, a social comparison process of an intergroup nature predominates.

3.1 Behavioural rhetoric and categorization

In order to develop a theory that integrates minority influence and intergroup research, it is nevertheless necessary to go beyond simply searching for the obstacles that intergroup dynamics create in the face of innovation. This has been the focal point of the greater part of recent research on minorities (cf. Doms, 1987; Maass and Clark, 1984; Moscovici, 1987; Papastamou, 1983, 1987a), in which it is generally agreed that minorities are usually socially perceived as outgroup, and negatively judged, degraded, ''psychologized', etc. Indeed, if we take a one-sided look at innovation through the ingroup favouritism and outgroup discrimination biases, and if we assume as a consequence that influence depends essentially on the favourable or unfavourable evaluations associated with the source, then we necessarily find ourselves in an impasse, since the very fact that minorities consistently break away from the dominant ideological norms and values nearly always results in their classification as outgroup in the category field. In short, minorities bring together the necessary and sufficient criteria to be the object of discrimination and stigmatization.

Yet we know that minorities still manage to obtain social impact and upset norms. Since this impact cannot result from social approval or target dependency upon the minority, then what explanation can be given of it? Note first of all that one of the characteristics of the intergroup model is that categorization and its resulting biases are considered in a somewhat static manner, as if categorizations were 'simple' (not overlapping), relatively stable, and impervious to new information. In reality, stereotypes can change, owing either to the gradual accumulation of data contradicting them or to the fact that subjects become suddenly and acutely aware of their inadequacy (cf. Weber and Crocker, 1983). The specificity of minorities is precisely that they actively intervene in the social field, perhaps in a somewhat unpredictable fashion, and that their rhetoric questions initial categorizations, sometimes going so far as to falsify certain prejudices (Roux, 1988). This framework may help us to understand why several experiments (cf. Personnaz and Personnaz, 1987) have shown that influence often sets in gradually, even during submission to the attempt to influence.

Although influence behaviours are indeed accounted for at certain levels by the model of intergroup relations, we must find the remaining links in the causality chain in order to genuinely interrelate the intergroup model and the interactionist model of influence. This will require going further, this time taking intergroup relations as dependent variables, and social influence as an independent variable.

Concretely speaking, the reciprocal effects of social influence on intergroup dynamics will be studied from two complementary angles. The first will consist of restoring to minorities their major device: behaviour and negotiation styles, i.e. their ability to generate and manage conflict (Moscovici and Mugny, 1983). The second will involve no longer considering minority impact where it is impeded, but rather where it is apt to be released: at the latent and indirect level typical of conversion.

In order to vary these intergroup dynamics, we must introduce the essential psychosocial resources available to minorities when expressing themselves and making themselves heard, namely styles of behaviour (Moscovici, 1976). If behaviour styles can cause resistance to the conflict they initiate, then they should in turn be able to act positively and induce influence. This implies acknowledging that minorities have the ability to introduce new meanings likely to break the social logic of prejudice and anti-minority discrimination. In other words, the notion of conflict must be reinstated in the intergroup model, in the same manner as it is formulated in the interactionist model of influence. This will allow us to consider other ways of treating intergroup conflict than just through ingroup favouritism and ethnocentrism, and to go beyond the principle of simple social reproduction. We shall see that the specificity of minority conflict resolution modes lies in social constructivism, manifested in particular in the potential occurrence of indirect influence, even in favour of sources that at the same time are discriminated against.

The outline of this chapter will be based on developments in recent research. We shall first demonstrate that neither ingroup favouritism nor outgroup discrimination is inevitable. By presenting a series of related studies, we shall show that a given minority does not exert influence simply because it is categorized as ingroup rather than outgroup, but that its impact also depends upon the negotiation styles it employs, its categorical identity only determining the range within which the intensity of the conflict it introduces must fall. The idea here is that when categorized as ingroup, a minority can use, and may even profit from using, an uncompromising style that increases the amount of conflict, whereas a minority categorized as outgroup may be better off employing a more negotiating style which attenuates the conflict (or at least does not increase it).

Past research (cf. Moscovici, Mugny, and Van Avermaet, 1985) has taken for established the fact that a minority, when consistent, is influential whenever its specificity and distinctiveness is recognized, which in our point of view means whenever it is categorized as outgroup. We shall show that this very same categorization has the paradoxical effect of increasing the amount of indirect and/or delayed influence, in short, of inducing a conversion process. The categorization of the minority as ingroup or outgroup can thus also have indirect influence effects that are the reverse of those predicted in the theory of intergroup relations. Another research trend will be used to show that even when categorized as outgroup and subject to 'open' discrimination, a minority is nevertheless capable of inducing influence, though of an indirect, private, or delayed nature.

This chapter will thus be devoted to presenting the ways in which our approach breaks away from the strict application of the intergroup model to minority studies (cf. Turner, 1981). Rather than aiming for in-depth coverage, we shall attempt to mark the main points, in view of proposing a genuine link between the direct influence of minorities and their latent impact. Moreover, the general model presented in the upcoming chapters is an attempt to account for all of the effects observed. But first, let us examine the reasons for doing so!

3.2 Categorization and degree of freedom

Let us begin by taking a look at the research dealing with the relationship between the intensity of the involved conflict, which generally varies as a function of the style employed by the minority, and the degree of influence it exerts when categorized as ingroup or outgroup in the context of an intergroup relationship.

3.2.1 Influence as a function of conflict intensity

According to the interactionist model, it is the conflict induced by a minority that is responsible for its impact. According to the intergroup model, the cause is the identification of the minority as ingroup, since intergroup conflict is supposed to oppose such influence. Although these two conceptions are radically opposed, we shall propose an initial reconciliation, which is only possible if rather than regarding influence as an increasing linear function of conflict intensity, we consider it in reality to be a quadratic function in which, after reaching the point of maximum influence corresponding to the point of optimal conflict, the curve begins to decrease. We shall see, moreover, that rather than representing a simple conflict rate, the curve has intensity thresholds, each corresponding to a different type of conflict. Most of the work done in the area of minority influence (cf. Moscovici and Mugny, 1987) suggests that a low level of source-initiated conflict is insufficient to produce influence. One proof of this is that minority inconsistency, manifested by a sort of avoidance or attenuation of the conflict, prevents the minority from imposing its views – all experiments comparing consistent and inconsistent styles converge in this respect (cf. in particular Moscovici, 1976; Mugny, 1975b).

In contrast, when at its maximum, the conflict is too intense to allow for any perceivable modification in favour of the minority position. Total blocking of negotiations was shown to be one of the possible outcomes of maximum conflict in Schachter's famous experiment (1951), and was again brought into the light by Doise and Moscovici (1969). In these examples, an obviously deviant accomplice who persevered consistently with the same attitude was nevertheless rejected in the end. Moreover, it was in view of explaining this paradoxical minority influence effect – paradoxical because consistency failed under these conditions to have the effect predicted in the conflict theory – that we first began our research in this area. And our first findings indeed showed that when the degree of consistency is kept constant, a rigid negotiation style can lead to the rejection of the minority by blocking negotiation and thus increasing the conflict (Mugny et al., 1972–3).

Thus, the minority influence process takes effect when the amount of conflict is optimal and intermediate. This is the idea that the discovery of flexibility effects led us to formulate (Mugny, 1982). We have often found that a minority not only is better off exhibiting behavioural consistency in its antagonism of the dominant norm, which already gives it the potential for creating considerable conflict, but also profits from negotiating to a certain extent with the population so as to attenuate the conflict inherent in its consistent opposition (Mugny, 1975a).

As we progressed through our research, however, we became aware of the danger of making hasty generalizations concerning these effects. For example, we found that over and above the fact that a flexible style tended to favour minority influence, flexibility effects, like rigidity effects, were sometimes positive and sometimes negative, depending on the meanings granted to the situations we designed (Mugny, 1982). All things considered, influence appears to be a quadratic function (an inverted U) of conflict intensity (Mugny and Pérez, 1985), as summarized in figure 3.1. This function suggests that in order for a minority to be influential, it must indeed induce conflict, neither too much nor too little.

Of course, the above curve is only a heuristic, and the problem becomes determining the significance of the inflection points on the curve before and after which minority influence decreases. Let us now take a look at a few examples.

3.2.2 Negotiation style and the feeling of shared identity

The styles employed by the minority (for an analysis of some available rhetoric styles, see Pérez, Roux, and Mugny, 1989) are relevant parameters for determining these inflection points, which depend on whether the targets identify or do not identify with the minority. As we initially suspected, accentuation of the conflict, and hence of psychological source–target distance, may promote the influence of a minority with which one identifies, while hindering that of a minority with which one does not. This is indeed what Nemeth and Endicott (1976) suggested when they showed that an increase in the distance between source and target increases the influence of sources on the same side of the ideological issue as that initially favoured by the subject (sources which may be perceived as more ingroup), and decreases the influence of sources taking the other side (apt to be categorized as outgroup).

Let us take an initial example! Remember that in one of the above experiments (Mugny and Papastamou, 1982; see point 2.3.3), we induced a strong feeling of minority-target shared category membership by making the targets believe they had five out of eight social identities in common, or

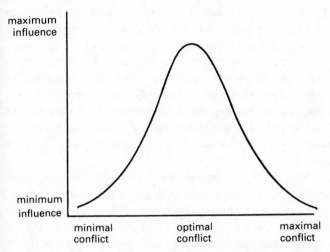

Figure 3.1 Hypothetical curve plotting influence as a function of conflict intensity

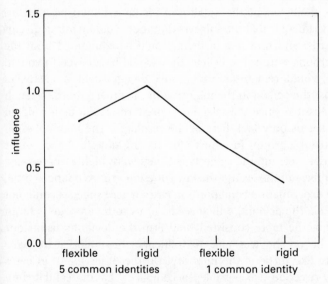

Figure 3.2 Opinion change (a higher number indicates more influence)

a weak feeling of identification by making them believe they only had one of the eight identities in common. Another variable was the negotiation style of the minority group, which was either more flexible or more rigid, i.e. more conflictual.

The results (see figure 3.2) indicate that these two variables interact. When the source was perceived as being more 'ingroup' (five common identities), it had more influence when its style was rigid than when it was flexible. However, when the source was perceived as more 'outgroup' (a single common identity), it was more influential with a flexible style than a rigid one. Even though in this experiment, the source perceived as ingroup was more influential on an overall basis than the source perceived as outgroup, the results suggest that ingroup minorities have a greater degree of freedom than outgroup minorities, since the former can present itself as more conflictual, while the latter has to rely on negotiation, in this case of an ideological nature, in order to attenuate the conflict induced by its outgroup identity.

We used this same reasoning to interpret the results of Wolf's experiment (1979), where negotiation was more formal: in jury simulation situations, groups of four were supposed to make a decision concerning the damages to be paid to a plaintiff. In each group, one 'accomplice' proposed a sum of money that was much smaller than the one recommended by the majority of subjects. In half of the cases, the 'accomplice' remained consistent until the end of the allotted time, whereas in the other half, he or she finished by expressing some doubt about the validity of his or her own position. In addition, the experimenter told the subjects that they would work in groups of three afterwards, and that one of them would be eliminated from the group; certain groups were led to believe they would be allowed to vote to determine who would remain in the group, giving them a means of retaliation against the person in the minority. In the other groups, no such retaliation was possible since the selection procedure was to be a random name drawing. Let us only look here at the results for the high-cohesion groups, which are the groups in which after having described each other following an initial meeting, the subjects felt they were highly appreciated by the other members of the group (the low cohesion groups changed little, regardless of the experimental condition). In cases where subjects could not voluntarily exclude the deviant, which seems to us to be analogous to an ingroup condition, the more consistent and firm the deviant's behaviour was, the more he or she was able to influence the majority to make judgements more like those of the minority. On the other hand, in cases where voluntary rejection was possible, 'accomplices' having exhibited an inclination to negotiate obtained more influence. Although this experiment was not conducted within the theoretical framework we are using here, and although the notions of ingroup and outgroup were not introduced, the response pattern obtained seems to provide a good argument in favour of the hypothesis that specific degrees of behavioural freedom can be granted in different situations.

3.2.3 Ideological negotiation and categorization

To convince ourselves of these effects, let us take another example. In this experiment, categorization as ingroup and outgroup was introduced in a dichotomous manner on the basis of the national identity of the subjects and of the minority; conflict intensity was controlled by varying the ideological argumentation supporting the claims. We asked (Mugny *et al.*, 1984) several hundred subjects to state to what extent they agreed with a few claims, all of which were favourable to foreigners and proposed by a minority source. The subjects were either native Swiss or foreign, as was the minority itself. Another variable considered was whether the claims were justified in humanitarian terms, which was supposed to constitute conflict-attenuating negotiation since humanitarianism is a widely recognized human value, or in sociopolitical terms, a source of more intense conflict since this ideology is not universally supported (see for example Appendix 7.2.2). The results are presented in Table 3.1.

One of the effects obtained was that foreign subjects stated they were more in favour of the claims pleading in their favour than native subjects were. This means that intergroup differentiation was obviously in effect here, and was the quite logical combination of an ingroup favouritism bias on the part of the foreigners and/or a discrimination bias on the part of the natives.

However, if we look at the results from the standpoint of influence source nationality, which is what interests us the most here, it is evident that we cannot conclude on an overall basis that the native minority obtained more influence than the foreign minority. At the influence behaviour level, then, no systematic favouritism or discrimination bias was observed in native subjects or foreign subjects, whose undeniable integration into Swiss society (these were young 'second generation' immigrants) explains why they tend to function like the native Swiss.

Some differences between conditions were found, however. First, the native source obtained more influence when it gave sociopolitical justifications to its claims, that is, when it increased the amount of conflict. The foreign source, on the contrary, obtained more influence when it negotiated the conflict by presenting humanitarian justifications, with which subjects already agreed. These results indeed replicate the findings of the experiment by Mugny and Papastamou (1982; see point 3.2.2), even though the experimental paradigms differ radically.

Finally, looking in detail at the data given in Table 3.1, we can see that these effects, which hold true on the whole, were particularly marked for certain subjects. Concretely speaking, the effects were stronger for native subjects and weaker for foreigners, who were torn between a *de facto* identification with Switzerland, where most of them had spent their entire childhood, and with their legal status as foreigners. Also, the effects were

Table 3.1. *Extent of agreement with xenophilous claims (the higher the number, the more xenophilous)*

		Subjects			
		Swiss	Foreign	Close	Far
Source	Claims				
Swiss	Humanitarian	3.84	5.19	4.95	3.97
	Sociopolitical	4.34	5.39	5.47	4.14
Foreign	Humanitarian	4.16	5.28	5.28	3.87
	Sociopolitical	3.88	5.11	4.99	3.71

Table 3.2. *Extent of agreement with xenophilous claims (the higher the number, the more xenophilous)*

		Claims	
		Humanitarian	Sociopolitical
Source			
Biblical	Desirable	4.89	5.35
	Imperative	5.76	5.22
Political	Desirable	5.55	5.20
	Imperative	4.96	5.40

very strong for subjects who were ideologically the closest to the source. What did these two kinds of subjects have in common? The effects can be considered to have been stronger when the salience of the identification issue was greater, placing the target subjects in a context of challenging intergroup conflict. This was true for the native subjects, for whom the source was more conflictual since it challenged them precisely with respect to their national identity. For these subjects, the social comparison was necessarily highly salient. For a reason which is slightly different, this was also true for the subjects who were ideologically closer the minority, since for them, the possibility of self-attribution of the minority characteristics was the most plausible due to the fact that their ideological proximity made 'categorical confusion' possible, the kind of confusion that should be avoided in cases where personal identity might be prejudiced.

Beyond all doubt, the striking fact revealed by this experiment is that there was no systematic bias favouring the minority in accordance with its categorization as ingroup or outgroup, but rather an interaction with the style it employed. This supports the idea that the degree of identification is not the only parameter of influence, and that it acts in conjunction with the intensity of the conflict introduced by the minority, an assertion which is consistent with the inverted U-curve model. These results suggest that source categorization cannot be treated as a frozen, mechanistic process: through their behavioural rhetoric, minorities can hinder the functioning of categorization.

3.2.4 Ideological discourse and psychosocial regulations

In the next experiment, identification with the minority (categorized as ingroup or outgroup) was induced in yet another manner. This was done by having the minority present a definitional or non-definitional argumentation of the identity of the group involved in the study. We also wanted to determine the effectiveness of negotiation, defined this time in more formal terms, since it concerned the flexibility of the regulation implicit in the minority discourse. The hypothesis was of course that formal negotiation would enable an outgroup minority to have an impact but not an ingroup, and vice versa for formal intransigence, which was introduced here by stating the restricting and obligating nature of membership in the group to which the discourse was assigned.

To create this set-up, all the subjects questioned were Christians (Mugny and Pérez, 1985). We might add that although our subjects are ordinarily young people, the sample in this experiment also included a large proportion of adults, some of whom were close to retirement. The subjects, all being challenged as Christians, read a text supposedly written by a xenophilous minority that was also Christian. However, in half of the conditions, the minority referred only to passages from the Bible, and can be considered to have been ingroup. In the other half, the minority who still claimed to be Christian, only relied on political arguments, which we can consider to be more outgroup, since political argumentation is generally disapproved in this milieu. The minority was therefore at the outskirts of the Christian ingroup, on the borderline of outgroup categorization.

In addition, in half of the cases, the minority defended humanitarian principles which were fundamentally definitional of Christian identity, being an explicit part of its ideological grounds. In the other half, the minority made sociopolitical claims, which were more radical and ideologically removed since, among other things, they advocated equality of political rights for foreigners.

This brings us finally to the third source of conflict. For half of the subjects, the minority presented its claims as simply 'desirable' (formal negotiation), a style which is in accordance with the typical constraints of the Christian circles under consideration. For the other half of the subjects, the claims were presented as 'absolutely indispensable to all Christians worthy of that title' (formal intransigence), a style which is more typical of political ideologies. The reader can get an idea of the texts by referring to Appendix 7.2.2.

The first series of results (cf. Table 3.2), obtained from the questionnaire on attitudes towards foreigners (cf. Appendix 7.2.5) that the subjects filled in following the experiment, confirms what we suggested above: on the whole, the 'biblical' source, more ingroup than the other, turned out to be more influential when it increased the conflict by insisting upon the strongly restricting nature of membership in the church group than when it attenuated the conflict by presenting it as simply desirable, allowing the individual the freedom to choose. However, the political source, a borderline case for outgroup categorization, was more effective if it did not mention this highly restricting nature and decreased conflict by its compromising style ('desirable') than when it held a peremptory discourse ('indispensable').

Note also that these effects, which are consistent with the quadratic function assumed to represent the relationship between influence and conflict intensity, only held true for the humanitarian claims. The differences were not as great in the conditions where the demands were sociopolitical and also highly conflictual, as indicated by other measures (cf. Mugny and Pérez, 1985). This finding is of interest in that, at a different level and in a different manner, the observed effects confirm those found in the previous experiment: the dynamics of integration or differentiation took effect here when the subjects – who, remember, were all Christians – were challenged by humanitarian and humanist claims that were more obviously definitional of the ideology of the church group to which they were affiliated. When this was not the case (sociopolitical demands), only the content of the message was significant, and the processes of identification resulting from the crossed effects of categorization and style did not modify the influence dynamics. We shall come back to this topic in a later chapter.

It is definitely true, then, that even direct or manifest minority influence can lead to diversified, yet coherent effects, and may or may not trigger an identification process of varying social costs for the subjects. These dynamics are indeed all the more complex when they involve social comparison that explicitly challenge the identity of the targets, a situation which exists whenever the attributes that are the object of the influence are clearly, almost consciously, definitional of some previously sought and desired identity (here, Christian) and whenever the psychologically and personally concerned or involved targets engage their identity and (re)define it through their new responses.

The outcome of an attempt to influence therefore does not depend irrevocably upon how the minority is categorized. In the classical approach – if we may call it that – two aspects are considered simultaneously:

ideological content, which functions by way of specific attributes, and the categorical division of the field. An anti-norm content classifies the minority in the deviant, ideological outgroup category. The magnitude of the deviation decreases whenever there is some shared category membership which somehow compensates for the differences in content, and increases whenever there is an additional categorization which reinforces ideological differentiation (see Maass and Clark's 'double minorities', 1983). To escape from the 'fatality' of these intergroup dynamics, a third element must be introduced: rhetorical behaviour. This means assuming that categorization does not function in a monolithic fashion, like a bias that is either purely cognitive, or due to some 'sociological load' that reproduces social differentiations.

It is behaviour style that effects and modifies categorizations, activating them or neutralizing them, if not recomposing them altogether. Through one's behaviour style, categorizations and contents, until then simply juxtaposed and unchangeable, are linked together and placed in full interaction. Behaviour styles, as we shall see in the next chapter, can falsify such juxtapositions and redefine new identity matrices, thus making intergroup relations dynamic.

3.3 The indirect effects of categorization

The argument we shall now develop will be simple, even if it goes against what is generally believed about influence and categorization: various experimental findings force us to conclude that minority influence, especially when indirect, can also paradoxically result from categorization of the minority as outgroup.

This paradox will in fact be considered as characteristic of the influence of minority groups: in order to appear as alternatives, minorities must necessarily exhibit consistency (Moscovici, 1976) and be recognized as such (Nemeth and Wachtler, 1974). And all alternatives, by definition, are perceived as being different, namely from the majority (in short, are necessarily categorized as outgroup), at least along the dimension upon which its distinctiveness is based. As such, alternatives prevent, or at the very least limit, their own direct influence, but can on the other hand exert indirect or delayed influence. But let us get on with some of the supporting arguments!

3.3.1 The private influence of outgroups

Let us first come back to the experiments conducted by Martin (1987b) who showed how responses expressed publicly are highly affected by an ingroup favouritism bias working in favour of the source whenever it is perceived as ingroup rather than outgroup. Remember that in these experiments (see point 2.3.1) subjects were to give their opinions as to the size of the scholarships to be granted to students wishing to continue their schooling, and were confronted with the position of a source belonging to either their same category or a different category and advocating a much higher amount than the subjects. In the public response conditions, the subjects thought they would participate later in a discussion in which their standpoint would necessarily become known. In the private response conditions, they thought their responses would remain unknown, since they placed them in a ballot box. Depending on the experiment, the categorization of the source as ingroup or outgroup was done on the basis of whether the source was said to be enrolled in the same school as the subjects or another negatively connoted school, according to the subjects' sex identity, or on the basis of some other minimal arbitrary criterion.

In all cases, the same dual effect occurred (cf. Martin, 1987b): when responses were given in public, the ingroup was preferred to the outgroup via the well-known favouritism bias. What is not familiar here is the disappearance of this effect when the responding was done in private, in which case the amount of influence actually observed was generally greater. Not only was an outgroup discrimination bias no longer in effect, but the outgroup even obtained more influence in this case than the ingroup. Granted, this effect was not statistically significant. However, its psychological significance is undeniable, and shows that although the favouritism bias takes effect in public, it does not necessarily do so in private, where an outgroup source may be more influential.

These surprising results, rarely found in the literature on persuasion or attitude change, are not isolated, as our own research has confirmed (see also Abrams and Hogg, 1990). Accordingly, Aebischer, Hewstone, and Henderson (1984) used aesthetic material to study the preferences of adolescents for hard rock (preferred by the subjects), new wave, and contemporary music. During the experimental phase, subjects were told that 80% of the students enrolled either in highschool (ingroup source, since all the subjects were highschool students) or in vocational school (preparing for less prestigious careers) preferred new-wave music, a different choice from that usually made by the type of subjects used in this experiment. Direct influence was considered to have been exerted when there was greater preference for new-wave music, and indirect influence, when there was greater preference for contemporary music, which is homologous to new-wave music along several parameters. The results of interest to us here are that although at the direct level, the percentage of influenced responses did not depend on the ingroup or outgroup nature of the new-wave alternative source, there was a difference at the indirect level, where the outgroup source obtained more responses favouring contemporary music than the ingroup source.

In another paradigm pertaining to aesthetic judgements, Doise *et al.* (1986) also found that although an anti-norm, ingroup source exerts more direct influence than an outgroup source, especially when the context brings out the intergroup nature of the influence relationship (cf. point 2.3.2), an outgroup source can nevertheless induce more latent influence. In short, a conflictual source, even if it is outgroup, is capable of having an impact, essentially manifested at the indirect level.

3.3.2 Outgroup minorities and delayed influence

Martin's research has shown that outgroup minorities obtain more private impact, despite the fact that they are rejected publicly. The research done by Aebischer *et al.* suggests that the influence of outgroup sources may also indeed be of an indirect nature. Before attempting to explain these effects, which are convergent despite the differences in the materials used, the experimental stimuli, and the induced categorizations, let us look at another way of observing the 'shifted' but existent impact of minorities categorized as outgroup, this time in the form of delayed influence, analogous to the phenomenon called the *sleeper effect* (cf. Cook and Flay, 1978; Moscovici, Mugny and Papastamou, 1981; Pratkanis, Greenwald, Leippe, and Baumgardner, 1988).

In this experiment which has already been discussed in regards to another topic (Mugny *et al.*, 1983), remember that subjects were confronted with an extremely pro-foreigner point of view. The only conditions we shall discuss at this point are those where there was no additional induced resistance and no psychologization. These conditions varied along two parameters: the minority was either native (i.e. ingroup) or foreign (i.e. outgroup), and it supported xenophilous demands by presenting arguments that tended to be either humanitarian and humanist (and thus less conflictual, as we have seen), or 'social' and sociopolitical (and thus more conflictual in the milieus under consideration).

As shown by the data given in Table 3.3 pertaining to the subjects' answers on an immediate post-test, an overall ingroup favouritism bias was found in the opinions expressed (that is, at the influence level) and in the image of the source, which will not be discussed in detail here (see point 2.4.3). In other words, on the whole the minority that was explicitly categorized as ingroup (native source) made a better impression and obtained more immediate influence than the minority that made the same claims but was categorized as outgroup (foreign source).

But, things changed with time. Two weeks later, we re-assessed the subjects' attitudes towards foreigners (without having them reread the

Table 3.3. *Agreement on first post-test, and delayed influence (the higher the number, the more xenophilous)*

	Ingroup minority		Outgroup minority	
	Humanitarian	Social	Humanitarian	Social
Post-test 1 agreement	5.48	5.43	5.15	4.98
Delayed influence	−0.33	−0.30	+0.11	−0.26

minority claims) in order to test for delayed influence. Delayed influence was indeed found, as can be seen in Table 3.3, which also reports shifts towards the minority standpoints occurring between the immediate post-test and the deferred post-test. Note that it was the foreign minority, i.e. the outgroup minority, despite its negative connotations and its weaker immediate influence, that was the beneficiary of such a *sleeper effect*. Granted, this was only true in cases where the minority argued for a not-too-conflictual position and defended humanitarian arguments (and where it also did not give rise to strong initial resistance, given that when psychologization was introduced, other dynamics thwarted conversion). This delayed effect did not occur with more conflictual sociopolitical argumentation, which suggests that the inverted U-curve may also apply to latent influence levels. Conversion, we may now conclude, also runs into obstacles!

Up until now, we have simply ascertained that a minority group, even when categorized as outgroup, is capable of exerting influence that is 'shifted' with respect to manifest influence, resulting in a private, indirect, or delayed impact. This phenomenon still remains to be explained, which we shall do in detail in the next chapter. Note however that the subjects' image of the minority in this experiment provides a clue for further study. Although as we have seen, outgroup minorities are the victims of an evaluation bias which is highly unfavourable to them on an overall basis (compared to the ingroup minority), some of their qualities are nevertheless recognized. Therefore, the outgroup minority that defended a humanitarian argument here – the one that produced delayed influence – was in fact deemed to state some element of the truth in the light of the current crisis situation and the need to express its national culture, as if it were somehow being ascribed a kind of 'social objectivity'. Except for its differentiation based on nationality, a minority may thus confront targets with its own 'truth', increasing its alternative value by challenging them on behalf of a principle (humanitarianism) that is definitional of the subjects (national identity), even though it takes time for this new value to find its means of expression. New dimensions for comparing ideological positions may then emerge, provided the amount of time required to break the barriers of intergroup differentiation is allotted. Denial does not exclude truth.

3.3.3 Beyond social costs: the alternative

A minority source, even categorized as outgroup, can obtain a conversion effect that an ingroup minority does not necessarily obtain. Let us take a final example to prove our point.

Take the case of an experiment based on the abortion and contraception paradigm. Since this paradigm is new for the reader, a few words should first be said about it. The subjects, all young people usually less than twenty years old, are asked to read a text highly in favour of voluntary abortion. Given that the experiments using this paradigm were conducted in Spain, the text obviously presents an anti-norm position, since not only is abortion still illegal in Spain, but at the time of the initial experimentation, the heated debate in parliament was limited to the possible legalization of so-called therapeutic abortion. Yet the text (see Appendix 7.3.1) argues in favour of completely legalizing abortion and making it absolutely free of charge, which without a doubt defines an alternative adopted by only a minority of the population. At the end of the experiment, and after having described the minority on several scales (like those given in Appendix 7.2.4), subjects fill in a questionnaire which is used to assess the degree of influence. Some of the items (see Appendix 7.3.2) pertain to abortion. These constitute the direct influence dimension since the minority explicitly took a stand in this matter. Other items pertain to contraception. These items constitute the indirect influence dimension since the minority did not take a stand on contraception. The two influence indexes are the factorial scores (output from a factorial analysis of the questionnaire) representing attitude towards abortion and attitude towards contraception, *relatively* higher scores being an indication of minority influence and reflecting a favourable attitude towards these two issues. The obvious highlight of this paradigm is that it enables the researcher to observe the dynamics of direct and indirect influence on an up-to-date social issue, in a context whose highly intergroup nature is most certainly evident to the reader.

In the experiment we are interested in here (Pérez and Mugny, in press), manipulation of the reference category was done in the following manner: subjects were to read a pro-abortion text supposedly written by a minority group whose identity was not revealed (other than the fact that it was a minority). In the conditions we shall examine here, subjects were asked immediately afterwards to imagine what would be the position (with respect to abortion and to the minority) of either young people (for the ingroup condition) or adults (for the outgroup condition). The idea was that referring to the ingroup was supposed to favour the expression of more 'progressive' opinions, while referring to the outgroup, more traditional or conservative opinions. Table 3.4 shows that in part, things went as expected.

When the subjects were induced to view the minority discourse through young people's eyes, which also corresponded to their own identity, they were more explicitly in favour of abortion than in the condition in which the filter was the adult and thus outgroup category. Reference to the adult outgroup, assumed to be more conservative and opposed to abortion, hindered the expression of the characteristic attitude of youth.

However, if we look at the indirect dimension, we can see that this attitude did not extend over to contraception. On the contrary! In the case of contraception, reference to the ingroup did not cause the positive attitude towards abortion to be accompanied by a positive attitude towards the liberalization of contraception. Instead, it was through the adult outgroup that indirect influence was possible and led the subjects to be more in favour of contraception.

Why? Some of the results showing the image the subjects formed of the minority provide us with a few interesting indications. First, two factors explain the lesser degree of direct influence obtained by the outgroup-filtered minority: subjects indeed recognized that the minority group would obviously be judged more negatively by adults than by youths, and also as less credible, since its members were not considered to be spokesmen for an alternative, nor were they viewed as sure of themselves, open-minded, realistic, or responsible. The lesser degree of direct outgroup influence may have been due to the fact that viewing the minority through what the subjects thought to be the eyes of adults made the conflictual nature of the minority position salient, and denied its social credibility. When as risky as that, social comparison would be conflictual and inhibit influence. And it would do so simply through the evocation of the judgements made by a social category legitimately able to establish the social costs linked to approving a counter-normative position.

However, as in the previous experiment, the image of the minority was not expressed in negative terms only, since from the adult point of view proposed to the subjects, the minority was also perceived as progressive and feminist, critical and committed, but tolerant. The distinctiveness of the minority stance, even though negatively connoted, was recognized.

In short, direct influence may be more marked when subjects are led to evaluate the minority positively by viewing it through young people's eyes, the ingroup category playing the role of social medium enabling the manifest expression of a progressive attitude towards abortion. Indirect influence, on the other hand, may be the most marked when conflict is generated through the negative connotations adults are assumed to apply

Table 3.4. *Direct and indirect influence (a + sign indicates positive influence)*

	Source	
	Ingroup	Outgroup
Influence		
Direct	+0.10	−0.31
Indirect	−0.38	+0.13

to the minority, provided, and in an ambivalent manner, the minority position (here progressive and feminist) is also made salient. In the next chapter, we shall see how this acknowledgement of the conflictual and distinctive nature of the minority brings together the conditions under which the typical minority influence pattern emerges, where indirect effects are contrasted to outward resistance at the manifest influence level.

3.3.4 Conversion: from the interpersonal to the intergroup

One last study will be examined here, and will enable us to confirm the generality of the observed effect: the indirect impact of outgroup sources. This will be done by showing that it may be the very insertion of the influence relationship into an explicitly intergroup context that gives rise to these indirect influence dynamics, which if nothing else, go against our intuition.

The theme of this study was pollution (Pérez and Mugny, 1985a). The subjects were all female adolescents, and the source was presented as belonging either to the ingroup (same sex identity) or outgroup (opposite sex identity). The text written by the minority group strongly questioned the subjects' sex identity itself, notably by accusing women of being the source of a number of forms of pollution.

In addition, the subjects were told either that the text had been written by a single individual or that it was representative of persons in his or her own category. In the former case, the experimenter pretended to have chosen a text at random among those written by members of the ingroup or outgroup, and emphasized the fact that the text was not representative; in the latter case, on the contrary, the text was supposedly written by a group of students who were said to perfectly represent the opinions of members in their category (ingroup or outgroup). Note once again that for the purpose of analysis, the direct and indirect influence dimensions on the opinion questionnaire were assessed separately. The direct influence dimension included those items upon which the minority had taken an explicit position, i.e. items accusing categories of individuals and taking the

Table 3.5. *Direct and indirect influence (a + sign indicates positive influence)*

	Source			
	Non-representative		Representative	
	Ingroup	Outgroup	Ingroup	Outgroup
Influence				
Direct	+0.40	+0.28	+0.16	−0.18
Indirect	+0.13	+0.09	+0.97	+0.68

blame off industry, the statements in the questionnaires being exact replicas of those in the minority text (cf. Appendix 7.1.1). The indirect influence dimension, on the other hand, included the items upon which the minority had not expressed an opinion; these accused industry and took all blame off categories of individuals.

The results we are interested in here (cf. Table 3.5) indicate that at the interindividual level (non-representative source), direct influence was greater, especially when the source was ingroup, whereas at the intergroup level (representative source), it was weak, especially when the source was outgroup. As to direct influence, the differentiation effects discussed in the previous chapter were also found here, in a coherent and evident manner.

However, it was the representative sources – the most conflictual at the direct level since a psychosocial identification process was involved to a greater extent – that exerted indirect influence, even quite strong, while the 'individualized' sources induced no notable change. This was true for both the ingroup minority and the outgroup minority.

It thus appears that a perceived conflict represented at the interpersonal level may be negotiable at the most socially explicit level, without necessarily implying a conversion effect. On the contrary, a conflict occurring within a category field or intergroup relationship, which implies a more salient definition of the minority as a collective entity involving more intense identification, would in this case be more conflictual at the direct level, although still leading the subject into a conversion process.

In order for conversion to take place, the minority group does not necessarily have to be explicitly presented as outgroup. In reality, it may be the very fact that the minority is placed in an intergroup context that leads to conversion. We shall have the occasion to come back to this crucial issue later, and shall contend that it is not actually *in spite of*, but rather *because of*, the categorization it induces that the minority becomes a source of conversion. We shall see, in fact, that even when the minority is presented experimentally as ingroup, it can generate a representation in which, even within the ingroup, it appears somehow as an outgroup or as a clearly definable sub-category.

One final note! Along the interpersonal-to-intergroup continuum (cf. Tajfel, 1978), we have known that the intergroup level is a source of conflict whose resolution involves an ingroup favouritism/outgroup discrimination bias manifested at the direct influence level. In the case of the private, indirect, or delayed evaluation of opinions and attitudes, minorities nevertheless induce paradoxical effects at that same intergroup level. Moreover, as Kelman (1958) showed, identification with the source of influence does in fact favour its approval, but only when the comparison is psychologically salient. In addition, non-identification does not mean the lack of indirect influence, a fact which updates an influence pattern unforeseen by Kelman.

3.4 Conclusions

It must be acknowledged that ingroup influence sources are not necessarily and unavoidably subject to favouritism, and that outgroup sources are not systematically discriminated against, as a strict interpretation of the model of identification might lead us to believe. We do hope to have convinced the reader that influence actually is governed by such dynamics. Inversely, influence processes themselves can bypass, even thwart, the intergroup discrimination dynamics to which active minorities are prone. These processes introduce some new dynamics into the field of intergroup relations, which otherwise function according to the categorical differentiation model described by Doise. As Moscovici (1976) contended, even minority sources and outgroup sources have an essential instrument at their disposal for inserting their plans into an intergroup relationship (even if this relationship partially determines the 'degrees of freedom' the minorities are allowed): behaviour and negotiation styles, their rhetoric in the expression of an alternative position.

These demonstrations illustrate what Moscovici (1976, p. 147) stated when commenting upon our studies on flexible (then qualified as 'equitable') and rigid styles, 'By extrapolating even more, one could say that within one's own group, if it is a minority, the dogmatic style of behavior is suitable. the "equitable" style only becomes important in the case of contact between majority and minority, or with another group. One can also say that the former style is compatible with ingroup relations and the latter style, with intergroup relations. In short, within a group, rigidity is effective: short of a few exceptions, the more rigid the style, the more influence it will exert. In external relations, however, the "equitable" style, equally firm and consistent, must be used in order to act upon the social environment.' Intuitions yes, but now backed by solid experimental support!

Finally, the indirect nature of the changes often observed presupposes the performance of a socio-cognitive activity on the part of the subjects, who are led to define themselves at the direct level and to mentally reconstruct both the categorizations they distinguish in the situation and the attributes defining those categorizations, as we have seen many times.

By providing evidence of this cognitive activity of a constructive nature, we have come to one of the central ideas in the study of minority influence, namely, that minority influence is not necessarily direct (like social learning), but also relies on a creative or generative process on the part of the targets, a process whose nature, conditions for induction, and underlying socio-cognitive mechanisms are yet to be clarified. The aim of the more recent studies, which are the main topic of the next few chapters, was to enable us to propose a single, unified model to account for these varied and complex dynamics.

If we had to sum up in one sentence what this chapter has contributed, we could say that it was aimed at proving the need to explain all possible patterns of minority influence. Indeed, everything appears to be possible, even if certain influence patterns are more common than others. Accordingly, in the previous chapter, we showed how identification with a minority source on the basis of some shared categorical identity can lead to an increase in its influence via an ingroup favouritism bias, and inversely, that categorization of a minority as outgroup can cause a discrimination bias against it. We had already noted when presenting our model, however, that social comparison can give rise to rejection of even an ingroup source, whenever that source induces an identification conflict.

Beyond this diversity, a single kind of reasoning nevertheless appeared necessary to account for the habitual influence pattern of minorities: inexistent or little direct influence, but indirect influence. In each case, it must be assumed that the minority has been mentally constructed as an alternative in the social field, as shown by our research on abortion and contraception. As such, it induces a sort of identification conflict that explains the weakness of its direct influence. But having been constructed as an alternative, it can exert indirect influence. In the next chapter, we shall present a model which, through the development of the notion of validation, will allow us to account for this cognitive activity performed by target subjects.

4 Validation and minority influence

Studies contrasting minority influence to majority influence converge in showing the specificity of each of these types of influence. In many of these studies, subjects are confronted with the same message, and thus, with the same alternative ideological content. Only the characteristics of the source are varied by the experimenter, the essential difference being that, in one case the source is a majority, usually a numerical one, assumed to be defending a position that diverges from the target subjects' position, whereas in the other case the source is a minority. The magnitude and nature of the conflict is also varied. It has repeatedly been shown (cf. Moscovici and Mugny, 1987) that compared to majority influence, minority influence is manifested by changes that are indirect rather than direct, private rather than public, and delayed rather than immediate.

In the preceding chapters, we showed two things by varying the identity of the minority source. We found out that categorization of the minority as an ingroup can lead to more influence, especially manifest influence. In addition, in studying the question of the anti-minority bias, we realized that a source that is mentally constructed as an outgroup can also exert influence, generally of a latent and indirect nature. In fact, the dynamics of minority influence can even be accentuated when the minority is categorized as an outgroup, whereas ingroup categorization may stimulate a majority source conflict.

Despite the apparent analogy between majority and ingroup on the one side, and minority and outgroup on the other, these two notions are not interchangeable. Although both involve an identification process of some type – and this is where the analogy lies – the specificity of the majority or minority nature of source group membership is that it also provides a social support for indicating proper conduct. In the first case, the control or resolution of the conflict is founded upon awareness of a psychological similarity (or difference), and also if not especially in the second case, upon how much pressure there is to conform. In addition, when these two complementary aspects of reality are crossed, other specific dynamics are found: being a minority within an ingroup, for example, does not have the same psychological implications as being a minority within an outgroup.

In this chapter, we shall see how the impact of minorities, in the twofold dynamics of direct and/or indirect influence, is the result of a validation activity, triggered by the intermingling of identification and resistance and defined by the generation of the new meanings required to resolve what becomes a genuine socio-cognitive conflict. The model to account for this can only be a constructivist model.

4.1 Learning by imitation or social constructivism?

4.1.1 Selective focusing on the source or on the object

Why then do majorities tend to obtain manifest influence, and minorities, latent influence? In an important article published in 1980, Moscovici and Personnaz presented a kind of reasoning which is now widely accepted by the research community in this field, and which we interpret as follows. Subjects may be led to consider the divergent attitudes (differences in perception or opinion) of a unanimous majority as socially 'true', as legitimatized by their commonness and their acceptance by a numerical majority, known to be so important to the definition of the 'social truth' (Festinger, 1954) in the 'epistemo-ideology' (Mugny and Doise, 1979) of common (and...scientific?) sense. In such a situation, the subjects themselves appear to deviate from the dominant, majority-supported, or allegedly most popular, response. In comparing their own responses with the majority's, subjects may feel different, and this feeling may lead them to adjust their responses. They may do so without necessarily considering the debated issue, and thus, without necessarily engaging in any particular perceptual or cognitive activity. In this case, it is only the social expression of the subjects' responses that has been modified, nothing more. This may explain why majorities or ingroups do indeed have more direct influence, as we have seen. In the terms of our model of identification, it can be assumed that subjects only engage in an activity of social comparison to the majority, especially since psychologically, they have no reason to distinguish or differentiate themselves from it. So far so good.

When the source is a minority, things change radically. The information minority sources convey may be considered as illegitimate, erroneous, socially 'false', especially when the context makes norms such as objectivity salient. In these conditions, it is the minority source that appears as deviant, thereby identifying the subject with the majority. The initial response towards the minority, which may be considered as an outgroup, would thus be rejection and discrimination; this is reflected by the lack of direct influence often observed.

However, since the subjects maintain their position, and the minority is consistent in maintaining its position, the conflict persists. The minority does not concede to pressure to conform, which may lead the targets to believe that it is right in some respects to act and think as it does. In the long run, the conflict leads subjects to focus their attention on the object and engage in a validation activity in which they attempt to apprehend the minority viewpoint in order to determine whether or not the deviant response masks some element of truth, and whether or not there is some ontological foundation in the properties of the object itself.

To conclude along with Moscovici and Personnaz, we must thus consider that during social interaction, target subjects avoid adopting the minority response in order to avoid being viewed as deviants, especially since in doing so they run the risk of being disapproved by the rest of the majority that provides them with direct social support (Doms, 1983, 1987). Expressing this in our terms, we would say that identification is impossible here because it is too conflictual. However, as the conflict gradually progresses, subjects may, in their attempt to verify the soundness of the minority claims, be led to consider the object of the debate more attentively, to judge it, and to perceive it differently than before the collective experience. It is thus while 'attempting to see or understand what the minority sees or understands that the majority begins to see and understand what the former sees and understands' (Moscovici and Personnaz, 1980, p. 272).

We do not intend to engage in a polemic to determine how the thorough examination of the debated object can alone lead to a change in favour of what the minority is advocating (objects do not speak!), especially since we know that such an interpretation was initially of undeniable heuristic value. However, this distinction between focusing on the source or content must be re-examined and revised, not only because it has been used over and over again in the literature on minority influence, but also because it is difficult to conceive of when formulated as such, for several reasons.

First, we must admit that it is not possible for target subjects to pay attention to the object without *also* considering (or having previously considered) the characteristics of the source. In other words, a comparison process necessarily takes place in *all* influence situations, regardless of the majority or minority identity of the source. Without it, we could not understand why the social expression of agreement with the minority position would be so difficult.

Hereafter, the validation and comparison activities are no longer to be considered as typical, one of minorities, the other of majorities. Both can be at work in majority and minority influence. The question, however, becomes determining the unfolding and outcome of each of these processes, while specifying above all the conditions under which the necessarily conflictual social comparison to the minority will still be accompanied by a validation process. (This will be the topic of Chapter 5.)

Before attempting to establish the above links, we must first pinpoint and further define the various cognitive operations that underlie the validation of minority positions, from which minority influence is assumed to be derived. This is what we shall now examine more deeply.

4.1.2 Indirect influence and social constructivism
Let us first take care of the problem of definitions. The epistemological status of the methodological distinctions made between public and private influence, immediate and delayed influence, and direct and indirect influence does indeed have theoretical consequences.

First, making the distinction between public and private responses leads to the assumption that the public aspect tends simply to cloud what the private aspect lets show through. The difference implied here is that responding in public increases the salience of the social costs incurred by a potential identification. Public responding thwarts any influence, which takes effect in private where the social comparison is less involving, the subject no longer being controlled to the same extent by the majority. The publicness of a response thus only acts as a brake on the social expression of minority viewpoint approval, and the outcome of the innovation process results from the strength of pressure to conform (even if that pressure is only implicit).

Making the distinction between immediate and delayed influence, on the other hand, implies two possible time-related processes: either the targets take time to further develop the cognitive validation activity, or with time the comparison to the source becomes less salient, as if the identity of those who entertained the minority viewpoint had been forgotten or at least masked.

Both of these distinctions implicitly involve the idea that at the manifest level (public and/or immediate), the blocking of responses can stem from the salience of the social comparison, and that the changes appearing in a latent manner (private and/or delayed) are not explicit, are somehow hidden, and only become external (cf. Personnaz, 1981) with an increase in the distance (spatial, temporal, or otherwise) separating response assessment from the position manifested by the minority. These, moreover, are some of the reasons why such distinctions are appropriate for studying the specificity of minority influence effects.

However, we prefer the more general distinction between *direct* influence and *indirect* influence, and the above operationalizations will in effect be included as particular cases, applicable in specific circumstances.

By *direct influence*, we mean the appropriation by subjects of the alternative position a minority proposed in its attempt to exert influence. This change in position is directly governed by the mechanisms involved in the social comparison process. It will thus occur to varying degrees, depending on whether it takes place immediately after the minority message has been issued or after a time lag, or whether it takes place in a public or private situation.

By *indirect influence*, we mean a change in the position of subjects on issues the minority did not explicitly address when delivering its message. Although the minority did not take a stand on these issues, its stand must nevertheless be inferable and must be indirectly, granted, but effectively linked to the explicit minority position. If a correspondence can be established between the influence exerted on these separate but related issues, then this implies that one and the same principle of a more general scope must underlie them. This principle will be referred to as an *organizing principle*.

Let us take the example of the abortion paradigm where the minority only states its pro-abortion position, whereas the subjects are also asked to state their position on contraception (cf. Appendix 7.3.2), which they can assume the minority would also advocate. In the final experiment reported in this book, subjects were also questioned on their attitudes towards the family, child obedience, the education system, and moral standards. A more tolerant or more progressive attitude towards these related issues is considered to indicate that the minority had a positive impact, namely in the form of indirect influence.

The reason we prefer this distinction between direct influence and indirect influence is that underlying it is a notion, even a conception, specific to the process of validation: social constructivism. Since the source does not take a stand on the issues indirectly linked to the discourse, the influence of the minority cannot be based on the laws of imitation and social learning, but implies that an inferential cognitive activity of a constructivist nature has been carried out.

This is not the case for the conventional distinctions made between public and private influence, or immediate and delayed influence. These types of influence do not exclude the possibility of proposing social learning or imitation as an explanation. In these cases, target subjects who exhibit the effects of minority influence in the end only go along with the position actually expressed by the minority, conforming to it in some way, even if only in private, even if only later on. Although these distinctions are useful and heuristic, and do not exclude a constructivist explanation, the advantage of the distinction between direct and indirect influence is that it is less apt to create ambiguity.

Another advantage of this distinction, which we shall develop in the next chapter, is that it will allow us to theoretically link direct and indirect influence, rather than simply allowing us to assume that private responding eliminates the obstacles of response externalization that publicity inhibits, or that time lets initially parenthetical information settle in for the amount of time needed to wear out the comparison process.

Note in addition that certain authors have contended that the study of private influence may be contaminated owing to the resistance brought on by the public expression mode in typical situations (cf. Personnaz and Personnaz, 1987) where subjects express themselves publicly in front of the minority source before answering in private. To avoid what had to be considered as a sort of experimental bias, between-subject designs were used to study these two 'purified' forms of influence *separately*, subjects responding only in public, or only in private (cf. Maass and Clark, 1984; Martin, 1987a), although the dynamics observed were not fundamentally different. This perspective leads to the assumption that we can theoretically separate the comparison process, which would hold for public influence, and the validation process, which would hold for private influence, as if the two operated autonomously. Once again, our position is that these two processes must not simply be juxtaposed, but rather interconnected at the theoretical level. This explains our experimental preference for within-subject designs, where measures at different levels are taken for *each* subject, to between-subject designs, where the public measure and the private measure are taken separately in different experimental conditions. The idea that social comparison and validation are in fact fundamentally inter-mingled in influence target activity will lead us in particular to consider that the very existence of direct, public, and/or immediate resistance may cause indirect, private, and/or delayed dynamics to take effect whenever validation occurs.

Our principal argument is indeed that for indirect influence to take place, target subjects must carry out a cognitive activity involving the examination of the various social definitions describing the objects under scrutiny and governing the influence relationship, which were not necessarily available to targets before they encountered the minority: at this level already, only recognition (recognition here meaning identification or ascertainment) of the innovative position taken by the minority can cause target subjects to review their own position, although this does *not necessarily* mean adopting it (even privately and/or after the fact). The resulting indirect influence is hypothesized to be derived from the integration of these various focal points, and thus cannot simply be reduced to the 'revelation' or externalization of a response identical to the majority's and previously inhibited by the social comparison. In the same manner as in our studies on cognitive development (Doise and Mugny, 1984), our conception is that minority influence does not result from a simple imitation process, but from a cognitive construction and coordination activity integrating divergent focal points.

This theoretical background must be kept in mind in the future whenever, by analogy, we use the terms public or immediate influence for direct influence, and private or delayed influence for indirect influence, since in our framework they are nothing more than different operationalizations of the same significations called upon to refer to the notions of direct and indirect influence.

Now that this distinction has been made, we can go ahead with this chapter, first illustrating how constructivism is the basis of the kind of divergent and creative thinking that is specifically triggered by the social revelation of minority viewpoints.

4.1.3 Minorities and creativity

It would be useful here to insist upon the parallelism of the hypothesis of minority-induced social constructivism and the main thesis of the theory of the social development of the intelligence (cf. Mugny, 1985; Mugny and Pérez, 1988b). In the same way as *alter*-induced socio-cognitive conflict appears to be indispensable to releasing children from an 'egocentric' perspective so that they might construct new cognitive tools, and in the same way as the conflict generated by a minority turns out to be indispensable to leading target subjects to reconsider points of view that were previously taken for granted, the prerequisite to change is indeed recognition of a difference, and recognition of a difference may already be a form of influence. It is also worth noting that this structuring function of conflict is at the very heart of the notion of consistency, whose action relies on conflict.

Several studies on minority influence have shown that one of the effects of minorities is to lead target subjects to respond in a way that is not only different from the majority's way, but also from the minority's (cf. Kimball and Hollander, 1974; Moscovici and Lage, 1978; Nemeth, 1986). This new response, which is no more due to conforming with the majority than it is to going along with the minority, necessarily implies that a creative process is under way. This particular approach to influence processes was more thoroughly developed in the recent research done by Nemeth and her collaborators (Nemeth, 1986, 1987) who showed that one of the specificities of minorities is that they lead subjects to *generate* new responses *themselves*, and even more, to devise more highly differentiated cognitive strategies. Thus, such phenomena are not the outcome of just any opposition. Let us quickly look at three illustrations!

In one experiment (Nemeth and Wachtler, 1983), subjects worked in groups of six on a task consisting of finding a standard figure hidden (or not hidden) in a series of six perceptual configurations varying in complexity, i.e. differing as to how easy it was to determine whether or not the hidden figure was present. In the majority conditions, four accomplices all gave the same answer to each item. In the minority conditions, only two of the accomplices gave the same answer. Also, in half of the conditions, they answered correctly, and in the other half, they answered incorrectly. Among the results obtained, the one that interests us here is that when faced with a unanimous majority, subjects tended to conform more often to the majority-supported answer. As easily suspected, this was not true for the minority conditions, where subjects generally tended to select figures that were different from those chosen by the minority, although also correct, regardless of whether the source's answer was right or wrong. With majority sources, different but correct answers were less frequent, and appeared especially when the majority was wrong, i.e. when the majority introduced a conflict. These findings confirm the fact that one of the capabilities specific to minorities is that they trigger a cognitive activity through which new solutions (and sometimes even 'correct' solutions at that) are sought.

This divergent cognitive activity was again illustrated by Nemeth and Kwan (1985) on a task consisting of distinguishing three-letter words in strings of five letters (for example, tDOGe). In all of the conditions, subjects were informed after a few trials that either three out of four persons (majority condition) or only one out of four persons (minority condition) systematically used a 'reverse' order strategy (reading from right to left: 'GOD'), while the rest of the group read in the ordinary fashion ('DOG'). In short, the subjects were given the same information (two possible strategies) with only the number of users having varied. Following this experimental manipulation, the subjects were asked to find as many words as possible in another series of letter strings.

The main finding here is that when the example was set by a minority, subjects used less reverse order strings than when the source was a majority. The minority source thus had less direct influence. However, subjects in the minority condition found more correct words since they used more diversified strategies, reading in the conventional direction, in the reverse direction, and even in both. When faced with a minority source, *all possible points of view* were considered and used, even in conjunction with each other.

In a third experiment (Nemeth and Kwan, 1985), subjects were to assess the colour and brightness of about twenty slides, all of which were obviously blue, while an accomplice answered 'green' on all trials. In the majority condition, the experimenter told the subjects that 80% of the people thought the slides were green, thus placing the accomplice in the majority. In the minority condition, they were told that 80% of the subjects said they were blue. The subjects' task was then to make free associations with the words 'blue' and 'green'. The results showed that the associations made were richer and more original (that is, less frequent and less conventional) in the minority condition. After interaction with the minority group member, more associations such as 'jazz' or 'jeans' were found, whereas after interaction with the majority group member the predominant associations were of the type 'sky' for blue and 'grass' for green.

In future studies, Nemeth was to expand upon this conception of minority influence to cover a whole range of cognitive mechanisms of diverse natures. Accordingly, Nemeth, Mayseless, Sherman and Brown (1990) showed how the conflict induced by a minority can aid targets in learning and memorizing information. It is not that subjects simply remembered more pieces of information here: above all, the organization of those pieces of information improved substantially, which again clearly indicates cognitive activity by the subjects following confrontation with a minority point of view.

Similarly, Nemeth and Chiles (1988) showed that targets of minority influence can be as daring as a daring minority. In an experiment using the blue–green paradigm, an accomplice incorrectly stated that blue slides were green. Following this minority influence phase, subjects were told they would undergo another experiment in which they would have to assess the colour of some slides that were quite obviously red. The other members of the group, all accomplices, incorrectly stated that the slides were orange. In this new situation, in fact a conformity situation, subjects who had previously been subjected to the dissident minority conformed less than the ones who had not. This means that not only can a minority induce divergent *thought*, but that it also, by setting an example of daringness, can induce the ability to *interact* in a divergent manner, that is, to resist pressure to conform.

Another example of 'behavioural conversion', as Joule calls it, is provided by a study using a compliance without pressure paradigm (Joule, 1987; Joule and Beauvois, 1987). Subjects, all smokers, accepted a small sum of money to take part in a study on concentration, only to find themselves asked to refrain from smoking for 18 hours so that their performance on the concentration test could be assessed, or so they thought, before and after tobacco withdrawal. Despite the fact that the experimenter also told them they would be paid less than expected, nearly all the subjects (92.31%) agreed to stay in the experiment anyway, although the experimenter made it very clear that they could still refuse. Most of them (91.67%) even agreed to participate in an experiment a few weeks later involving three days of tobacco deprivation. However, it was shown that this snowball effect could be combated by the intervention of an accomplice belonging to a minority group. Indeed, in one experimental condition, the author introduced an accomplice who, after having first accepted to play the game and take the concentration tests, announced that he had thought about it, and had changed his mind. He told the experimenter he no longer wished to participate in the experiment, and did not want to stop smoking for a day as he had just agreed to do. After the accomplice had left the laboratory, the experimenter repeated to the subjects that he would understand if some of them decided not to follow through with the experiment. Yet none of the subjects followed suit with the accomplice by breaking the contract. The accomplice therefore did not have any direct influence on contract breaking. However, less than half of the subjects (48%; cf. Joule, Mugny, and Pérez, 1988) volunteered for the next experiment involving refraining from tobacco for three days, while this same compliance without pressure technique had convinced virtually all of the subjects when the accomplice had not been involved. Obviously, minority influence did not lead to the immediate imitation of the deviant act, but was reflected in a delayed manner in this experiment, namely, by a behavioural conversion.

In such experiments, we repeatedly find that when an explicitly minority point of view is introduced, subjects are far from conforming to it, but carry out an original creative cognitive activity which is the outcome of a divergent mode of functioning involving richer cognitive problem-solving strategies, ones that are more varied and more complex. Moreover, this is why 'the way of the minorities' constitutes one of the ways of avoiding the harmful effects of 'groupthink' (Janis, 1972).

These studies amply illustrate the kind of activity subjects can be led to carry out when faced with a minority point of view. This activity is not restricted to the approval or rejection of the behaviour and discourse specific to the minority, but presupposes the ascertainment or construction of the organizing principles underlying the minority positions, which can even lead to the development of other new strategies, both cognitive and behavioural. This indeed is what makes the validation process a fundamentally constructive and creative process.

4.2 The model of validation

The above studies have convinced us that minority influence, because it is secret and private, follows winding and obscure paths. We have set out to clarify these paths, with experimentation as our support. These studies have basically revealed the existence of such phenomena, but have not provided real explanations of their psychosocial origins. As an example, let us take the notion of conflict which underlies all of the effects considered so far.

There is a genuine consensus about the assertion that one of the essential prerogatives of minorities is their power to generate conflict. From a social point of view, such conflict is easy to observe, even measure. Its parameters are the existing difference between the content of the minority position and that of the majority or predominant position, and the strength of the resistance initiated by reaction to the minority. But a psychosociological model cannot be limited to these measures, which are *external to the target subject*. It must account for the mechanisms through which minority confrontation has the observed latent repercussions. The fundamental principle of our approach is that in order to have such an impact, the conflict maintained socially by the minority must be mentally re-transcribed and then reconstructed, and must therefore be incorporated into the subject's representations of the field of innovation.

We shall describe these mechanisms in detail by positing that the constructive activity induced by the revelation of a minority viewpoint involves a cognitive activity affecting at least three levels: the (re)-construction of categorizations, the (re-)definition of attributes, and the (re-)analysis and (re-)working of the actual content of the minority's message. (Nemeth's work reported above is indeed a remarkable illustration of this third level.) The rest of this chapter will deal with recent research that develops the three complementary levels underlying minority influence, which in our mind are its constituents.

One of the aspects of this constructivism can be found in the socio-cognitive definition of the source via the attributes assigned to it. The central hypothesis here is that one of the effects of minorities is the *modification* of the attributes used to define the source. Beyond the application of initial stereotypical images (which moreover are culturally predetermined by dominant norms) whose function is obviously to justify and anticipate resistance to innovation, the intervention of the minority may cause targets to re-examine these stereotypes and discover in the minority new, initially unfamiliar or even unknown dimensions likely to transform the minority position into a legitimate point of view or focal point, even into an alternative.

This change-generating cognitive activity that modifies representations in the social field is also carried out at the categorization level. The minority can lead targets to re-examine the relationships they hold with various social entities, including the minority itself, and to define a new set of boundaries by eliminating some old ones and setting up some new ones. The appearance of the minority viewpoint cannot leave the social category map unchanged, especially insofar as it explicitly introduces the intergroup dimension into the innovation context, and even creates subdivisions within the outgroup, which until then was apparently subject to consensus. By denying the universality of norms, the minority reveals the existence of as many underlying social divisions as there are ideological divisions, among which the dominant norm now only appears as a specific focal point – unless of course the targets totally deny the existence of the minority, which consistency across time renders difficult, as we shall see further on.

The dynamics of influence thus do not stem only from the evaluative connotations ascribed to the self-attributable characteristics of the minority during the social comparison process involving subject-to-source identification. For such connotations are not fixed. They depend on the transformations that the identity matrices, inclusive of categorizations and attributes, undergo following the action of the minority.

But why do targets change the data in these identity matrices? The basic reason is that the social conflict has been transposed to the psychological level. The fundamental hypothesis here is that authentic socio-cognitive conflicts are in effect introduced, stemming namely from the incongruities that appear between categorizations and attributes (Roux, 1989). Indeed, the dynamics of change appear whenever the categorization of the source and its indexation are contradictory, i.e. whenever the principle underlying the categorical differentiation becomes questionable. In other words, new attributes may become incompatible with old attributes, creating a state of in-depth *ambivalence*. We shall see how the behaviour style of the minority plays a preponderant role in this respect, since it breaks the barriers of categorization and points out new attributes likely to validate minority positions.

This diversity, this sort of dispersion of the representations involved in an innovation context explains why minority influence rarely takes on the form of a simple yielding to the minority position, and why it is expressed in an indirect manner. The fact is that minority influence acts through these transformations, which are representational or definitional of new identifications, without however implying or requiring compliance with the minority positions.

We are bordering here on what one particular view of innovation, the 'reductionist' (and somewhat 'paranoid') view, considers as 'recuperation'. We often find that the ideas of a minority *gradually* filter into the ranks of the majority and power groups. This in fact is what gives us the illusion that change is always the outcome of decisions generated from within the system (cf. Ibàñez, 1987), and that it does not stem, or if so only in a peripheral manner, from the conflictual interactions that minorities introduce. The fact is that change can only be the outcome of a reconstruction process brought on by conflict. Insofar as the conflictual state prevents the approval of the minority, the nearly unconscious changes resulting from the validation activity are not and cannot be ascribed to the exertion of minority influence, even though they in fact *are* attributable to it, via a social cryptomnesia effect (Mugny and Pérez, 1989b). It is true that majorities do not necessarily have a psychosociological model of change at their disposal.

The last question developed will be the following: How can minorities rejected at the direct influence level exert indirect influence that is so strongly in their favour? Our answer is that among all the possible attributes apt to describe the minority, one particular type is of primary importance: for indirect influence to come about, the target must necessarily have been able to cognitively ascertain or construct the organizing principle(s) of the minority positions, considered here as definitional attributes of the specificity of the ideological positions behind the direct and indirect dimensions of influence.

We must therefore admit that the complex activities involved in the validation process pertain as much to the source of influence as to the actual controversial ideologies under debate. It is never ideological content alone that gives rise to change, but rather its social and conflictual insertion into the networks of categorizations and attributes. In other words, it is the fact that each position (including the new one introduced by the minority) corresponds to specific positions in the social field, to which in turn particular meanings are associated and become more and more contradictory as the minority or the resistance context intensifies the conflict. Change, whether direct or indirect, is always the psychosocial resolution of a conflict.

We shall even go farther in showing that striving for the social denial of the minority viewpoint, which corresponds psychologically or subjectively to social resistance to change, can lead to the construction of a representation in which this denial paradoxically ends up outlining an alternative and consequently re-defining the relationship the targets maintain with the minority. In order to deny the validity of a minority's message, targets do not have to assert and thus reinforce their own position, but rather must try to falsify the counter-position: resistance is not indifference. And to falsify, the reality of the other point of view must necessarily be constructed – one must put oneself in the other person's shoes. This already involves decentering, withdrawing from one's own point of view. This is the best demonstration of the fact that minority influence is not based on approval, but on the constructive handling of the conflict triggered by the minority: validating is not approving; it is psychosocially reconstructing the experience of the conflict inherent in social reality as it is defined by others. As the philosopher Alain said, 'To think is to say no.' And in order to think, someone must indeed say no.

This outline of our constructivist model of validation served as a basis for several experiments which give it some empirical foundation, further illustrate the notions set forth so far in general terms, and deepen our understanding of them. So let us thoroughly develop each of these aspects of minority-induced constructivism.

4.3 Psychosocial construction of the minority

Let us first consider the construction of the attributes of the source before going into more specific detail about source categorization. The occurrence of indirect influence presupposes the recognition of the fact that the minority constitutes an autonomous and distinct entity in the social field, and not just that it is deviant, marginal, and negatively defined with respect to the dominant norm. In other words, it is necessary that the minority be represented cognitively as an alternative in its own right, that it be recognized as an anchor point in its role as a specific social entity, even if as such it is initially disapproved.

In short, the dynamics underlying the representation of the minority are twofold. The minority group's attributes are first constructed in reference to the norm and the majority group, then in reference to the relationship between the minority and the object under debate. The first construction process is more stereotyped and is based on intergroup prejudices, while the second involves the recognition of the minority in its own right. The former accounts for manifest resistance to change, the latter, for latent impact. Let us give several illustrations of the way in which this *ambivalent* representation works, and how it is connected to influence dynamics.

4.3.1 The ambivalence of minority representation

Using a paradigm dealing with aesthetic judgements (Mugny, Gachoud, Doms, and Pérez, 1988) subjects were asked to state their preferences for either one-coloured stimuli (blue checks on a white background) or multicoloured stimuli (checkerboards of eight colours). In a very systematic manner, a norm was revealed: most subjects preferred the blue and white checkerboards. They were then asked to compare each of the one-coloured stimuli with each of the multicoloured stimuli while being informed of the preferences of the other persons. In two of the conditions, other people systematically preferred the blue and white stimuli: these were thus *pro-normative* sources, who polarized the dominant norm to the utmost. In two other conditions, which naturally interest us the most, other people consistently expressed a preference for the multicoloured figures, a *counter-normative* position.

The minority or majority identity of the source was also varied. Before each pair of stimuli were presented, the subjects in the minority conditions

were told that 18 % of the people previously questioned preferred either the
one-coloured figure (pro-normative minority) or the multicoloured figure
(counter-normative minority). In the majority conditions, this percentage
was set at 82 %.

Three series of measures were taken. First, direct influence was assessed
through the preferences shown for one-coloured or multicoloured stimuli
before and after the influence phase. A measure of indirect influence was
made using black and white figures that varied in complexity, where
complexity was defined by how redundant they were (reproducibility of the
figure) and how many elements they were composed of. In the counter-
normative conditions (which best simulated innovation), since the
multicoloured figures preferred by the source were in fact more complex
(due to the greater number of colours), indirect influence would be
manifested by an increase in the number of also more complex black and
white figures. Finally, subjects were to judge the minority on a series of
seven-point scales. Our analysis will focus on these ratings first. The main
findings are given in Table 4.1.

Let us compare the representations of the counter-normative and pro-
normative sources. One initial difference is evident: the counter-normative
sources were more *conflictual*. Specifically, they were judged to be unfriendly,
less sociable, more unpleasant, less well-liked, in short, as being rejected
more at the relational level. Construed more as a minority, they were
thought to have bad taste and to know nothing about art, to be less
objective, less competent, less realistic and credible, and less convincing. In
short, the characteristics ascribed to the counter-normative source were
based on the dominant norm, and were consistent with rejection at the
relational level. Negative representation of sources that break away from
the norm is thus quite evident here.

Nevertheless, some ambivalence existed since the counter-normative
sources were also viewed as more extreme, more eccentric, more original,
and more progressive. In other words, these sources were indeed thought to
be capable of defending their own alternative point of view on the basis of
an originality norm.

Let us focus now on the counter-normative sources alone, since only they
introduced a genuinely innovative point of view. And let us look at how
majority- or minority-group membership affected the representation of the
source. Since the position being defended was one and the same, any
differences observed indicate prejudice against one of the groups. It should
not be forgotten, moreover, that the counter-normative status of these
sources already gave targets a more conflictual image of them (with respect
to the norm they were breaking away from), but also granted them that air
of originality we discovered above. The data show that compared to the

Table 4.1. *Source image* (*the higher the number, the more the characteristic fits the source*)

	Anti-norm source		Pro-norm source	
	Majority	Minority	Majority	Minority
Friendly	4.00	4.10	4.74	4.92
Unsociable	4.02	3.98	3.40	3.68
Unpleasant	4.18	3.92	3.30	3.40
Majority member	5.00	2.70	5.70	4.12
Accepted	3.90	3.74	5.26	4.56
Disliked	4.92	4.54	3.42	3.50
Objective	2.86	3.56	4.08	4.38
Incompetent	4.40	3.90	3.38	3.60
Indifferent to art	4.24	4.24	3.82	3.82
Poor taste	4.84	4.62	3.34	3.36
Ignorant about art	4.84	4.42	4.24	4.12
Unrealistic	4.24	4.70	3.04	3.26
Not credible	4.54	4.32	3.48	3.72
Unconvincing	5.02	4.64	3.86	4.24
Progressive	4.04	4.48	3.30	3.50
Not eccentric	3.92	3.88	5.24	4.84
Submissive	4.56	3.96	3.78	3.60
Extreme	3.62	4.26	3.44	3.70
Original	3.36	4.02	3.02	3.56
Coherent	3.38	3.74	5.28	4.80
Self-confident	4.22	4.10	4.84	4.68
Indecisive	4.48	3.66	3.14	3.42
Open-minded	3.56	4.08	3.60	4.26
Flexible	4.04	4.38	3.64	3.64
Unimaginative	3.60	3.76	4.68	4.04

majority, the numerical minority was indeed perceived as having many more of the 'minority' characteristics. It was deemed to be more extreme and original (the proof being that it was also viewed as unrealistic), less submissive and without prejudice, and less progressive. The minority identity, while accentuating the deviant nature of the sources simultaneously accentuated the originality and novelty of the alternative that the counter-normative minority was setting forth.

Thus, a minority does not necessarily trigger a monolithic representation (Ricateau, 1970–1) with a single, negative aura. Profound ambivalence exists due to the fact that the representation may actually be multidimensional. Indeed, a minority's image is only negative when its stand is compared with that generally taken by targets. Considered alone, minority positions lead to the recognition of the specificity and originality of the innovative point of view. Note on this subject that other authors have defended this same idea. In a factor-analytic approach to the perception of minorities, Bassili and Provençal (1988) found that the image of minorities is characterized by a high degree of assertiveness, conviction, integrity, and consistency, even though they are obviously disliked.

From the social comparison standpoint (the minority–majority relational aspect), this ambivalence is reflected by the opposing yet simultaneous occurrence of *disapproval* of the minority point of view, and the reconstruction of that point of view as *judgemental independence* or resistance to submission. *From the standpoint of the relationship with the object*, the ambivalence is reflected by the *denial of source credibility*, accompanied nevertheless by its reconstruction as *the carrier of a new and original definition* of the object. In each case, then, the image of the minority is a reflection, quite simply we might say, of the social distance that the minority keeps from the dominant norm, while also being a manifestation of the construction of a viewpoint specific to the minority-advocated options. From the former standpoint, the *dominant norm* constitutes the anchor point of a social comparison which is unfavourable to the minority. From the latter standpoint, the *alternative proposed by the minority* is the anchor point of the social validation of the opinion it is expressing. In one case, a new social entity is constructed, an outgroup of sorts; in the other, a new possibility for defining the object or the norm is generated.

This ambivalence in the representation of a minority is the source of an internal conflict manifested at the influence level. The results obtained in this experiment indeed show that the influence of the counter-normative majority was exerted at the direct level, whereas the influence of the counter-normative minority was exerted at the indirect level, as indicated by the fact that the minority did influence targets to transfer the minority's preference for more complex stimuli to the black and white figures, even though it did not exert any influence at the direct level. This again is additional evidence of the usual minority effect.

To better understand this effect, we calculated the correlations between the image of the minority and both direct and indirect influence, for the counter-normative majority and minority taken together. This was aimed at determining what proportion of the dual representation of the source accounts for what proportion of the twofold dynamics of influence.

Concerning direct influence, it was above all highly correlated to the description of the source as belonging to the majority, accepted, likeable, and convincing, in short, to its social approval. Moreover, direct influence was also correlated here to the recognition of the source as tolerant, open-minded, appreciative of art, having good taste, and credible. Approval of the source coincided here with approval of its view of things. Given that the minority was perceived as more conflictual from both of these standpoints, we can understand why its direct influence was not very strong.

The picture changed, as we could have imagined, with indirect influence, which was directly proportional to the recognition of the source as a minority, also construed as incompetent, and reluctant. The source was sure to have an impact here insofar as it was defined as progressive, open-minded, and eccentric, that is to say, because of its alternative qualities.

4.3.2 From a stereotype to a dual representation

In order for the recognition of this dual representation of the minority to emerge, several prerequisite conditions must be satisfied. The first pertains to the conflict that the minority induces by breaking away from prevailing norms – the difference we just found between pro-normative and counter-normative sources was a good demonstration of this. We must indeed admit that a conversion effect can only take place if the specific contents of the minority positions are made public and challenge the targets by introducing a new point of view opposing the one that prevails in targets, a point of view that could serve as an anchor point in the redefinition of norms and values. This is one of the *sine qua non* conditions enabling minority positions to trigger a validation activity and to be assigned new and specific attributes.

This is what a very simple experiment on abortion suggests. In the first condition, subjects were simply to express their opinion about abortion. Before doing so, though, they were to state what impression they had of a fictitious minority supposedly in favour of abortion. This simulated a condition involving the simple activation of a stereotype generated by the minority label. In the second condition, subjects were to read a text attributed to the minority group before filling out two questionnaires, one concerning the image of the minority group that had written the message, the other concerning their opinions on abortion. These subjects thus underwent an attempt at minority influence. The results showed that on both an immediate post-test and a deferred post-test taken three weeks later, subjects expressed a more favourable opinion on abortion in the condition in which they had been subjected to minority influence than in the one where they had not. The minority thus did have an impact.

The important thing here, however, is the transformation of the minority image. We can see indeed (cf. Table 4.2, which reports the scores output from the factorial analysis of the minority image assessed directly after the attempted influence, and then three weeks later) that the active minority introduced something new into the field: its image was systematically more positive than the stereotyped image the subjects assigned to the fictitious pro-abortion minority, as it was evaluated higher, was considered to present more of an alternative, and its consistent but flexible style was recognized. Its image did not match the rigidity attributed to the fictitious minority. And except in one case, all this was maintained even after the three-week time

Table 4.2 *Immediate and delayed image (the higher the number, the closer to the label)*

	Immediate		Delayed	
	Control	Text	Control	Text
'Evaluation'	−0.21	+0.24	−0.12	+0.07
'Alternative'	−0.34	+0.17	−0.30	+0.22
'Flexibility'	−0.17	+0.26	−0.19	+0.32

lag. Although the active minority was no longer present and became as fictitious as in the control condition, the targets remembered it as representing more of an alternative and as being more flexible. On the other hand, the difference along the evaluative dimension decreased and was no longer significant. This suggests that the lasting effect of the influence was not based on an evaluation bias, which can only last as long as the discourse of the minority remains salient.

Almost paradoxically, a minority that expresses itself and acts in the social field can thus partially modify its image to its own advantage more than a minority that does not express itself and only exists in the imaginary and collective world of stereotypes. The power of minorities does indeed reside in their ability to act. And the instrument of their action is consistency. Let us take a look at this idea now.

4.3.3 Consistency

The dynamics of the gradual conversion to minority positions are partially rooted in the fundamental ambivalence that also characterizes consistency. The fact is that consistency has a two-faceted meaning. As we have seen, it reflects an attitude within a conflictual relationship at the same time as it expresses a way of looking at things. Exclusive centering on the conflictual, relational aspect may underlie the dynamics that thwart the impact of minorities. Socio-cognitive focusing on their views, on the other hand, may be the origin of their hidden impact. To find out if this is true, rather than measuring these two dimensions after the fact, as has been done up until now, we could explicitly define them experimentally as independent variables by placing minority consistency in a context which would make salient either its relational dimension relative to the conflict, or its socio-cognitive dimension relative to the content of the minority standpoint.

In a series of experiments using the paradigm on attitudes towards foreigners, Kaiser (1989) simulated various forms of diachronic consistency. In the eight conditions in the experiment we shall report here (cf. Kaiser and

Mugny, 1987), subjects read the usual xenophilous text attributed to a minority group. However, the text was divided into two parts that had supposedly been published two months apart. In half of the conditions, the minority was said to be intervening in the social field in order to present a xenophilous alternative whose value had been reinforced by an alleged significant xenophobic social event, namely, the firing of all the foreign workers in a given Swiss firm. The second part of the text explicitly stressed this event. In the other half of the conditions, the minority's diachronic consistency was justified by the fact that it had supposedly been the object of scathing criticism during its initial intervention. Its second plea explicitly served as a retort to these reprimands, and thus focused target attention on the relational aspect of the intergroup conflict in which the minority was involved.

The consistent advocacy of the minority took on one of two different negotiation styles with which the reader is now quite familiar: the message was either presented in a more compromising manner as being 'desirable', or in an uncompromising manner as being 'absolutely imperative'. In half of the cases, the minority first used either the desirable style or the imperative style, and likewise for the second text. Crossing these two manipulations made four distinct conditions. In two of the conditions, the style did not vary, the minority remaining either compromising or uncompromising form start to finish. In the other two conditions, the style varied: either initial flexibility was followed by hardening (desirable style first, then imperative style), or inversely, the uncompromising style was followed by the more compromising style, thus slackening the conflict. The influence measure (cf. Appendix 7.2.5) was taken immediately after these inductions, and then again a few weeks later. Let us look at the amount of delayed change, which represents variations in indirect minority influence, given in Figure 4.1.

What happened in the more relational context when the minority appeared to be reacting to the pressure of other groups? The most marked effect was the low degree of influence exerted by the minority when the first message was delivered in an uncompromising manner. In a conflictual intergroup relationship, it is therefore not to the minority's advantage to show itself as conflictual at the onset: in doing so, it makes the criticism of the belittling parties seem justified. The relational motive of the discourse would in this case mask the potential validity of its content.

In this relational context, however, one of the conditions did lead to a high degree of delayed influence. This occurred when the minority first exhibited a 'clean slate' through its compromising behaviour, and then defended its positions rigidly, only after having been attacked. The minority's perseverance in maintaining its own stance may have been taken as

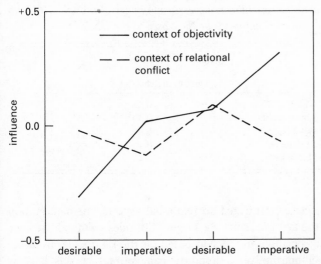

Figure 4.1   Delayed change (a + sign indicates more influence)

evidence of its self-affirmation capability, since it did not give in to social pressure, thus proving the validity of the defended positions, even if defending them meant incurring the social risks inherent in the confrontation of antagonistic points of view. As such, it maintained the conflict, but was allowed to do so in the light of the provocative context. Since discrimination failed to hush the minority and deny its social existence, it may have stealthily shifted the attention of targets towards the analysis of the minority's characteristics, including the meanings associated with the position being so strongly advocated.

This indeed is also what the observed effects lead us to believe in the case where the setting for the minority's consistency was an aroused social context by a xenophobic act independent of the prior stand taken by the minority. In this case, the influence exerted was weak when the minority was compromising at both stages. When the minority yielded in the face of social reality, it was only showing the weakness of its position, especially since the attentuation of the conflict was not perceived in this case as a simple strategy to decrease conflict (Nemeth and Brilmayer, 1987). Due to its inability to assert its position to the extent called for by the evolution of social events (cf. also Nemeth, Swedlund, and Kanki, 1974), it lost its status as a potential alternative.

In this 'objective' context, delayed influence was all the more pronounced when the minority affirmed its xenophilous position in an uncompromising manner, especially when issuing its second message. It pays to be firm when the facts make firmness legitimate.

Table 4.3. *Direct and indirect influence scores, and image of the minority (the higher the number, the more influence or the closer to the label)*

	Without	With
	Cognitive activity	
Abortion	−0.07	+0.01
Contraception	−0.12	+0.30
'Evaluation'	+0.04	+0.05
'Tolerance'	−0.07	+0.12
'Feminism'	−0.19	+0.27

When the subjects concentrated on relational aspects, the determinant message became the first one, since the targets' attitudes seem to have been set by their initial, negative impression based on the rigid style. By being consistent and self-affirmative, a minority can counteract this bias by manifesting uncompromising behaviour in the future, provided it first proves its flexibility. In a relational context, then, consistency can sometimes reinforce minority influence.

When the objective aspects of the social situation took precedence over the interpretation of the minority's consistency, the final intervention was the most important one insofar as it did not appear to be *justifying* an uncompromising attitude, but *requiring* one. Thus, there are truths that may not lend themselves to negotiation. In other studies, it has indeed been found that indirect minority influence often occurs in conjunction with a firm and imperative rhetoric, but is perceived and interpreted as stemming from a sort of 'social objectivity' founded on the current social conditions (namely, for this xenophilous minority, on the crisis situation and on national values; cf. Roux, Mugny, and Pérez, 1989).

4.3.4 Validation implies focusing on the source
In the above experiment, the targets were provided with the contextual elements needed to interpret the conflict induced by minority consistency. This was done by means of experimentally induced orientation of this interpretation towards one of the poles characterizing the ambivalent image of the minority. The involved contexts either did (or did not) enable the validation of the minority position, depending on whether (or not) they justified the conflictual nature of that position, which thus appeared (or did not appear) as an authentic alternative containing its own element of truth. Indirect impact thus appeared to be the outcome of a process involving the mental construction of the minority position and the shifting of the

cognitive activity of targets away from relational aspects and towards consideration of the objective reasons for adopting the divergent positions.

This dimension of social constructivism instigated by the intervention of a minority group is based on the fact that targets can be led to actively build new meanings (which were purposely provided in the preceding experiment), and in particular, to discover or imagine new attributes to define or redefine the initial or prior stereotype of the minority.

In a preliminary explanation of indirect minority influence, the definition of validation was limited to the simple focusing upon the object, and not the source (Moscovici and Personnaz, 1980). We have been led to postulate, on the contrary, that the validation of a position also implies redefining the minority group that is advocating that alternative position. At this point, we must demonstrate that the occurrence of the semantic activity subjects are led to carry out in regards to the characteristics of the source is indeed one of the necessary conditions for the exertion of indirect influence. One way of proceeding would be to provide the targets with the means for engaging in this activity. This can be shown by comparing two of the conditions in an experimental study on abortion (Pérez, 1985, experiment 1). The only difference between them is that in one condition the subjects filled in the opinion questionnaire immediately after reading the minority text and described the minority afterwards, whereas in the other condition – as in virtually all of our studies (for reasons which will become evident) – after having read the minority text, they started by stating the characteristics of the minority on the usual image questionnaire, only to answer the opinion questionnaire measuring minority influence at the very end of the experiment. In the former condition, the targets had to directly take a stand concerning the conflict induced by the minority, whose image must have been close to the usual stereotype of the minority; in the latter condition, they were given the opportunity to generate a more elaborate representation of the minority.

The results are clear (cf. Table 4.3): the conventional kind of minority influence (weak at the direct level, strong at the indirect level) only appeared when the subjects were first led to reflect upon the characteristics of the minority, and to express their attitudes afterwards.

The image measures obtained here are indicative of what happened: when the subjects described the source before expressing their opinions, they presented a clear image of the minority, defined as young, feminist, and progressive on the one side, and open-minded, tolerant, and democratic on the other. This was not the case for subjects having answered the opinion questionnaire outright. Is it surprising then that no influence was observed? Note also, as we have already seen on several occasions, that this indirect effect was not due to an 'evaluative' difference, since the two conditions under consideration here did not differ in this respect. This explains why the amount of direct influence, which has been shown to be correlated to general approval of the minority, did not change across conditions. Whatever the case may be, it is evident that cognitive construction by the subjects does in fact serve as a causal go-between which accounts for influence. It is the interface between social conflict and attitude change.

4.3.5 From intergroup conflict to intragroup change

We are familiar with the idea that the world is organized in a balanced and coherent fashion. Since Heider (1958) and Festinger (1957), the theorists of social psychology have devised numerous models explaining how such mental orders are established and re-established, even though social psychology has obviously provided arguments supporting the idea that humans often exhibit irrationality and are prisoners of bias in their judgement and assessment of reality (cf. Markus and Zajonc, 1985; Nisbett and Ross, 1980; Tversky and Kahneman, 1973). In influence or persuasion processes, individuals often do not examine the content of messages, preferring to limit themselves to the use of highly simplifying heuristics (cf. Chaiken, 1987).

We have just seen that intervening minorities introduce new elements apt to create a state of ambivalence that may be the source of specific conflicts leading to the restructuring of attitudes and social field representations. How do these socio-cognitive incoherencies operate? Without attempting to consider all of the possible cases, we shall look in particular at the one that comes to mind first, namely when the new attributes assigned to the minority (due to its consistent insertion in the social field) contradict other attributes resulting from the categorization of the source (the initial attributes justifying discrimination).

Validation thus may involve the unobtrusive transition from a conflict first sensed and represented at the 'relational' level to the examination of the relationships maintained between the involved social entities and the object under debate. First, social comparison leads to the consideration of message content solely on the basis of negative attributes assigned to the minority as deviant from the norm. Afterwards or simultaneously, validation leads to the consideration of the content for its own sake, by virtue of its status as a counter-normative alternative. It is at this point that socio-cognitive incongruities appear, initiating a mental activity aimed at reconstructing the meanings associated with the minority position.

Another example of what will form the gist of this chapter is an experiment already discussed in the preceding chapter and dealing with attitudes towards foreigners expressed in a Christian milieu (Mugny and Pérez, 1985). Again, a substantial amount of influence was exerted in this experiment by the minority taking an essentially biblical approach (ingroup) when it used an uncompromising discursive style (using the mandatory tone: 'it is absolutely imperative'), and by the minority who took a political approach (thus borderline outgroup) when it made its message sound less constraining ('it would be desirable'). Less influence was obtained, on the other hand, when the biblically-oriented minority was compromising and when the politically-oriented minority was uncompromising.

Can these results be interpreted in terms of potential socio-cognitive incoherencies? To do so, we must of course assume that in reality, different styles can define specific ideological positions and identities. On the basis of this premise, the freedom of opinion implicit in the word 'desirable' would be typical (or at the very least more typical) of the biblical source, since this idea is clearly established in the milieu under consideration in this experiment. Inversely, and by contrast, the intransigence associated with the word 'imperative', more typical of political ideologies, would be more coherent with a source arguing on the grounds of an explicitly political principle. A particular way of interpreting the influence effects obtained here can now be suggested: influence appeared when the compromising or uncompromising style and the biblical or political categorization of the minority were contradictory.

The dynamics of change were indeed at work when the biblical source showed itself to be uncompromising, inducing more social conflict and simultaneously introducing some degree of incoherency between its categorization and its style. The same was true for the political minority which, granted, attenuated the conflict by using a flexible style, but which at the same time introduced some sort of incoherency between the attributes of flexibility, known to qualify the minority due to the style it actually utilized, and the expectation, if existent of course, of the more uncompromising style assumed to correspond to a clearly ideological discourse without political circumlocutions.

The other conditions, where influence was weak, were the ones where there was complete 'coherency' between the style expected for that category and the actual behaviour of the minority, in which case there was confirmation of normative expectations. This homology may also partially explain the lesser degree of influence obtained in these conditions, as if there were nothing to change since each social actor in the end was acting in accordance with the position he/she occupied in the social field, manifesting – we might say in a completely natural fashion – the predictable behaviour (Roux, 1989). Under such conditions, no cognitive reconstruction activity would have to take place.

If this analysis has any heuristic value, it is obviously because it allows us to assume that one of the major devices of minorities is exhibiting a

Table 4.4. *Immediate agreement, attitude score, and minority image (the higher the number, the more influence or the closer to the label)*

	Control	Sociopolitical claims
Immediate agreement	5.40	4.84
Post-questionnaire	4.89	5.29
Image		
'Credibility'	+0.11	−0.12
'Progressiveness'	−0.19	+0.00
'Generosity'	−0.02	+0.11

behaviour or negotiation style that goes against the expectations derived from the application of the homology principle by target subjects. In short, minorities break the laws of this psychosocial logic by forcing targets to modify, complete, and in any case more finely develop their representation of the minority.

An additional cue to such potential socio-cognitive conflicts can be found in another finding from the same experiment. To pinpoint it, let us compare the least conflictual condition (biblically-oriented, desirable style, humanitarian claims) with the four conditions (taken together) involving political claims. As shown in Table 4.4, subjects clearly did not accept the claims as much when, immediately after having read the minority text, they were asked to express to what extent they agreed with it as a whole (cf. Appendix 7.2.3). However, at the end of the experiment, when they were asked to express themselves on various points (opinion questionnaire; cf. Appendix 7.2.5), it became evident that, in spite of their original rejection (compared to the condition considered here as the control condition), a high degree of influence was observed, as if within the short lapse of time during which the experiment took place, we had managed to reproduce highly direct influence (explicit agreement) as well as indirect influence (opinions about the claims). Why?

Another result to be retained here is that the minority defending the least acceptable claims (since they were undeniably the most extremely pro-foreigner) acquired an ambivalent image which in effect was formed between the time when agreement was expressed and when attitudes towards the claims were stated (cf. Table 4.4). On the one hand, its progressive and somewhat excessive position would indeed merit its being judged negatively as more incompetent and less credible. Its initial rejection was in fact accompanied by evaluative discrimination, as described in the model of categorical differentiation. On the other hand, despite this categorization and discrimination, the minority saw itself being granted some qualities: it was quite reasonably construed as more progressive, but was also viewed as more generous, more humanitarian, etc., as having all the characteristics thought to qualify ... the subjects themselves as confirmed Christians. Thus, by their extremism, these minorities may have exerted influence (on the final questionnaire) in spite of their initial rejection, because in the end, their claims were viewed as being inspired by biblical texts to an even greater extent than the claims expressed by the biblically-oriented minority.

These dynamics again result from opposing attributes, which introduce a sort of contradictory state into the influence situation and falsify the presuppositions of homology conveyed by the identity matrices initially used. The resolution of a conflict of this nature, namely through a change in attitude, must necessarily involve a construction process by means of which a subject readapts his or her identity matrix to redefine all of the attributes and category networks characteristic of it.

To deal with a source obviously inspired by a principle which turns out to be political, Christian subjects were indeed faced with the following dilemma: 'How can I, a Christian, be less generous towards foreigners than an extremist, sectarian minority whose political grounds I am moreover supposed to condemn?' This is a nice example – in the terms of the Self-Categorization Theory (Turner *et al.*, 1987; Turner and Oakes, 1989) – of a case in which, via its intervention, the minority modifies or re-defines the prototypicality of the positions in its own favour.

This dual action, on the one side involving intergroup differentiation, and on the other, integration into the very definition of the ingroup, implies what in the preceding chapter we considered to be the dissociation of social comparison and validation. Indeed, no one response, whether exhibiting discrimination or favouritism, sufficed to resolve this *now internal conflict* in that it challenged targets as members of the ingroup (here, Christian). First of all, at the social comparison level, the subjects could not outwardly show approval of the minority without running the risk of being identified with an ideologically unacceptable position. However, neither could they fail to recognize the alternative value, since this value in the end was indicative of fundamentally biblical inspiration, which until that point was assumed to be one of their own values, now appropriated by the minority. There are truths that can not be eluded. By denying the minority, these subjects would in effect be denying themselves.

4.3.6 *Homologies and their negation*
Let us more clearly incorporate these diverse dynamics into our under-standing of intergroup relations. The theory of categorical differentiation (Doise, 1978) illustrates how, in intergroup relations, differentiations tend

to affect representations, behaviours, and evaluations in a coherent manner: individuals who sense a difference between their own category membership and that of another person are thought to act towards that person in a discriminatory fashion and evaluate him or her negatively, and individuals considering themselves to be close to another person are thought to evaluate that person positively and act in his or her favour. The same would be true for behaviours and evaluations that are at the root of differentiation. In short, individuals set things up so that all differentiations at a given level correspond in a homologous manner to other differentiations at other levels, forming a balanced and coherent view, one which generates and justifies social differences. This model accounts remarkably for the vicious circle of prejudice and discrimination, which end up justifying each other, and in effect, ensuring the symbolic and concrete reproduction of social divisions.

Because of their ideological positions, minorities appear in the social field as negatively connoted outgroups. If the above functionings were to constitute the sole response to a minority's attempt to innovate, we could obviously not understand how any change, defined by any mode of appropriation of innovative positions, could ever come to be. It must therefore be assumed that minorities manage to break the laws of this differentiation logic at some point.

In the same manner as it can lead to the indexation of attributes other than those justifying discrimination, the validation activity should, according to how it situates the minority in the representation of the category field, allow for other categorizations, other social 'nooks' where the minority is perceived in its distinctiveness rather than simply as an outgroup that must be differentiated.

It is precisely this vicious circle that consistency manages to interrupt. As we have said, via its consistency, the minority scorns the discriminations directed towards it, placing itself above them. The minority forces targets to go beyond discrimination, since discrimination does not suffice to diminish the conflict that lingers on. The rhetoric of minority consistency thus constitutes the antidote of the rhetoric of discrimination, notably forcing the targets to consider new arguments to handle the conflict (cf. Billig, 1985; Maass and Clark, 1983).

Accordingly, we must also examine the social and cognitive dynamics likely to question the validity of the principle of homology, that is, the extension of discrimination to various levels. A break of this sort means that various significations regarding representations, evaluations, and behaviours have been introduced and are incompatible with each other, in short, that a sort of 'incoherency' may have come to prevail.

Now, various studies on social representations have shown that their socio-cognitive function is to make the strange familiar (Moscovici, 1981), to explain whatever does not correspond to 'social logic' (Bolzman, Mugny, and Roux, 1987), or to explain the unexplainable (Mugny and Carugati, 1989). In short, their purpose is to allow subjects to cope with such 'socio-cognitive incoherencies'. We shall propose here a kind of extension to this conception based on the same line of thinking whereby we contend that minorities, particularly via their behaviour styles, can introduce such deviations from the social logic of minority discrimination by introducing something unusual (Roux, 1989) likely to trigger the specific cognitive activity needed to handle it.

Naturally, several cases are possible, as we have already seen on various occasions. By means of an *ad hoc* experimental induction, we shall examine at this point the more specific hypothesis wherein indirect influence (that is, conversion) depends on a conflict founded on the opposition between categorizations and evaluative connotations, and on the cognitive activity that this opposition initiates.

In the previous experiment, we took advantage of the fact that the minority's ideological position, in conjunction with its rhetoric, led to the restructuring of the innovative viewpoint due to intergroup conflict. In the next experiment, we shall combine categorizations and evaluative connotations (with the same ideological content in each case) in such a way that sometimes they support each other and sometimes they contradict each other.

Consider the study on abortion (Pérez and Mugny, 1986a) in which the same pro-abortion text was distributed to young men and women. In certain conditions, we said the text had been written by a minority group that was young. This was designed to reinforce its categorization as an ingroup. In other conditions, the text was attributed to adults, a non-trivial outgroup for the subjects.

The minority text was read after the subjects had rated 'people in favour of abortion' on ten characteristics among which they were to choose six. In half of the conditions, all of the characteristics were negatively connoted (irresponsible, intolerant, reactionary, unrealistic, immoral, selfish, uncritical, unconvincing, dependent, authoritarian), thus necessarily limiting the subjects to a solely negative view of the position which would turn out to be that of the minority, either ingroup or outgroup. This therefore threatened the identity of those who might be slightly in favour of the minority. In the other half of the conditions, and in a symmetrical fashion, subjects were to state their mind using the same characteristics, but this time, only the positively connoted pole was given.

The subjects were thus presented with congruent situations wherein the identity of the source was consistent with either the favouritism bias (ingroup minority, positive connotations) or the discrimination bias

Table 4.5. *Direct and indirect influence* (*a* + *sign indicates more influence*)

Categorization	Ingroup		Outgroup	
Connotation	Positive	Negative	Positive	Negative
Abortion	−0.15	+0.05	+0.29	−0.17
Contraception	−0.19	+0.39	−0.06	−0.11

(outgroup minority, negative connotations), which we compared with incongruent situations wherein the evaluative connotations were in contradiction with the categorization of the source (ingroup minority, negative connotations; outgroup minority, positive connotations).

The results (see Table 4.5) speak for themselves: the ingroup minority exerted more influence (granted, indirect – we shall come back to this later) when the normative context stressed the negativeness of the connotations associated with the source, whereas for the outgroup minority, more influence was exerted (granted, at the direct level) when it had positive connotations (which is consistent with one of Martin's findings, 1987a; cf. section 3.3.1).

Thus, the dynamics of attitude change were activated, not when the connotations endorsed or coincided with the ingroup or outgroup identity of the minority in accordance with the principle of ingroup favouritism and outgroup discrimination, but when, in effect, the categorization of the source and the indexation of the attributes associated to it were contradictory. Without a doubt, it may be in a socio-cognitive conflict and not in a state of 'concordance' that the dynamics of minority influence originate. This was indeed true here, since whenever the social logic of homology was followed, i.e. when the ingroup was accredited or the outgroup was discredited, the dynamics of influence do not seem to have been set off at any level (in comparison to the other conditions, of course). This can be explained by the fact that in these conditions, no validation activity could have taken place, at least not to the same degree. We shall consider other data below that support this assertion, which will enable us to take a closer look at what occurs between the various levels of influence.

4.3.7 Conversion: not 'in spite of' but 'thanks to' categorization

Insofar as the attributes of the source that have been constructed cognitively are generally projected onto the identity matrix, social constructivism should also contribute to the categorization of the social field. The innovative nature of the minority position may lead targets to cognitively (re-)construct new categorizations in the social field that do not necessarily correspond to the categorizations existing before the minority intervened or at the very beginning of its intervention. Note that although the initial categorization of the minority tends to increase the distance between the targets and the minority source, these new categorizations are thought to cause the re-definition of the field of possibles and hence to trigger the re-definition of the previously assigned categories, thus leading to new potential definitions.

But let us go one step further. Given that, by definition, an alternative can only be distinct in the socio-cognitive field if it is defined as 'other', and if in some sense it is categorized as an outgroup with its own special attributes, we must acknowledge that what makes validation of its message possible is the very fact that the minority is placed in an intergroup context. We have seen examples of this in the preceding chapter on the limits of discrimination.

This brings us to formulate a hypothesis that goes against our intuition in the current state of the art. We must indeed admit that it is not actually *in spite of* but *thanks to* the minority's categorization as outgroup that it becomes a source of conversion. The more conflictual the minority, the more it is discriminated against, like an outgroup. And the more it is 'particularized', the more it is recognized as distinct, and thus paradoxically, the wider the range of possibles becomes. This complementary nature is one of the aspects of the categorization mechanism that intergroup research has not yet sufficiently investigated (as other authors have stressed: Billig, 1985; Doise, 1987), and that the study of minority influence demands.

To illustrate these assertions, let us look at one of the other results of the experiment discussed above (Pérez and Mugny, 1986) in which positive or negative characteristics (congruent or incongruent) were crossed with categorization of the minority as either ingroup or outgroup, and direct influence (abortion) and indirect influence (contraception) were measured. The effect of interest to us here, which we saw above but did not elaborate upon, is that when influence was found, it did not act at the same level in the ingroup case as in the outgroup case (cf. Table 4.5).

First of all, the positively connoted outgroup minority was influential at the direct level. In effect, we can consider paradoxically that the minority as an outgroup did not involve identification to as great an extent since it was located outside the field of all possible identifications, and that being positively connoted, subjects may have felt they would run the minimal risk by yielding to the source. The impression this minority made indeed shows that it was evaluated positively in all respects: it was described as flexible, less feminist, and less sectarian.

Furthermore – and this is the essential part of our demonstration here – the minority with the same category membership as the subjects (i.e.

ingroup) exerted mostly indirect influence, that is, when negative connotations were associated with it. But indirect influence nevertheless does not appear by virtue of an ingroup favouritism bias, as if the subjects were protecting their own identity by defending the threatened identity (cf. Breakwell, 1983) of a minority source, granted, but nevertheless an ingroup source.

This conversion is indeed a corollary effect of a validation process which is manifested by constructivism at the categorization level, a new distinction being set up in the ingroup itself. The source was not simply described as 'young' (compared to adults), as the experimenter had presented it, but was defined, that is, categorized as feminist and described as rigid and sectarian. This new categorization of the minority source was constructed cognitively by subjects as they attempted to give meaning to the influence situation, and in effect implies the acknowledgement of the specificity of the alternative ideological positions of the minority. As a source of conflict, the minority thus induced change in spite of this categorization.

Categorization as 'us' or 'them' (cf. Zavalloni, 1971; Zavalloni and Louis-Guérin, 1984) can give rise to paradoxical effects when we consider the indirect influence actually granted to the minority. This brings us back to what appeared to be a categorization paradox: a minority, even a negatively connoted one, even an outgroup one, can exert influence, although of an indirect nature. The influence does not result from positive connotations, which as we have seen are not assigned to it, nor from an ingroup favouritism bias since it is not categorized as ingroup, but rather from its categorization as 'other', and thus of the fact that it is recognized as an alternative in the social field.

4.4 Validation and recognition of an organizing principle

Let us approach the question of the indirect nature of the influence of minorities in another manner. Insofar as indirect minority influence affects matters upon which the minority did not explicitly take a stand, we must exclude the hypothesis, as seen above, that imitation and social learning are its underlying mechanisms, since at best they can account for direct influence. The specificity of our studies in this area, as in developmental social psychology, is the acknowledgement of the fact that minority influence relies on social constructivism, i.e. that it is based on a complex cognitive activity (Nemeth, 1986). We have just seen this to be true in the case of the psychosocial construction of the source on the basis of its attributes and categorizations. Another facet of this cognitive activity should also be considered: targets of influence are led to reflect not only upon the specific content of the message presented by the minority in its attempt to influence, but also upon a larger set of contents and positions made cognitively salient by the minority. Let us now take a look at the constructivism that operates on minority message content.

In the circumstances we shall discuss in the next chapter, targets confronted with a minority may be led consciously or unconsciously to *infer the organizing principle* of the minority position, i.e. the principle underlying the positions manifestly stated by the minority as well as others. This organizing principle can be reactivated at other times, as in the case of indirect influence, even if targets do not openly endorse the claims made by the minority. It also enables targets, if the case may be, to *transpose* the explicit positions of the minority to other (indirect) responses, behaviours, attitudes, or contents that are different from the ones involved in the actual attempt to influence but also underlain by the same organizing principle.

4.4.1 Organizing principle and perceptual context

The target's ascertainment of an organizing principle that is common to both indirect influence responses and direct influence responses can be revealed in various ways, and with different paradigms.

We addressed this question in regards to Asch's paradigm (1956) using what we might call a 'negative' approach (Mugny, 1984) involving an *ad hoc* manipulation to counteract the indirect influence the minority would otherwise be in a position to exert. To do so, the experiment (which, remember, consists of judging which of three variable-height bars is the same height as a sample bar) was presented to part of the subjects as a study in perceptual illusions. Using examples for support (the inverted T illusion and the Müller–Lyer illusion ←——→——<), these subjects were informed of the fact that they might give in to illusions like those in the examples, although the two segments compared each time were shown to be the same length, despite their appearance.

The (Asch-type) influence phase then began. The incorrect response given by the influence source consisted of systematically underestimating the variable-height bars in comparison to the sample bar (the source always choosing a bar that was in fact taller instead of one that was the same height as the sample). In half of the cases, this incorrect answer was said to have been given by a minority, namely 12% of the people who had supposedly been questioned. In the other cases, it was attributed to an 88% majority.

The direct influence of the source was assessed by counting the number of times the subjects adopted the source's response system by choosing a bar that was actually too tall. Indirect influence was assessed on a series of about 30 items, shown before and after the interaction phase, where only one variable-height bar was presented along with the sample bar. The subjects were supposed to decide which of the two bars was the tallest, and

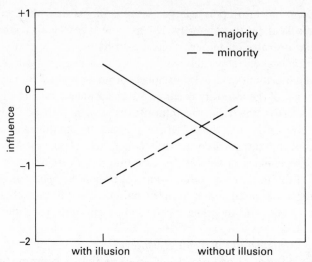

Figure 4.2   Indirect change (a + sign indicates more influence)

were not allowed to answer that they were the same height (the answer used during the influence phase). If indirect influence occurred on this measure, then the subjects would be assumed to have inferred the principle of underestimation of variable-height bars which underlaid the explicit choices of the source, and to have transferred it to this other set of questions. Figure 4.2 shows the changes undergone in each condition between the pre-test and the post-test for the indirect influence measure.

These results reveal a significant interaction between the two variables. The minority exerted indirected influence when the subjects were not informed of the possibility of an illusion, a typical finding in this kind of study. However, when they were led to think that an illusion might be hidden in the experimental materials, no indirect influence was observed, as if the possible existence of an illusion invalidated the responses of the minority, assumed necessarily to be wrong and to have yielded to the illusions. The indirect influence resulted from the inference of the organizing principle of the minority response (in this case, the underestimation of variable-height bars) when nothing in the situation opposed such an inference (the subjects indeed had no reason to suspect that the material might induce illusions in some subjects). Minorities therefore can exert indirect influence when the situation does not furnish a 'reductionist' explanation of their behaviour, which is thus examined and analyzed in its own right.

The mapping systems used to establish a correspondence between message content or source behaviour and the characteristics of the source have been widely studied in regards to the phenomenon of psychologization

(Mugny and Papastamou, 1980; Papastamou, 1983), which we shall come back to in the last chapter. Psychologization causes a reduction in the amount of minority influence and consists of leading targets, for one reason or another, to explain and, if the case may be, reduce a minority's behaviour to the psychological reasons responsible for that behaviour. Such socio-cognitive 'reductionism' is based, moreover, on the social norms of internality (cf. Beauvois, 1984; Beauvois, Joule, and Monteil, 1987; Leyens, 1983). Validation, and hence conversion, is thought to be defused (Papastamou, 1987) when, instead of being interested in what is being said, targets restrict the interpretation of the divergence to the question of who said it, and for what subjective reasons that have nothing at all to do with reality, even some hidden reality. In contrast, these effects provide evidence of the fact that validation involves the inference of an organizing principle backing the expressed positions, one that has some real, if not objective foundation.

Let us consider what happened when the counter-norm was thought to be supported by the majority. The majority did not obtain any indirect influence when the notion of illusion had not been introduced, in conditions which were indeed like those used in the conventional paradigm of minority and majority influence studies (cf. Personnaz and Personnaz, 1987). However, it did obtain influence when the subjects thought there might be an illusion. This is a new and important observation that goes against the 'creed' of the minority influence model, which generally predicts a lack of indirect majority influence. How can this apparent contradiction be explained?

In an influence situation, explanation and interpretation systems for understanding the behaviour of others are activated in target subjects whenever that behaviour is divergent from the behaviour the targets manifest spontaneously and expect other social actors to manifest. Roughly speaking, there would in this case be two fundamental landmarks for finding such explanations. The characteristics of the source, here its membership in a majority group, take precedence outright. The direct influence measure shows moreover that the majority exerted nearly twice as much influence as the minority, as could be expected. The heuristic (Chaiken, 1987) that dominated was the consensus heuristic. Thus, in the condition conventionally used in majority and minority studies, i.e. without illusion, only comparison guided the targets' reactions, and the compliance observed was greater than in any of the other experimental conditions.

Then, a cognitive validation activity can nevertheless be added to the pro-majority social comparison, provided the context itself allowed for presupposing the existence of an organizing principle which may have escaped the targets' attention. In this case, subjects no longer relied simply on a consensus, which furthermore was beyond comprehension (the responses of the majority were false). They examined the behaviours for their own sake, in an attempt to determine their causes. This happened when the largely consensual majority adopted an unexpected behaviour in the illusion context. Therefore, the object is what 'dictated' the response, not just the desire to reach a consensus. The subjects in this case were motivated, over and above their conformity to the dominant response, to determine the organizing principle (which necessarily existed since it underlaid an illusion, perhaps that of the subjects themselves). Thus, in certain conditions, validation and conversion can also be caused by 'majorities', and the compliance generally attributed to them is not necessarily only surface-level influence (cf. Brandstaetter, Ellemers, *et al.*, 1989; Cialdini, 1987; Mackie, 1987).

The results of an experiment based on the same paradigm (Mugny, 1985b) confirm the fact that 'inferiorized' sources can nevertheless trigger the ascertainment of the principle that underlies their responses. In this experiment, subjects (age 15–17) were exposed to a source that responded in accordance with the same principle as above. They were told that the experimenters were studying the development of visual acuity in ado-lescents, and that to this end, they had already questioned other individuals of either the same age, younger, or older (three distinct experimental conditions). Indirect influence was observed for a third of the subjects in the same-age or older conditions. The most striking finding is that with the younger source, 46% of the subjects exhibited the effects of indirect influence, even though the credibility of the source had in some sense been denied by the simple fact that younger sources can be assumed to be less 'credible' on the development scale. Moreover, it was in this condition that the subjects most often exhibited the usual minority influence patterns: no direct influence, yet indirect influence. It is therefore possible to be influenced by an organizing principle of a source that one has good reasons to judge as inferior.

4.4.2 *Inferential cognitive activity and validation*

In the studies examined so far, the subjects must be assumed to have discovered the organizing principle backing the minority positions insofar as they relied on it, in the conditions predictable by the theory, to formulate their responses with respect to other behaviours, other objects, or other attitudes.

A fundamental question is raised here. It pertains to the transfer of the explicit content of the minority message to the content or set of contents indirectly linked to it, a transposition which the influenced subject must actually make at some time or another, either consciously or even – and most likely – unconsciously, as shown by the studies on the chromatic after-image effect (cf. Personnaz, 1981; Personnaz and Personnaz, 1987). Otherwise, we could not understand why the change would occur in the same direction as that underlying the explicit message of the minority. An indirect impact favouring the ideological or perceptual position the minority would most likely have invoked, had it taken a stand on that dimension, in fact implies the activation of a cognitive process of a fundamentally constructive nature. It is indeed the targets themselves that must construct or ascertain this orientation or perspective, and then later apply it to other contents.

Thus, in order for target subjects to furnish responses that comply more with the (implicit) minority stance along an indirect dimension, they must carry out an *inferential cognitive activity* through which they ascertain or deduce, from the message issued by the minority, the *organizing principle* likely to be the basis of the positions both indirectly and directly related to the minority's claims. This inference is necessary for the establishment of a correspondence between what the minority is asserting and the position it is assumed to advocate at the indirect level. The ascertainment of such an organizing principle may be what enables indirect minority influence to occur, provided of course it is taken into account. For indirect influence to be exerted, then, the targets do not have to yield to the minority at the direct level, but only have to discover its underlying principles.

However, finding a means of observing whether an organizing principle is inferred is difficult to do *a posteriori*. Granted, we could examine the various aspects of the image of the minority as we did in several studies. This image is likely to tell us something about how the minority was represented. But we generally end up *assuming* that the subjects *must indeed have inferred* such an organizing principle, in a somewhat tautological manner, since the existence of the effect is what suggests the existence of the cause. To make sure that this is actually what happens, we decided to experimentally introduce this hypothetical principle *a priori*, once it had been ascertained. We will examine this ascertainment process first.

4.4.3 *Consensus about the specificity of a minority norm*
Let us take the example of our paradigm on abortion, where we have regularly found indirect influence on the contraception dimension. In the many studies using this paradigm, a factorial analysis of the source image quite systematically shows that morality is one of the most highly saturating items of the first factor of the minority image, a factor which is fundamentally evaluative in nature (and is highly correlated to the expression of attitude towards abortion). Another factor is represented by tolerance, which may account for indirect influence. Our hypothesis is that

in this paradigm, the principle that links the minority's stand on abortion to changes in the subjects' opinions about contraception is *tolerance* more than morality. Why?

We might first reason by assuming that both the advocates and opponents of abortion would claim to have good morals, even if the definition of morality is not necessarily the same in each case. This would logically imply that morality is not a specific attribute of the pro-abortion stance. This is not true for tolerance. Being against abortion in effect implies refusing others the right to resort to abortion, which constitutes a unilateral, even dogmatic normative regulation which precisely rejects tolerance. By contrast, being in favour of abortion (which does not mean intrinsically valuing abortion for its own sake, as an ethical and social finality) amounts to demanding open normative regulation, in effect democratic, allowing each person to freely choose to resort to abortion in certain circumstances, without however involving any obligation. If recognized and adopted, this principle could also be applied to a more open-minded attitude towards contraception or towards other attitude realms likely to be regulated by a norm of tolerance or intolerance, as we shall see in the last chapter.

Before providing an experimental demonstration of these assertions, let us first consider several findings which suggest that tolerance may indeed be one of the recognized organizing principles specific to the pro-abortion point of view, at least more than morality would be. Subjects were asked (Pérez, 1985; experiment 6) to state what they felt people in favour of abortion would be like by ordering (from 1 to 8) the eight triplets formed from the following three dichotomous criteria: progressive vs. conservative, tolerant vs. intolerant, and moral vs. immoral (for example, people who are in favour of abortion are progressive, intolerant, and immoral). The values obtained for the index used (ranging from -20 to $+20$, where $+20$ means a positively connoted description) showed that pro-abortionists were most often judged as progressive ($m = +7.34$) and tolerant ($m = +2.27$), but also as immoral ($m = -2.96$). In other words, whenever a representation of the pro-abortion position had to be constructed from these three dimensions, the attributes describing persons in favour of loosening up social regulations were the ones rated positively, and not those describing moral persons.

The prominence of tolerance as a definitional feature of the minority position becomes even more marked when the opposition of the ideological positions is brought to light. Accordingly, we asked subjects to judge the pro-abortion position by placing themselves in two types of conditions. In the first, they were supposed to imagine what might be the opinion of young people in general, whereas in the second, they were to imagine what might be the opinion of either conservative young people or progressive young people. Among the results (Mugny and Pérez, 1988a), what interests us here is that when the subjects were more or less forced to recognize the alternative and progressive nature of the minority source in contrast to conservative young people, the source was construed as more tolerant, flexible, compromising, and democratic, descriptors which qualify both the attitude of the source and the organizing principle underlying what it was saying. Indeed, it was when we added minority-induced conflict to a context of ideological opposition that tolerance, far from being withdrawn from the minority, was attributed to it even more.

In another study already mentioned in this chapter (Pérez and Mugny, 1986a), the subjects were asked to describe people in favour of abortion in terms that were either all positively connoted or all negatively connoted, the subjects being forced to choose 6 out of 10 adjectives alleged to describe such people adequately (the adjectives used are presented in point 4.3.6). What did the subjects do? When the connotations were all positive, more than 70% of them chose to qualify pro-abortionists as democratic, progressive, and tolerant, three items describing a principle of open social regulation. When the connotations were all negative, more than 70% of the subjects chose to qualify pro-abortionists as irresponsible, immoral, and selfish, all characteristics involving a value judgement.

Thus, when choosing exclusively among attributes that upgrade the pro-abortion viewpoint, subjects qualified it as tolerant, not as moral. When choosing only among attributes that degrade the pro-abortion viewpoint, they deemed it to be immoral, not intolerant. Tolerance, then, is indeed the specific organizing principle of the pro-abortion stance. This easily leads to the idea that the tolerance principle is highly likely to be 'generalizable' to attitudes towards contraception, where the progressive minority position also presupposes openness and tolerance in personal choice.

Let us now apply a more direct approach to test the hypothesis that tolerance is generally agreed to be the specific organizing principle of the minority position in the paradigm on abortion and contraception. We asked 168 teenagers to use bipolar, 7-point scales to judge either people in favour of abortion or people against abortion. On the basis of their answers on a short pre-test, the subjects were divided into two groups, those more or less in favour of abortion ('pro' subjects, for the sake of brevity) and those more or less against abortion ('con' subjects). To make our point here, only the outcomes of the factorial analysis for the first two factors will be discussed.

The first factor describes people for or against abortion as younger or older, more or less atheist, feminist, audacious, flexible, tolerant, progressive, democratic, open-minded, realistic, objective, independent, and compromising. From Table 4.6, we can see that all subjects agreed that the pro-abortion attitude was more feminist and more tolerant (this is how we shall summarize this first factor) than the anti-abortion attitude (cf. Pérez and Mugny, 1989). This was true, moreover, for both the con subjects ($m = +0.67$) and the pro subjects ($m = +0.78$). The interaction between type of subject and target, however, indicates that the pro subjects judged the anti-abortion attitude to be lacking in these qualities ($m = -1.11$); the con subjects, on the other hand ($m = -0.40$), were more reluctant to highlight what for them constituted a sort of self-criticism. These findings tell us which attributes specifically characterize the attitude we shall present in the next few experiments as the minority position. In summary, the pro-abortion position can be defined as being represented by a categorical entity (namely, feminist) that conveys a specific alternative norm of its own (tolerance).

The second factor describes the individuals as more or less responsible, moral, generous, convincing, objective, competent, and integrated. For this factor, a certain amount of credibility was attributed to these individuals, in this case by virtue of their evaluation as moral and responsible. Among the results shown in Table 4.6, we are interested here in the fact that the specificity of the pro-abortion position does not emerge on this factor. Indeed, as indicated by the interaction between these two variables, each person tended to judge his or her own ideological position as more moral: con subjects favoured the anti-abortion stance, and pro subjects tended to favour the pro-abortion stance (which also validates the distinction made between the two types of subjects). This factor thus represents an evaluative dimension along which the twofold intergroup bias takes effect. Note also that this morality-based credibility is not characteristic of any one categorization of the differing positions. The morality dimension therefore gives rise to intergroup competition, unlike the tolerance dimension which is subject to a sort of intergroup consensus (cf. Van Knippenberg, 1978).

Another finding appears to support this interpretation. An overall significant difference was indeed found between the pro and con subjects, for both factors under consideration. The two factors showed the opposite tendency, however. The pro subjects ($m = -0.16$) chose tolerance (first factor) less often than the con subjects ($m = +0.16$), whereas inversely, the con subjects ($m = -0.16$) chose morality (second factor) less often than the pro subjects ($m = +0.16$). Wouldn't this suggest that subjects more sparingly choose the attributes they consider to be definitional of their own position? Whatever the case may be, tolerance more than morality should be regarded as defining the specificity of the ideological position supported by our pro-abortion minority.

The above evidence will be advantageously applied to several studies reported below. Indeed, our aim will be to render various attributes

Table 4.6. *Factorial scores for tolerance and morality (a + sign indicates that the label applies more)*

	Attitude towards abortion			
	of judges			
	Against		For	
	of judged target			
	Against	For	Against	For
Tolerance/Feminism	−0.40	+0.67	−1.11	+0.78
Morality/Responsibility	+0.30	−0.57	−0.30	+0.62

cognitively salient. In certain conditions, the judgements made of the minority will be oriented towards the attributes shown to be consensually specific to the pro-abortion position (tolerance will be selected). We shall then compare these conditions with those in which the attributes used (namely, morality) are not subject to such a consensus, and thus where the judgements made cannot do justice to the distinctiveness of the invoked position.

4.4.4. *Experimental induction of the organizing principle*
We therefore imagined explicitly making the cognitive activity of the subjects deal with the organizing principle, or, in contrasting conditions, deal with some other principle that does not underlie the minority position. Our hypothesis, of course, was that for indirect influence to occur, there must be a validation activity through which subjects are led to employ such an organizing principle. As a corollary, less indirect influence must be assumed to be exerted whenever for one reason or another such a validation process is not activated, or whenever the subjects' cognitive activity is directed towards a principle that is not a potential organizing principle of the positions expressed on either direct or indirect scales. This was the specific purpose of one of our studies (Pérez and Mugny, 1986b).

In this study, the message proposed to subjects was attributed to either an ingroup or outgroup minority on the basis of its sex identity. The variable we are interested in here was manipulated by varying the normative filter through which the source's ideological positions would be interpreted: the filter proposed was either morality or tolerance. After reading the message, the subjects were to judge the five main arguments summarizing the stand taken by the minority, either on moral–immoral and responsible–irresponsible scales, or on tolerant–intolerant and compromising–

Table 4.7. *Direct and indirect influence (a + sign indicates more influence)*

	Principle			
	Morality		Tolerance	
	Categorization			
	Ingroup	Outgroup	Ingroup	Outgroup
Abortion	+0.02	+0.11	−0.05	−0.08
Contraception	−0.14	−0.15	+0.12	+0.17

uncompromising scales. The latter scales were supposed to explicitly center the targets' attention on the organizing principle underlying the minority position, i.e. tolerance.

The first finding discussed here (Table 4.7) will be the fact that when judged along the tolerance dimension, the minority did tend in fact to be perceived as more tolerant, which proves that the experimental induction was effective. In addition – and here the outcome is even more interesting – the minority was categorized as more feminist, introducing the ambivalence with which we are now familiar. Moreover, its direct influence tended to be weaker here than when it was being judged as to its morality, whereas its indirect influence was greater, regardless of the source's identity, and despite the fact that it was more strongly categorized as feminist. Thus, explicitly orienting the subjects towards the organizing principle (in this case tolerance) can favour recognition of the minority's point of view. This does not appear to be true for the morality norm, which indeed could hardly account for the pro-abortion and pro-contraception positions of the minority since it does not specifically underlie these positions.

We now have all the pieces of the puzzle: the fact that target subjects are led to focus on the principle of tolerance underlying the stand taken by the minority, although it does not ensure explicit conformity with the minority (on the contrary even), nevertheless leads to a conversion effect, manifested here by the expression of a more favourable attitude towards contraception. In a complementary fashion, the minority tends in this case to actually be perceived as more tolerant, but also to be categorized as more feminist. This means that the minority may present more of an alternative since its categorization includes tolerance as a distinct attribute. Could it be precisely for this reason that the effect of the tolerance filter is not direct, and is only observed on the indirect influence measure? If this were indeed true, it would be by virtue of the implementation of a twofold process: the weak direct influence would be the result of a social comparison process involving identification with the minority and causing a potential identification conflict; the strong indirect influence would be linked on the contrary to a validation process involving a cognitive activity based on the organizing principle underlying the content of the minority message.

To demonstrate this, we must provide evidence of the fact that direct influence can indeed be explained by the variables reflecting the identification process, i.e. the 'psychosocial proximity' of the target and the source. Indirect influence, on the other hand, should be explainable in terms of the variables reflecting the cognitive activity of the subject in regards to the minority position itself, namely by their ascertainment of the organizing principle which bridges the gap between message content and indirect influence.

To this end, we simply conducted two regression analyses (*stepwise* solution) pooling all subjects in order to bring to light the variables that predict attitudes towards abortion and contraception. The predicting variables of the analysis were the following. Concerning social comparison, the initial position of the subjects was selected (mean response on a short pre-test questionnaire), based on the fact that the ideological distance between source and target is known to be an important variable. The evaluative factor of the minority image (the first factor above) was also chosen, a factor which moreover is highly saturated by the morality component. Concerning validation, we selected the mean response given during the induction (of either morality or tolerance), which reflects the degree to which subjects agreed to use the proposed normative filter to interpret the content of the message. We also chose the three factors describing the source image, which differentiate the conditions from each other (tolerance, feminism, and self-interest).

The results pertaining to direct influence indicate its significant dependence upon two of the variables introduced. The ideological position of the subjects as assessed by the pre-test was the most determining factor (β: 0.49). The evaluative factor was second (β: 0.43): the more the source was evaluated positively, the more the expressed attitudes favoured abortion. Thus, a social comparison process did indeed govern the dynamics of influence at the direct level along two well-known parameters: the initial ideological commonality of target and source, and the evaluative connotations assigned to the source.

The results pertaining to indirect influence indicate that it too depended on both of the variables introduced. This time, however, other parameters played a more predominant role. The most determining factor was the degree to which the subjects actually used the suggested normative principle during the morality or tolerance induction phase (β: 0.43): the more positively the subjects judged the content of the minority position through the proposed filter, the more they expressed a favourable opinion about contraception. The second most determining factor was the subject's cognitive activity involving the categorization of the source as feminist (β: 0.23): the more the subjects mentally reconstructed the minority as being feminist, the more favourable their attitude towards contraception was.

Thus, the cognitive activity validating the content of the message on the basis of available filters and their projection onto the field of social categorizations are the roots of indirect influence, and not the dimensions involved in social comparison. We must admit that this was true here for both morality and tolerance, and fact which emphasizes the important effect of the cognitive activity per se as it acts upon the content of the minority's arguments. Nevertheless, given that the analysis of variance unambiguously showed that the tolerance filter induced this conversion process to an even greater extent, we must also admit that the increase in the cognitive activity constructing the minority alternative was indeed due to the proposed filter, which we have seen renders salient the tolerance attributed to the minority and defines it as belonging to the new feminism category. This in turn may enable the perhaps unconscious inference of a specific attitude relative to a whole range of other attributes, including attitude towards abortion. In other words, the activity involving the mental construction of the minority position ranges over an extended 'field of possibles', and does so even more when founded on the principle of tolerance in social regulation.

4.4.5 To validate is not to approve
The inference of an organizing principle by targets is thus crucial to a minority's effectiveness at exerting influence. Since minority influence appears in particular when the source is perceived as an outgroup, it must be acknowledged that this inference may very well originate in active resistance to minority influence. The regularity with which minorities are found to have little direct influence but some indirect influence indeed suggests that such resistance may cause this inferential activity to come about. This is not the least bit paradoxical.

This question leads to a new assertion, accompanied by a new demonstration: the validation process does not imply the acceptance of the theses set forth by a minority, but may even result from their active denial. We have already noticed this in regards to the paradoxical effects of categorization. Thus, an attempt to disprove a position may be what enables the organizing principle of the minority position to be inferred: in order to deny the validity of a position, its grounds must be understood. This idea is supported by some previous demonstrations which were not necessarily based on a postulate of this sort.

Collier's (1944) findings will be interpreted in this manner. This author showed that American students who had been asked to critically examine Nazi propaganda, precisely for the purpose of denying its validity, were caught in the trap, later expressing views that were not as anti-Nazi as before. In another perspective, it has also been shown that provocative, hardly plausible ideas may be more effectively stored in memory than plausible ones (cf. Wyer and Hartwick, 1980). It is understandable, then, that they have an impact of their own.

Isn't this also what Billig (1985, p. 99) meant when he said 'Novel arguments, and novel situations, might elicit novel, previously unformulated, responses. As such, it is not surprising that extreme minority opinions can produce effects on majority attitudes ... for the minority opinion will be setting up new topics for debate, to be countered, or at least examined, by new arguments. Thus even if the minority views are rejected, they will not leave the majority attitudes unchanged, for new stocks of arguments will have been formed. In this way, one might find oneself formulating views in the course of a debate; thus, rather than the attitude determining in a strict sense what is said, the attitude in a real sense might only be discovered through argumentation.'

There is another framework in which such a hypothesis appears to have some degree of plausibility. Recently, Wegner, Schneider, Carter, and White (1987) experimentally demonstrated the paradoxical effects of thought suppression. They showed that when subjects were asked not to think about something (in this case, a white bear), not only did they not think less frequently about it, they in fact reported even more thoughts concerning it. When people are asked to think about something, they may actually think about it by exploring less ideas pertaining to it, thus implementing a sort of convergent thought process. By contrast, a prohibited idea may lead subjects to involuntarily associate a greater number of ideas to it, thus implementing a sort of divergent thought process. These effects are not really surprising in the light of the paradoxical effects we have pointed out so far.

An experiment on abortion illustrates this issue more directly (Moscovici, Mugny, and Pérez, 1984–5). This experiment took place in two phases. The first, during which the experimental manipulations were introduced, progressed in the customary manner. The first-phase measures were thus taken on a questionnaire (first post-test). Three weeks later during the second phase of the experiment, subjects were asked to answer the same questionnaire (second post-test), without re-reading the minority's statement, and without any other experimental induction. We thus had measures of direct, indirect, immediate, and delayed influence.

Now let us get on with the experimental manipulations. The main induction was aimed at introducing the denial of the validity of the minority

Table 4.8. *Direct and indirect influence, immediate and delayed influence, and image (a + sign indicates more influence or closer to the label)*

	Text	Denial
Immediate		
Abortion	4.81	4.52
Contraception	5.45	4.88
Delayed		
Abortion	−0.02	+0.21
Contraception	−0.18	+0.31
'Evaluation'	+0.24	−0.04
'Flexibility	+0.26	−0.10
'Alternative'	+0.17	+0.17

stance, which could be done for example by qualifying it as illusory or utopian. This denial was operationalized by highlighting the implausible nature of the claims the subjects were going to read. Subjects in the denial condition were given the following information:

We have conducted a series of studies on the various arguments used to deal with the question of abortion. Our goal is to find out which arguments are not worth taking into account, are not valid, in other words, which arguments are not reasonable today. According to the results of previous studies, four of the five arguments presented below are not worth taking into account, i.e. are not generally considered to be reasonable.

Then the subjects were presented with the following four demands taken from the text supposedly written by the minority group, which they would read afterwards:

It is indispensable that we legalize abortion immediately.
It is indispensable that we legalize abortion immediately.
It is indispensable that National Health Care pay for all the costs of abortion, just like it does for diseases.
The legalization of abortion is an absolute requirement of democracy.

To these four arguments, we added a fifth which was not taken from the minority text, and which expressed a less clear-cut view apt to be considered as more valid: 'One should be able to have an abortion in the case of rape.'
The subjects' task in the denial condition was to select and indicate in writing the four implausible arguments, i.e. the ones that were 'not valid' and were 'not worth taking into account'. Another condition enabled us to assess the effects of the denial itself. These subjects were asked to read the text attributed to the minority, but no denial was explicitly introduced. They

simply filled in a questionnaire about the impression they had of the minority that had made the statements, and a questionnaire about their opinions on abortion and contraception.

Let us start with the results for the experimental induction of denial. They show that on the average, subjects chose 3.59 claims, which means that they did in fact agree that the majority of the arguments were invalid. Denial was thus possible, and was actually exercised.

The results (cf. Table 4.8) show that on the immediate post-test, opinions were more in favour of abortion in the condition where the subjects had undergone minority influence (text condition) but had not had to deny the validity of the minority's demands. An analogous result was obtained in the case of contraception. On the whole, denial thus induced overall resistance to the minority. This is not surprising if we consider the ease with which the subjects agreed to the denial. The overall resistance on both dimensions can thus be interpreted here as indicating that the induced denial acted upon the inference of the organizing principle itself. Can denial thus cancel all influence effects? No!

If we look at the delayed influence found here, we can see that after three weeks, the subjects who had read the message that had been qualified as invalid became more in favour of the attitudes in question. This was true, moreover, for both abortion and contraception, although the effect was more marked at the indirect level. Again, the hypothesis of organizing principle inference still proved true here. An even finer analysis of the effects of indirect influence also showed not only that more subjects changed in the denial condition, but also that they changed more.

The subjects' image of the minority here indicates two things. When they had to deny the source, subjects judged it less positively, regarding it as more rigid, in short, as relating in a more conflictual way to targets. This evaluative discrimination and the construed conflictual nature of the minority still did not prevent it from being recognized as a spokesman, sure of itself, competent, objective, and worthy of faith, in short, as an alternative which in all plausibility demanded reflection due to the very denial of its validity.

By means of other conditions, we aimed to determine whether recalling the minority position and denial on the second post-test would affect the minority's impact. We therefore retained the denial condition in the above experimental design and added three other conditions. The new experimental manipulations were as follows. Just before taking the second post-test, we had the subjects simply re-read the minority text, without additional explanation. The observed delayed influence effects (abortion: $m = +0.16$; contraception $m = +0.37$) were not greater than in the simple denial condition: recalling the minority position did not add anything to the paradoxical effects of denial, which can therefore be considered sufficient to produce them.

In the other two conditions, the subjects were reminded of the denial to which the demands had allegedly been subjected by being asked (or not asked) to read the minority text again. The effects obtained are clear. Recalling the denial prevented the occurrence of the denial effects found in the previous experiment, particularly when the subjects did not re-read the text (delayed influence: $m = -0.08$ for abortion; $m = -0.27$ for contraception), whereas this immunization effect was not as great when the subjects re-read the text (abortion: $m = +0.18$; contraception: $m = -0.01$). These results remind us of two things. First, resistance or denial should not be underestimated, and a context in which such resistance is constantly renewed can mask, weaken, or prevent the dynamics of change (Pagès, 1987). Second, repeatedly exposing targets to a message advocated by a minority (which is a possibility) can in turn at least partially counteract the effects of resistance. Kaiser's studies (1989) in which the significations of such consistency on the part of a minority group were more highly controlled have already sensitized us to the above.

Whatever the case may be, when individuals make every effort to deny the validity of a point of view, to explicitly oppose it, they may be involuntarily led to acknowledge its soundness, its truth. This is not a trivial paradox. The next two chapters will demonstrate this in an even more convincing manner.

4.5 Conclusions

In this chapter, we have shed some light on an entire range of conditions, variables, and situations which cause the emergence of the mechanisms responsible for latent minority influence. These indirect, sometimes delayed changes are the outcome of a validation process rooted in the psychological re-transcription of a social conflict affecting the representations of the whole field of innovation. This process acts through mechanisms of a constructive nature by means of which subjects establish new meanings and features to qualify the minority, new definitions of objects and norms, new behaviours and attitudes, and new categorizations in a more highly differentiated social field.

The most striking thing in the end is that these social creativity phenomena, made up of re-definitions of objects, are the product of individuals and groups that at the onset are less socially credible and approved, are 'poorly brought up' and on the fringes of society, are the most strongly against the norms, the most often denied, and usually categorized as outgroup, to use our main illustrations.

These recurrent effects, which take on various forms depending on the paradigm, are not due to oversight, as if targets did not perceive such characteristics or forgot them. On the contrary, this constructive activity results from a greater degree of concentration on the source and the content of its message, and from a greater inclination to resist change at the manifest level.

We are now dealing with psychosocial functionings that are not one-dimensional, monolithic, or static. When confronted with a minority, individuals discriminate and particularize, disapprove and validate, resist and change. Only a constructivist approach to social influence could suggest searching for such tensions and opposition, and could lead to devising experimental proofs of what indeed simulates the ecological reality of the spread of minority-originated innovations.

These complex dynamics, where everything and its opposite are true, situate the process of comparison on the resistance side and the process of validation on the change side, both intricately interleaved, as we discovered each time we focused our reflection upon one or the other. Now that all the puzzle pieces have been laid out and turned over, the time has come to put the puzzle back together by proposing a model of their psychosociological interrelationships.

5 Comparison and validation in minority influence

5.1 Explaining the possible

In the preceding chapters, we discussed the mechanisms underlying the processes of social comparison and validation in minority influence phenomena. Although our initial aim was to analyze them in an independent manner, we soon realized that they always overlap, and that in order to understand a given effect, it is often necessary to rely simultaneously on certain notions taken from the model of psychosocial identification and on others borrowed from the model of validation. Thus, little by little, as we attempted to understand the minority phenomenon in all its complexity, the need to theoretically interconnect these two processes became apparent. After having stated once again the reasons why this theoretical framework is required, we shall propose some new and necessary notions, developed in order to integrate social comparison and validation into one psychosocial model.

5.1.1 Resistance and/or change

The studies discussed so far have shown us that, when faced with a conflict induced by a minority, target subjects are rarely passive. They mentally reconstruct their experience of the social conflict, with two goals in mind. From a more motivational, relational, or affective point of view, they attempt to protect their own psychosocial identity, for it may be involved in the manifest expression of influence. From a more socio-cognitive point of view, they are led – particularly at the latent level – to adjust their mental representation of the field of ideological positions and social relations, for its validity may be questioned by the emergence of the position taken by a minority.

From the former point of view, influence relationships involving a position explicitly recognized as a minority position force target subjects to compare themselves socially with the minority and to (re-)define their psychosocial identity, now psychologically salient, by directly and manifestly yielding to or avoiding the minority positions, depending essentially on how conflictual the connotations attached to them appear to be.

120

| | indirect influence | |
	null or negative	positive
direct influence null or negative	0 0	0 +
positive	+ 0	+ +

Figure 5.1   Possible combinations of direct and/or indirect influence

From the latter point of view, these conflictual relationships may cause target subjects to engage in a cognitive validation activity, a complex, intense, and sometimes creative activity through which they mentally construct or reconstruct a specific representation of the source, and redefine the meanings attached to the various positions and entities newly distinguished in the influence field.

We have gradually seen the following idea take shape: a conflict is always at the root of the diverse dynamics of identification, which we managed to explain by applying an intergroup approach to the minority phenomenon. Only when it is compatible with a socially gratifying identity is identification with the minority as a group or collective entity allowed, in which case the self-attribution mechanism accounts psychologically for direct influence. Conflict is also what triggers the socio-cognitive validation activity by means of which targets define the field of ideological positions, introduce new arguments, and construct new, previously unforeseen meanings, in which case the indirect social impact typical of minorities is observed. We have seen that deviations from the principle of homology, notably the disproving of certain prejudices, are also sources of mental restructuring.

The problem posed by the complexity of minority-related phenomena is that such conflicts can call for regulations affecting both the validation activity and the social comparison activity, just like in developmental social psychology where we found that socio-cognitive conflict can result in regulations that are either purely 'socio-cognitive', or purely 'relational' (cf. De Paolis and Mugny, 1985). Depending on the nature of the conflict-resolving activity, influence effects will occur in different forms, at different levels, and at different times. They may or may not activate resistance and may or may not express a change in favour of the minority positions, since all cases of direct and/or indirect influence, as shown in figure 5.1, are possible in the end. Granted, this is only a typology that as such can be completed at will (cf. Nail, 1986), but it is nevertheless based on the two acting processes whose interrelationships enable us to predict the conditions under which such and such an influence pattern will be activated.

Among the four possible patterns, we have seen that the 0+ pattern (inexistent or negative direct influence, positive indirect influence) is the one that is in fact prototypical of minorities. This does not mean, however, that the other patterns are impossible, not at all; and they too should be explained. To do so, the minority influence model must be extended by 'particularizing' minority group phenomena.

On this subject, we have seen that two outlooks are possible for the researcher: for some, 'simultaneously' evaluating direct and indirect influence constitutes an experimental bias in which explanation via the validation activity and explanation via the comparison activity run the risk of being confused, one of the two activities potentially 'contaminating' the other. Indeed the O+ response pattern can be broken down, since some subjects in some conditions are led to yield to the minority, while others in other conditions are led to keep their distance or move away from the minority. By breaking down these dynamics, whose intricately overlapping structure is apparent, we in fact oppose the validation activity and the comparison activity.

We shall thus proceed in a different manner, which is more complex, but is more suited to the problem posed by the diversity of minority-related phenomena and is closer to the real contexts in which innovation spreads. Rather than opposing the comparison activity and the validation activity, we contend that they must instead be integrated theoretically, an approach that is all the more necessary since throughout our experimentation, these two activities have appeared to occur simultaneously in subjects. Thus, defining the *interrelationships* between these two types of regulation in minority influence dynamics will be the ultimate stage of our model.

The first conclusion that must be drawn in the light of the facts described so far is that all patterns of influence necessarily presuppose the involvement of a comparison process. In other words, all ideological positions specified in the field, whether upheld by a majority or a minority, require a response based on a comparison involving some degree of identification. An interpersonal or intergroup comparison is thus thought to be made 'spontaneously', like a sort of socially rooted motivation (analogous to that studied by Festinger, 1954), unavoidably invoked by any divergence in the field.

The same would not be true for the validation process, assumed to be able to act *or* not to act, at least not in the same form, depending namely upon the load and cost incurred by the comparison. Unlike the social comparison activity, the validation process does not necessarily occur automatically, and may in particular be modulated by the outcome of the social comparison. Let us look a little more closely at the hypotheses required by such a model of social influence in its direct and indirect forms.

5.1.2 *Comparison and validation: their theoretical link*

We now have all the necessary elements to synthesize the various facets of our model and summarize its conceptual foundation. From the psychological point of view of target subjects, it is the interdependency of the social comparison process (notably with the identifications and identification conflicts that set it in motion) and the validation process (notably involving the recognition of the specific organizing principle and alternative value of the source, presupposed through the subjects' socio-cognitive activity) that accounts for the diverse patterns of influence a source is likely to induce. Four fundamental postulates can be set forth at this point.

The first is that whenever a situation of influence induces a very strong identification conflict (due to the inferred or invoked categorization of the source, to its behaviour styles, to the normative context, or to resistance to change) and prevents validation from taking place, no direct influence will be observed, nor will there be conversion. This particular case, where influence fails to be exerted, is without a doubt the one that has been predominant in the functionalist view of minorities.

The second postulate is that whenever a situation of influence induces a moderately intense identification conflict (identification with a divergent source is always loaded with some conflict) and prevents the validation process from taking place, direct influence will be observed, but not conversion. This is the typical kind of identification in Kelman's conception (1958) and of compliance or conformity with the majority (Asch, 1956), where interpersonal divergence is resolved solely by social comparison to sources that are either socially attractive or provide support. In minority influence, this response pattern will exist whenever for one reason or another comparing oneself to a minority source is socially gratifying.

Let us now consider the case in which indirect influence is exerted. The third postulate is thus that whenever a situation of influence induces a very strong identification conflict, but allows the validation process to take place, no direct influence will be observed, although a conversion effect will occur. There is no need here to stress that this is the most characteristic pattern of minority influence!

Finally, the fourth postulate hypothesizes that whenever a situation of influence induces a moderately intense identification conflict but allows the validation process to take place, both direct influence and indirect influence will be observed. Kelman's (1958) internalization falls into this category. We also saw in the preceding chapter that this was true for the numerical majority in the Asch paradigm, where the potential existence of an illusion triggered a cognitive activity on the part of the subjects. Although the ecological likelihood of this case in minority influence is low – at least during the phase in which the existence of the minority point of view is being revealed, known to be ridden with conflict (Moscovici, 1985a) – we still cannot exclude it, notably if a change in the spirit of the times comes about (due to the preceding influence pattern!) and the context becomes favourable to innovation, i.e. if initial resistance to change is bypassed and pluralistic ignorance gives in to social evidence.

To understand how societies function, we must consider these dynamics to be coexistent, even if some are more typical of certain stages in their development, depending on the tensions that set societies off from time to time as they maintain, instigate, or diffuse social change. In reality, the varied manifestations of comparison and validation are linked together in succession to form a chain of reciprocal causalities. This is because comparison and validation are two sides of one and the same reality, in perpetual motion. Every social comparison is projected onto the representation of the social field, which is organized and indexed with meanings through validation. Each validation is dependent upon identifications and identification conflicts, and on the social games of integration and differentiation. The processes involved at one level are the source of new dynamics at other levels, in accordance with the specific logic of sociocognitive conflict we pointed out in the preceding chapter. In another area but also from a constructivist perspective, Monteil (1985) gave us a very accurate idea of the circularity of such dynamics in the development of professional education programmes.

In other words, these four postulates necessarily constitute abstractions, in some sense 'slices' taken out of a continuously evolving reality of which they are but particular manifestations dependent upon the time or stage under consideration. Moreover, it is this kind of abstraction that enables us to experimentally study the conditions and mechanisms involved at various points in time. Their theorization makes their reconstruction, their experimental synthesis, possible.

5.2 The paradox of identification

We shall now illustrate the possible direct and indirect influence patterns, starting with situations where only a symbolically costly social comparison predominates, in which case direct minority influence and indirect minority influence are thwarted. We shall take advantage of this opportunity to discuss one of the paradoxes of categorization in minority influence, one that is not of lesser importance either: the identification paradox.

5.2.1 Comparison versus validation

Let us look at three of the conditions in one of our first experiments on abortion (Pérez, 1985, experiment 1). The subjects, all young women, were asked to read a pro-abortion text supposedly written by a minority group.

Table 5.1. *Direct and indirect influence (a + sign indicates more influence)*

		Minority identity	
	No identity	Ingroup	Outgroup
Abortion	+0.01	−0.15	+0.35
Contraception	+0.30	−0.17	+0.03

In one of the conditions, the identity of the minority was not specified, other than the fact that it was a minority. (This set-up, where subjects are not explicitly informed of whether the minority is ingroup or outgroup, is the most common condition for examining minority effects.) In another condition, we pretended the text had been written by a minority group with the same sex identity as the subjects, thus making salient its ingroup identity. In the third condition, finally, subjects were told that the minority was of the opposite sex, thus making its outgroup identity salient. The results for direct and indirect influence, given in Table 5.1, speak for themselves.

Three effects are of interest to use here. First, when the question of the source's identity was not explicitly raised, the ordinary minority influence pattern was obtained: no particular direct influence, but indirect influence indeed. Analysis of the image the subjects had of the minority showed that it was perceived as young, feminist, and progressive, i.e. as a clearly categorized, alternative subgroup, also viewed positively as flexible and as upholding positions based on the principle of tolerance.

What happened when the source was explicitly categorized as ingroup? The results show undeniably that the overall amount of influence exerted decreased, at both the direct and indirect levels (00), which leads us to believe that the favouritism bias did not take effect. What happened then? Analysis of the minority's image reveals that it too was perceived as feminist, but that this time it was assigned all the negative characteristics made available to the subjects, namely, it was viewed as rigid, acting in its own interest, and extremist. In short, it was attributed no positive qualities. Discriminated against at the representational and evaluative level, it is not surprising that this minority was also discriminated against at the influence behaviour level. It is true that the self-attributions involved in a potential identification would have entailed a real symbolic social cost, and all the more so because the subjects had the same identity as the minority and ran a greater risk of categorical confusion. The social comparison, made salient and particularly risky, predominated to the extent here that the subjects did everything in their power to distinguish themselves from the minority, causing an effect of the black sheep type (Marques *et al.*, 1988).

This indeed is a paradoxical identification effect: when the subjects were not informed of the minority's ingroup identity, the image they formed of it was feminist, an alternative with which they certainly did not identify (at the direct level) but from which they drew some inspiration to reformulate their attitudes (at the indirect level) by adopting the principles of tolerance and open-mindedness that constitute the recognized inner core of the minority position. On the other hand, when the ingroup identity was stated, the social comparison became both salient and somehow threatening, to the extent that the subjects may have focused on it totally, striving exclusively in both their influence behaviour and judgements of the minority to differentiate themselves from it. But as we already know, the identification conflict increases in salience as the psychological involvement of the subject in the social comparison increases. We can understand why in the ingroup (female) the minority would profit from being explicitly defined as outgroup (feminist alternative). The condition for the emergence of the 0+ pattern would indeed be that the psychological salience of the social comparison not be too great, and that it let a state of ambivalence appear to allow a validation process to take place, through which the minority would be defined as an alternative in the social field.

Finally, this paradoxical effect becomes the most apparent when we compare the effects of the ingroup minority with those of the outgroup minority. The latter exerted a great deal of influence at the direct level, but had no specific effect at the indirect level, which completes the identification paradox. The source image found here indicates that unlike the other two minorities, this minority was not perceived as feminist, but for the most part was evaluated very positively. As in an experiment we shall describe later, it appears that categorization of the source as an outgroup sometimes triggers manifest influence, as if there were less risk of identification, or as if the question had become irrelevant. It should also be noted that the inexistence or weakness of such an identification conflict is a corollary to a lack of indirect or latent effects, which in turn presupposes the lack of a validation activity. This in effect illustrates the third case we imagined (+0). If in addition we consider that the outgroup, here male, may have been construed as socially 'superior', then we would have to admit that its status would induce a process similar to compliance. And the very fact that the source thus becomes attractive prevents the alternative value of its advocacy from being recognized.

On the whole, these effects suggest two things. First, as far as direct influence is concerned, specifying the categorization of the minority may reinforce the social comparison, as we might expect. Slightly less evident is the fact that this comparison may result in a dual action: differentiation and refusal to be influenced when the source is an ingroup, and its acceptance when it is an outgroup. In the former case, the subject's activity may be completely oriented towards creating or accentuating the differences in order to avoid any categorical confusion. The need to establish boundaries may indeed be all the more pressing when the social actors consider themselves to be closer to the source. Whenever outgroup categorization is done outright, the boundaries are already available and are in some sense sure, so that the differentiation activity need not be carried out, at least not to the same degree.

Finally, we must admit that the indirect influence observed here did indeed result from the sub-categorization of the source as feminist, and from the assignment of what we considered in the previous chapter to be its organizing principle: tolerance, open-mindedness, which implies a certain amount of constructiveness in the categorization and indexation of the source. Such categorization, we must remember, is not primarily located at the social comparison level. Indeed, no indirect influence occurred when the minority source was perceived as feminist but the anchor point was defined by the ingroup. In addition, it also did not occur in the conditions where the outgroup source exerted direct influence, perhaps precisely because the conflict created by the divergence and its resolution was limited solely to the social comparison level, which was not highly conflictual. Validation thus may only have taken place when there was social comparison, but – since the comparison was not anchored in the ingroup – only when the identification conflict was less strong, and did not monopolize the cognitive activity of the targets, thus allowing for the recognition of the minority as an alternative.

5.2.2 The dual dynamics of social cost

Social comparison, even conflictual, is not necessarily opposed to a conversion effect. We have seen, however, that this may only be true provided 'dis-identification' with the minority (here, the ingroup) is not the sole preoccupation of the targets. The effects observed in the preceding experiment having been challenging at the least, it became necessary to more closely examine the dynamics of the social costs of identification. This is exactly what we set out to do in a study conducted in conjunction with our colleagues at the Laboratory of Experimental Social Psychology at the Autonomous University of Barcelona (cf. Mugny, Ibáñez, Elejabarrieta, Iñiguez, and Pérez, 1986), in which we once again examined this identification paradox in situations where it was explicitly introduced as an independent variable.

To do so, we recorded the attitudes of subjects (young men and women) about abortion and contraception, after having suggested they read the conventional minority source text. Four of the experimental conditions will be considered here, obtained by crossing two factors, one inducing a variable social cost, the other involving or not involving the *de facto* identification of the subjects with the minority.

To force the subjects to identify with the minority and to engage in a social comparison process, we led them to believe (as in the Mugny and Papastamou experiment, 1982, discussed in Chapter 2) that a sociological study had revealed that their school and a certain minority group highly in favour of abortion had many general characteristics in common. In each condition, the subjects were to choose 5 out of the following 6 categories possibly common to both: social milieu, type of education, family, political tendencies, professional activity, and religious background. The subjects also had to choose four other characteristics out of the five proposed, this time pertaining more to traits likely to be common to both: degree of sensitivity, value system, degree of sociability, type of personality, and level of intelligence. The subjects did indeed choose 5 of the 6 categories and 4 of the 5 general traits (the categories and traits being broad enough to make that feasible). In the conditions without identification, this induction simply did not take place.

The induction of the social cost of the identification was done in the following manner. Just before reading the minority claims, the subjects were informed of one thing. In the low social-cost condition, they were told: 'Before reading the text, we would like to remind you that the Church is totally against abortion.' This was considered as a low social cost since this information was nothing more than a reminder of something the subjects knew perfectly well. In the high social-cost condition, the subjects were told: 'The Church condemns abortion as a crime and considers those in favour of it to be immoral, irresponsible, and selfish.' This obviously involved a high symbolic cost, since advocating the minority positions would explicitly imply the self-attribution of negatively connoted characteristics.

What were the results? From the data reported in Table 5.2, several points should be considered. First, little change appeared when the social cost was low, identification with the minority slightly increasing the amount of influence, but not significantly. The introduction of a high social cost, however, accentuated the differential effects the explicit identification with the minority had upon the influence it was granted. The conventional minority influence pattern appeared when the conflict was accentuated by the high symbolic cost but when the subjects did not have to assume a common identity with the minority: direct influence did not differ significantly from in the low-cost conditions, which provides evidence of the same degree of resistance at the direct level; indirect influence increased significantly, however. Resistance to the minority, in this case the symbolic social cost, may be the source of paradoxical effects causing the influence of

Table 5.2. *Direct and indirect influence (a + sign indicates more influence)*

	Without identification		With identification	
	Low cost	High cost	Low cost	High cost
Abortion	+0.03	+0.12	+0.10	−0.21
Contraception	−0.09	+0.30	+0.12	−0.34

the minority to increase at the indirect level, as we saw in the preceding chapter in a denial situation.

Finally, when the social cost was high and the subjects were explicitly identified with the minority, they engaged in a process of dissimilation or differentiation, as we have already noted in the analogous condition in the preceding experiment where the minority was said to belong to the ingroup. The subjects' influence scores, always negative, emphasize their efforts to avoid a threatening social comparison, threatening because it implied the self-attribution of negatively connoted characteristics: immorality, irresponsibility, and egoism, made salient by the evocation of the moral power of the Church. This effort may have clouded their minds to the extent that it cancelled any potential influence, both indirect and manifest.

Thus, the effects of social cost are two-faced, just like ingroup minority identity. It is known that when target subjects are convinced of the fact that they are like the minority as to what categories they belong to and what general traits they share, and thus when they have more ingroup commonality with the source, influence is far from being governed by the ingroup favouritism bias, and is the reflection of psychosocial differentiation. In other words, when the social cost associated with the minority position is high, being perceived as ingroup reduces the minority's chances of exerting any influence: and what is more, even indirect influence is thwarted.

An innovation resistance strategy may thus be effective when the targets are identified with the group or category towards which resistance is directed. Since minorities are often categorized as outgroup, we now have another explanation of why such resistance can turn out to be ineffective in the long run. It is indeed when the social cost of its positions is acknowledged, and its value as an alternative is thus recognized, that a minority has its 'usual' latent effect, provided however the identification process, the 'dis-identification' process we should say, does not dominate the entire cognitive activity of the targets.

5.3 Beyond comparison, validation

At the beginning of this chapter, we set forth four general hypotheses to account for the various possible patterns of influence. The above data inform us about the conditions that cause the overall failure of the type of minority influence covered by our first general hypothesis. In contrast, they also inform us about the conditions under which the typical minority influence pattern emerges. In order for an indirect minority effect to occur in spite of the lack of manifest influence, two conditions must be satisfied: first, there must be an identification conflict, and second, target subjects must not feel bound by this identification conflict. We shall now develop the hypothesis that these two conditions are in fact satisfied whenever the target can *dissociate* the comparison activity and the validation activity, that is, whenever the potential validation does not depend on the comparison. But let us first see in a more intuitive manner how we might observe the action of this kind of 'decentering' from the comparison process.

5.3.1 *The cognitive way to conversion*

The above can be demonstrated by one of the experiments already discussed (in point 4.4.4) in which subjects were asked to judge the degree of tolerance or morality in the main arguments contained in a minority message. Remember that indirect influence was found in the tolerance conditions. In order to capture the dynamics linking comparison and validation, two regression analyses were conducted separately on the tolerance and morality conditions, while retaining only the most significant parameter for social comparison (in this case, the subject's initial position on the pre-test) and for validation (the degree to which subjects used the proposed normative principle during experimental induction). In the first analysis, the pre-test data were input first, followed by the induction measure, whereas in the other analysis, the order for inputting the predictors was reversed. In both cases, indirect influence was the dependent variable.

For the morality conditions, the pre-test measure was clearly shown to play an essential role (β: 0.30) since it explains a significant part of the variance, regardless of whether it was introduced first or second. In contrast, the induction measure (β: 0.23) only accounts for a significant part of the variance when entered into the analysis before the pre-test measure. Thus, the judgements made through the morality filter did not have an indirect influence prediction value of their own, since the subject's position on the pre-test suffices to account for it. The degree to which subjects agreed to define the minority position as moral depended directly upon the social comparison, which is based on the ideological proximity (or remoteness) that unites (or separates) the targets and the source. The socio-cognitive process would in this case be 'convergent' and one-dimensional: the initial positions of the subjects were as much a determinant of (1) their judgements about the morality inherent in the minority claims during induction as of (2) the indirect influence actually exerted. Quite trivially, then, subjects in favour of abortion judged the minority position to be moral and also expressed a favourable attitude towards contraception, and vice versa for those who opposed abortion. The validation activity did not turn out to be dissociated from the social comparison activity. Since the morality filter did not induce genuine constructivism, we can understand why the conversion effect was smaller.

On the other hand, the effects observed in the tolerance conditions suggest the occurrence of an authentic construction process. Indeed, the pre-test measure (β: 0.05) only accounts for a significant part of the variance when it was input before the induction measure, while the induction measure (β: 0.41) explains a significant part no matter when it was entered into the analysis. Thus, it is the degree to which the subjects where challenged by and consequently recognized the tolerance conveyed by the minority's message that explains the conversion effect to the greatest extent, regardless of the subjects' initial positions regarding abortion. In other words, an individual can apply (here, to the contraception assessment scale) the tolerance principle granted to the pro-abortion minority, without necessarily sharing the same attitude towards it. These dynamics imply that the judgements made of the minority position were *decentered* from the subject's initial positions on abortion, and thus that the validation process and the social comparison process were dissociated or orthogonalized.

5.3.2 *Dimensionality of judgements and validation*
When is this orthogonalization possible, and to start with, when is it not possible? The experiments presented at the beginning of this chapter suggest how this question might be approached. An overall lack of influence has been shown to be due to the fact that the comparison is *limited* to the search for a difference. This implies that the comparison is made in a *one-dimensional* manner, being based solely on the judgement dimension governing the comparison. Yet, if only one dimension is considered, only one norm or one view of the world can prevail, at the expense and to the exclusion of all others. Since the comparison is necessarily located along a dimension defined by, and definitional of, the majority position, minority influence becomes impossible, for no 'social nook' is available for inserting the minority, viewed only as the 'negative' of the majority. The ideological debate is then reduced to the identity conflict, comparison contaminating validation.

Table 5.3. *Direct and indirect influence (a + sign indicates more influence)*

Minority	Majority	Abortion	Contraception
Ingroup	Ingroup	−0.07	−0.02
Ingroup	Outgroup	−0.04	+0.19
Outgroup	Ingroup	−0.10	+0.07
Outgroup	Outgroup	+0.23	−0.25

In order for the specificity of the minority position to be recognized, it can be assumed on the contrary that the judgements must be *multidimensional*. In this case, the comparison would be made, sometimes at the expense of the minority, along the 'majority' dimension; but validation could also take place in that the minority would also be defined for its own sake, along a judgement dimension of its own. Only at this cost can direct influence be absent while indirect influence is still present. Targets can then start thinking in terms of the minority, but without betraying the majority.

How can such hypotheses be tested experimentally? In the experiments that follow, our aim was to create situations that would simulate these various cases of minority influence. Some were aimed at restricting the minority–majority comparison space by enclosing it within a single referent, thus hopefully introducing interdependency of comparison and validation in a forced one-dimensional universe. The aim of the other experiments was to introduce several dimensions along which majority and minority were nevertheless to be compared, but where each could be defined in its own specific terms. These conditions should allow for validation of the minority position, despite the conflictual comparison, by dissociating the two processes.

5.3.3 Salience of the intergroup context and validation
An experiment (Pérez and Mugny, 1987) on abortion attempted to answer these questions by making the intergroup context salient. In all conditions, for the purpose of reinforcing the conflictual comparison of the antagonistic entities present, the ideological positions of the majority were also stated, not just those of the minority. In addition, so as to vary the dimensionality of the comparison space, both majority and minority were explicitly given either an ingroup identity or an outgroup identity on the basis of their sex category membership.

To restrict the subjects (young women) to a one-dimensional comparison process in some of the conditions, our idea was to make salient the categorical identity common to both the majority and the minority. These two groups differed in their ideological positions, the minority being in favour of abortion and the majority being strongly opposed to it, 'like it should be'. However, minority and majority were both located within one and the same categorical universe. In two of the conditions, they were both presented as belonging to either the ingroup or the outgroup on the basis of their sex identity. In these two conditions, their ideological divergence was projected onto a single, one-dimensional social space where judgements made of each were mutually dependent and exclusive, diverging views being incompatible within a single reference category. Approval of one source thus implied disapproval of the other, a condition which should work against constructivism.

In the other experimental conditions, designed to leave room for a validation process and to allow for the recognition of both the specificity of the positions defended by the minority and the distinctiveness of its attributes, we contrasted the categorization of the majority to that of the minority. Either the minority was presented as ingroup and the majority as outgroup, or vice versa. In both cases, the ideological difference was based on differing category memberships in a multi-categorical and multidimensional universe. Two independent dimensions were provided to the subjects to differentiate the majority from the minority, enabling them to recognize the specificity of the minority position. Let us see to what extent the results, given in Table 5.3, support our ideas.

The results for direct influence show that the amount of influence the minority exerted decreased when it was opposed to the contradictory position of the ingroup majority, the outgroup majority thus inducing less resistance. The breakdown of the analysis further showed that the greatest amount of direct influence was exerted when the subjects were located outside the comparison field, i.e. when the outgroup minority was opposed to the outgroup majority, and identification was less committing.

This provides additional evidence supporting several of our assertions. The ingroup majority position may indeed tend to exert a great deal of pressure to maintain some sort of orthodoxy. In a complementary fashion – and this is a somewhat unexpected demonstration – innovation at this level can be conveyed by the outgroup. In this case, ingroup identity may be especially advantageous for majority groups and not for minority groups, for which outgroup identity facilitates the social expression of approval, provided it frees that expression from social costs.

The indirect influence results show that the two manipulated variables interacted. Indirect minority influence was greater when the majority and minority were of contrasting identities, i.e. when the ingroup minority opposed the outgroup majority, or although to a lesser degree, the outgroup minority opposed the ingroup majority. What about the image of the minority? Limiting ourselves here to the two conditions having produced indirect influence, note that the minority was evaluated more negatively, but was also perceived as more representative of an autonomous and independent alternative. Indirect minority influence thus appeared when the intergroup context showed through in a more conspicuous manner, setting itself up as an obstacle to the social comparison (direct influence), but also when the minority position was nevertheless validated, i.e. perceived in its specificity (indirect influence).

Identification with the minority, which obviously determined direct influence, thus became increasingly difficult as the subjects became more and more involved in the comparison and had to choose between the majority and the minority. This is what is implied by the finding that as soon as reference was made to an ingroup entity (whether the minority or the majority), direct influence decreased. By coming closer to the minority, the target subjects indeed ran the risk of seeing a 'categorical confusion' set in, causing their identity to suffer.

But let us get on to the link between comparison and validation, taking the conditions one by one! First, the lack of direct influence in the case where both minority and majority were ingroup was due to the intensity of the identification conflict, all the more marked when the minority–majority comparison space explicitly included the subjects themselves. Their appropriation of the source's ideological position obviously involved the self-attribution of the characteristics of the source, whether majority or minority, that they were to approve outwardly. Faced with this dilemma, it is not surprising to find out that the subjects tended to choose the majority, in order to attribute themselves the symbolic advantages connected to it, or and perhaps especially to avoid costly identification with the minority. As to the lack of indirect influence, it can be explained by the fact that in a one-dimensional space as constraining as this one, subjects may not have inferred any other organizing principle when examining the minority position than its 'deviation' from the model set by the majority and made salient by the social comparison. In this case, validation was inhibited by the comparison, and the one-dimensionality governing the representation of the antagonistic sources made the former dependent upon the latter.

Such an inhibition on validation also appeared when the comparison was made between two outgroup sources. This accounts for the fact that indirect influence did not appear here, although the subjects did undergo some direct minority influence. This was made possible by the fact that the explicit appropriation of the ideological position did not involve the self-attribution of the minority's characteristics, or if so to a lesser degree, since the subjects were in some sense only simple observers, psychologically less involved in the intergroup comparison. Moreover, the minority was evaluated very positively here. The influence observed, which was direct, only expressed the momentary attractiveness of a minority that was less conflictual after all, as we saw at the beginning of this chapter.

Let us keep going! The fact that the majority and minority differed also by one categorical identity did not cause an increase in the discrimination against or rejection of the minority, at least not at the indirect level. the idea here is that the stratagem used resulted in two inferences occurring at different levels. First, the increase in the difference between majority and minority due to their opposing memberships further emphasized the particularity of the minority position. This was true of the minority image, where its distinctiveness was shown to predominate. Second, the subjects were led to cognitively dissociate the social comparison and the consideration of the minority's alternative positions *per se*. They first compared categorical identities, which proves that at the direct or manifest level the majority's identity is what dominates. We have seen indeed that the ingroup majority induced stronger direct resistance than the outgroup majority. The comparison issue was 'settled' on the intergroup dimension opposing majority and minority in terms of their respective identities, at the expense of the minority, moreover. This may have given the subjects the chance to examine their now ideological differences on their own accord. It must therefore be to the organizing principle of the minority positions that they reacted, i.e. to the principle of tolerance, doing so all the more since the minority's autonomy of judgement and distinctiveness were recognized.

True, this is but hypothetical reasoning. We indeed do not have an available measure enabling us to guarantee the actual recognition of such an organizing principle or the reality of such a dissociation. Moreover, it is precisely to make sure they do in fact exist that we experimentally induced these comparison and validation dynamics by explicitly introducing such an operation in the next few experiments in this chapter.

5.3.4 *Interdependent or independent judgements, and dissociation*
Under what conditions is the dissociation of comparison and validation possible? In the preceding experiment, we manipulated the way in which innovation would be represented in the category field by enclosing or not enclosing the concerned ideological positions within a single categorical universe where a monolithic comparison inhibited validation, and a multiple comparison released it (and indirect influence besides). Now let us address this problem by directly and explicitly causing the comparison and validation to be based upon the organizing principle of the minority positions, and by inducing their dissociation as an independent variable. The procedure used is now familiar to the reader.

The methodological foundations of the next experiment were derived from the intergroup research conducted by Mummendey and Schreiber

(1983, 1984), and Mummendey and Simon (1989), for whom the well-known ingroup favouritism bias results from the fact that the comparison of the ingroup and outgroup is done in an independent and one-dimensional manner. Indeed, categorization is thought to be rooted in discrimination, especially when the intergroup comparison implies the *interdependence* of symbolic resources, where that which is symbolically won by one of the groups is lost by the other, as in a zero sum game. In such a highly limited comparison universe, intergroup competition would inevitably lead to outgroup discrimination, a necessary condition for preserving social identity. Such discrimination, however, would have no *raison d'être* if the intergroup comparison were made independently. This would be the case whenever for a given dimension the ingroup and outgroup are evaluated separately, or whenever the subject can judge (and favour if the case may be) both the ingroup *and* the outgroup along different, 'orthogonal' dimensions, some of which can be specific to the ingroup, others, to the outgroup, constituting a sort of mutual validation (Rijsman, 1984; Van Knippenberg and Ellemers, 1990).

This analysis is directly applicable to minority influence, and allows us, by analogy, to make a few predictions about some of the conditions which ought or ought not to allow a minority to be influential. Thus, whenever for one reason or another the social comparison of the minority and majority position is done in an interdependent, one-dimensional mode, the subjects' self-comparison with the minority can be assumed to render psychologically salient the compelling need for differentiation. In such a case, since the distance separating the subjects from the minority becomes the most important implication of the situation, any cognitive validation or recognition of the alternative proposed by the minority is excluded, for the very reason that judgement interdependence implies that the symbolic value assigned to one position is necessarily subtracted from the other, in a complementary fashion.

Indeed, a one-dimensional comparison is necessarily located in the dominant normative field exclusively defined by the majority and power structures (cf. Guillaumin, 1972), and would by definition be in the minority's disfavour. The minority's image can only be negative in this case (since it is the complement of the majority's positive image) and makes its deviant nature salient. Interdependence and one-dimensionality thus contribute to open discrimination against the minority, but also to preventing the minority from looking like a valid alternative, and preventing any organizing principle from being recognized as the minority's. These two aspects may also inhibit the establishment of ambivalence in the representation of the minority, which as we have seen, mediates the induction of the influence pattern typical of minorities.

As a corollary, this line of reasoning can be used to discern the conditions under which a validation process will on the contrary allow the minority group to exert indirect influence, even beyond any potential discrimination. It will be posited here that whenever a comparison is made in a multidimensional universe and in an independent mode, the attributes specific to the minority, including the organizing principle which is the basis of the particularity of its alternative, can also be recognized.

It is indeed conceivable that the various entities involved in a situation of influence are evaluated via a multidimensional matrix of identities and attributes. If so, the specificities of each entity distinguished in the category field can be recognized and can contribute in a constructive way to the redefinition of the field of positions and attributes associated with them.

Consider the experiment on abortion and contraception which expressly confirms these assertions. This experiment was based on several assumptions which in fact were findings obtained in previous experiments. The first is that the pro-abortion position (and the pro-contraception position for that matter) is based on the principle of tolerance, while the opposing position is based instead on the principle of morality. The first assumption, then, is that the existence of indirect minority influence implies that the tolerance filter be ascertained, an effect which would not occur if the morality principle is made evident. This was shown to be true, moreover, in one of the experiments presented in the preceding chapter.

The second assumption is that the recognition of an organizing principle specific to a minority (in this case, the principle of tolerance) implies that the judgements comparing the minority and the majority be made independently. Minority influence would not occur if this comparison is done in an interdependent mode.

By combining these two assumptions, we can guess the prediction we are now in a position to test experimentally: indirect minority influence should be greater when (1) subjects have the tolerance filter at their disposal (rather than the morality filter) and (2) they independently judge the minority and majority.

The experimental design to test this hypothesis could not be simpler. In the following experiment, again on abortion (direct influence) and contraception (indirect influence), subjects (young men and women) first read the same text in favour of abortion, and were then asked to judge the minority, and also to judge people in general, explicitly presented as the anti-abortion majority. To do so, we had them re-read the five statements that best summarized the content of the minority message. For each of the statements, the targets were to assess to what extent the pro-abortion minority and the anti-abortion majority were either tolerant (for half of the conditions in which the principle of tolerance underlying the minority viewpoint was made salient) or moral (for the other half of the conditions in which the salient principle was the organizing principle of the majority viewpoint). This was the first variable.

The second variable amounted to modifying the way in which the degree of tolerance or morality in the majority *and* minority positions was assessed for each of the five statements summarizing the minority message. Accordingly, in the conditions involving the interdependence of majority and minority judgements, subjects had a total of 100 'points' of tolerance or 100 'points' of morality, depending on the condition. These 100 points were supposed to be divided up between the pro-abortion minority position *and* the anti-abortion majority position, in such a way that the total number of points to be used was exactly 100, 'no more, no less' (cf. Appendix 7.3.4). In other words, the conditions were indeed set up so that the points 'given' in tolerance (or morality) to one of the entities were automatically and complementarily 'taken away' from the other entity, thus establishing perfect judgement interdependence.

It was quite simple to introduce judgement independence into the other conditions. To do so, we simply gave the subjects 100 points of tolerance (or morality of course) for the minority, and another 100 points of tolerance (or morality) for the majority, making it very clear that they could use all 100 points for each source independently. Let us see what the results tell us (cf. Pérez and Mugny, 1989) by looking at Table 5.4.

First, note the difference between the number of points attributed to the minority and the number attributed to the majority, an index of intergroup differentiation. The first result of interest here is that on the whole, the minority tended to obtain a few more points than the majority, which is consistent with the fact that in general the subjects themselves were basically in favour of abortion. (In the next paragraph we shall consider only those subjects who were the most opposed to it.) The essential fact, however, is that the judgements favoured the minority more strongly in the independence conditions than in the interdependence conditions. The specificity of the minority position (its tolerance) was thus more salient in the independent judgement condition, in addition to the fact that it was construed as more moral.

The results obtained for the influence measures are easy to summarize. Although no difference was significant at the direct level, two effects occurred at the indirect level. First, it is evident that tolerance induced a stronger conversion effect than morality, which supports our hypotheses as to the attitude-structuring function of the tolerance filter (cf. point 4.4.4). The observed interaction of these two variables confirms the fact that it was indeed when the tolerance principle was available *and* the judgements of the minority and majority were independent that the conversion effect was the

Table 5.4. *Difference in number of points, and direct and indirect influence (a + sign indicates more influence)*

	Morality		Tolerance	
	Interdependence	Independence	Interdependence	Independence
Difference in allocated points	+5.70	+21.30	+11.46	+20.14
Abortion	−0.01	+0.07	+0.06	−0.12
Contraception	−0.20	+0.20	+0.01	+0.40

greatest ($m = +0.40$). In this respect, the dissociation hypothesis is largely validated.

5.3.5 Comparison, validation, and ideological distance

Let us take a closer look at the effects found in the preceding experiment for those subjects who were the farthest away from the minority in their initial opinions, and for whom the effects were particularly strong. This procedure is legitimate, moreover, since these subjects were indeed the ones who were on the majority's side and whose resulting ideological commonality with the majority led them to perceive the minority as more of an outgroup of sorts.

The number of points attributed to the majority and the minority during the induction phase (cf. Table 5.5) is proof of the above. It appears indeed that on the whole, these subjects attributed more points to the majority, both tolerance points and morality points. These targets, then, were biased in favour of their own positions. Although there was discrimination against the minority at this level, two things must be noted.

First, discrimination was not as strong when the subjects had to judge the majority and minority in terms of tolerance (for them, a relevant organizing principle and thus a valid alternative) *and* when their judgements were independent of each other.

Second, because of this very fact, we can understand why the influence effects were quite strong for these subjects, who were far removed from the minority. In fact, although the subjects in the tolerance/independence condition granted the sources the lowest amount of direct influence, their opinions on contraception indicated that they were radically in favour of the minority. Thus, even a high degree of discrimination like that observed for the subjects in this condition (where direct influence was the lowest in the experiment) does not necessarily inhibit validation, provided the dissociation of the comparison process and the validation process can take place by some means or another.

Table 5.5. *Direct and indirect influence and image for the subjects most far-removed from the source (a + sign indicates closer to the label)*

	Morality		Tolerance	
	Interdependence	Independence	Interdependence	Independence
Allocated points				
Minority	32.67	35.99	34.59	42.43
Majority	67.29	59.69	65.41	50.02
Influence				
Abortion	−0.58	−0.63	−0.65	−0.81
Contraception	−0.71	−0.75	−0.24	+0.37
Image				
'Consistency'	−0.20	−0.15	−0.15	+0.15
'Feminism'	−0.06	−0.14	−0.06	+0.11
'Tolerance'	−0.43	−0.22	−0.34	−0.05

This conversion effect can in fact be explained by a process involving the construction of the minority as an alternative. Indeed, these subjects more than the others perceived the source (cf. Table 5.5) as more consistent (coherent, critical, competent, self-assured), more feminist, and finally, more tolerant (tolerant, compromising, flexible, democratic, and open-minded).

These results of course support our interpretation of the categorizations and ideological contents that undergo social and cognitive validation, induced through dissociation, as we saw in the preceding chapter. But also, if not especially – it is useful to stress this while on the subject – these findings guarantee us that the processes of change we are studying do indeed account for the conversion of as-yet-unconverted individuals.

5.3.6 Conflict and dissociation: from discrimination to conversion

One question still remains at this point. Does the conversion effect made possible by the independence of the involved judgements result solely from the fact that the comparison is less conflictual when such independence exists, and thus from the fact that the minority can be evaluated more positively regardless of what is attributed to the majority? This seems highly unlikely since morality, recognized just as much as tolerance, did not induce such a conversion effect. Furthermore, our previous experimental data has led us to believe that this is not necessarily true, and that conversion occurs even in cases of strong conflict, provided however that the involved judgements are independent so as to avoid exclusive centering on the conflictual social comparison. In the following experiments, we decided accordingly to vary the intensity of the conflict associated with the minority position.

Making salient the feminist categorization of the minority position may in fact lead to constructivism in categorizing, while at the same time convey the negative connotations attached to that category. By inducing a potential identification conflict, these connotations may thwart any direct influence without necessarily preventing conversion. If this is true, then we may assume that evaluative discrimination – if it does not monopolize all of the subject's cognitive activity – should paradoxically be the very source of the most common minority influence pattern: manifest discrimination and latent change.

In all of the experimental conditions that will now be presented (Pérez and Mugny, 1989), the subjects were first asked to judge the *pro-abortion minority* and the *anti-abortion majority* as to their degree of feminism. Then they were asked to make judgements qualified as either 'descriptive' (for lack of a better term) or 'evaluative'. Concretely speaking, they were to state to what degree they considered the majority and the minority to be young and then progressive, or attractive and then pleasant. The first condition thus stressed the categorical characteristics describing the source as 'young-feminist-progressive'. The second condition stressed the more evaluative dimension: 'feminist-attractive-pleasant' (in effect, this represented social (dis)approval, known to often be subject to the anti-minority bias; cf. for example Mugny *et al.*, 1988).

In half of the conditions, the judgements were expressed in an independent context, and in the other half, in an interdependent context, the manipulations made in this respect being identical to those in the preceding experiment (cf. Appendix 7.3.4). The results given in Table 5.6 pertain to two indexes: the difference between the number of points attributed to the majority and the minority, and the measures regarding abortion and contraception.

The results of the intergroup comparison indicate two things. First, we can see that the minority was quite obviously construed as more feminist than the majority, regardless of the experimental condition. On the other hand, a difference appeared depending on whether the consecutive judgements were more 'descriptive' or more 'evaluative'. Although the minority was indeed considered as younger and more progressive than the majority (the index shown is the mean of the two responses), it was nevertheless discriminated against on the evaluative dimension in comparison to the majority. In other words, the feminist minority was indeed perceived as young and progressive, but in contrast, also as less pleasant and less attractive. In the latter case, the feminist label meant conflict and more negative evaluation, and can be assumed to have more strongly introduced the ambivalence characteristic into the representation of minority sources.

Table 5.6. *Difference in number of points, and direct and indirect influence (a + sign indicates more influence)*

	Judgements			
	Interdependent		Independent	
	Dimensions			
	'Descriptive'	'Evaluative'	'Descriptive'	'Evaluative'
Difference % feminist	+9.21	+24.55	+13.30	+23.14
Difference % dimensions	+5.73	−5.53	−9.15	−6.43
Abortion	−0.05	+0.14	−0.03	−0.07
Contraception	−0.28	0.00	+0.01	+0.24

Table 5.7. *Difference in number of points, and direct and indirect infuence (a + sign indicates more influence)*

	'Dimensions'			
	'Descriptive'		'Evaluative'	
	Normative filter			
	Morality	Tolerance	Morality	Tolerance
Difference % feminist	+20.43	+23.05	+22.19	+26.63
Difference % dimensions	+26.19	+21.35	−5.34	−4.00
Abortion	+0.09	0.00	+0.02	−0.11
Contraception	+0.04	−0.12	−0.16	+0.24

What influence effects were observed? Two simple effects are of interest here for indirect influence. First, judgement independence was indeed particularly favourable to the occurrence of conversion, as we already saw in the preceding experiment. Second, indirect influence was more marked in the evaluative context, which nevertheless ended up giving rise to more discrimination. Thus, for the same alternative categorization of the source, the conversion effect was more pronounced when the source's conflictual nature was made more salient. This obviously confirms the apparently paradoxical effects of categorization in minority influence: indeed, it is evidently when one discriminates the most, when one resists the most, that the conversion effect occurs to the greatest extent.

Once again, however, this presupposes the independence of the majority–minority comparison. This indeed is what the cumulative effect of the two factors indicates: conversion was more intense ($m = +0.24$) when the intergroup context highlighted the conflictual nature of the minority and when the intergroup comparison was done in the independent mode. Conversion here was indeed the paradoxical effect of open discrimination, precisely in a highly conflictual context. As we suggested above, validating is not approving.

At this point, we can draw the following conclusion: individuals discriminate but then adopt the minority's organizing principle. This states once again that fundamentally, conversion is the outcome of conflict (see also Mugny, Sanchez-Mazas, Roux, and Pérez, 1991). But not in just any context: this would only be true in a context of judgement independence (we shall consider this fact to be established, and in the next experiment, this variable modality will be held constant) where on the one hand, the conflict is made salient, and on the other hand, the tolerance filter is available. Let us now go on to another experiment in which these various factors were combined.

5.3.7 Independence, dissociation, and organizing principle

The gist of this experiment (Pérez and Mugny, 1989) is the same as above. After reading the text written by a minority, the subjects were to give points to the minority group and to the majority group. They had 100 points for each source, which they thus attributed independently to each (independence of intergroup judgements). Half of the subjects were to rate the majority and minority using 'descriptive' qualifiers (young and progressive) to describe the feminist category, while the other half had to use evaluative qualifiers (attractive and agreeable) assumed to apply more to the majority. Following this rating step, the normative filter (either tolerance or morality) was made available to the subjects in the same manner as described in point 4.4.4. The subjects thus had to judge each of the five main arguments of the text on either a tolerant–intolerant and compromising–uncompromising scale, or on a moral–immoral and responsible–irresponsible scale. Results are given in Table 5.7.

The difference between the points attributed to the minority and the majority largely confirms the effects found in the preceding experiment: the minority, generally judged to be more feminist than the majority, was also thought to be younger and more progressive. This was not true for the evaluative dimension, where the majority was rated more positively than the minority.

As to influence, there was an interaction between the two variables, again for indirect influence: the most marked effect is that the condition with the most indirect influence ($m = +0.24$) was the one where after having strongly discriminated against the minority (on the evaluative dimension, in contrast to the more descriptive dimension of the feminist category), subjects still centered on the organizing principle of the minority position, tolerance.

5.4 Conclusions

We have now gone through the entire loop. The theoretical problem posed in this chapter was the following: under what conditions does a validation activity occur in conjunction with the comparison process, or in other words, how can we account for the conditions allowing for the emergence of one influence pattern rather than another? And above all, how can we account for the fact that indirect influence can occur even when direct influence is inexistent or negative following a particularly strong identification conflict?

Understanding these paradoxical effects called for several complementary theories. Namely, we postulated manifest influence to be underlain by an intergroup, social comparison process (with its inherent identifications and identification conflicts) so as to account for intergroup differentiations. To explain conversion effects, we proposed the further specification of the validation process to include the performance by minority influence targets of a constructive activity involving categorizations, indexations, and recognition of an organizing principle.

To go even further, we needed a theory that could incorporate discrimination and the 'on beyonds' of discrimination. The notion of dissociation enabled us to make the required psychosociological link. One can discriminate, maintain the status quo, and then change after all. The necessary conditions were then specified: the intergroup conflict must be constructed via a dual cognitive activity, so that beyond the inevitable social comparison, a validation activity can take place. And this is sometimes possible, provided as we have seen that three conditions are satisfied: recognition of the conflict explicitly induced by the minority, categorized as such; independence of the judgements of the various social entities recognized in a now multidimensional universe; and recognition of an organizing principle underlying the minority positions that is both relevant and transferable to a wider range of attitudes.

Indirect influence thus implies that subjects carry out two separate cognitive activities, comparison of themselves to the source, and validation of the minority positions proper. First, a comparison bearing on category identity is made, wherein it can be assumed that at the direct or manifest level, the identity of the normatively dominant entity and/or that of the minority is a determinant. Then once this comparison issue, generally detrimental to the minority, is 'settled', subjects can focus their attention on the content of the minority message itself. At this point, they react to the organizing principle underlying the message, provided they are able to ascertain or construct it. This was established here by showing with the paradigm on abortion and contraception that validation leads to indirect minority influence, provided the dissociation of the minority–majority judgements bears on the organizing principle, in this case, the tolerance norm, which indeed underlies both the alternative proposed by the minority and the various attitude domains in its range of influence.

We can now better understand how the views of minority groups can be diffused and spread through the network of social relations, even following initial discrimination. Since their impact is based on conflict, however, this is only possible if the socio-cognitive operations the members of a society implement in order to psychosocially resolve this conflict are dissociated. As we saw at the beginning of this chapter, such social constructivism can be quite difficult to attain, particularly when the identification conflicts involved are too salient due to the ever-present resistance to change exhibited by all groups and societies. Nevertheless, sooner or later, dissociation will become necessary and the minority viewpoints will even come to be a part of the spirit of the times, the new social reality. This will be demonstrated in the final chapter of this book.

6 Resistance and change

At the end of the presentation of our approach to minority influence processes and the many experiments that support this approach, it might have appeared as though everything had been said and shown. This is not quite true, however, although most of the support for our 'case' has been submitted, exposed, and interconnected. To conclude this book, we would like to apply the proposed model to the question of the psychosocial effects of resistance to change.

The preceding chapters have provided quite convincing proof of the following: minority influence is dependent upon the conflict a minority group introduces into the social field of innovation. The most obvious parameters of this conflict are the different types of resistance elicited by the emergence of a point of view that goes against a norm, which we have treated as 'counter-majority influence'. For the sake of simplicity, we may consider active resistance on the part of targets to stem either from the definition of the source or from the characteristics of the actual normative content of the minority message. In studies on minority influence, *psychologization* is a prototype of the former kind of resistance, while *denial* is one of the forms of the latter. As we shall see, resisting while focusing on the psychological characteristics of the source and resisting while centering on the credibility of the message content do not have the same psychosocial implications.

6.1 Psychologization as a form of resistance

Faced with the emergence of a minority point of view, the initial reaction of individuals is generally to refute the very existence of any potential alternative (cf. Mugny and Papastamou, 1984). When the new point of view cannot be recognized as such because it falls outside the 'range of credibility' defined by the ideological background of the targets, they account for it by using one form or another of *naturalization*. The divergent point of view is explained in terms of the intrinsic characteristics of the source. The potentially innovative content of the message is reduced to some biological, psychological, or sociological aberration. We are all familiar with

146

these attribution modes. The cause of such socio-cognitive functioning is most likely the exclusive focusing upon the social comparison process, and its effect is preventing the activation of the validation process.

Psychologization (cf. Papastamou, 1983) is a form of resistance which consists somehow of implicitly or explicitly mapping the psychological properties of the source to the innovative behaviours or contents it employs or advocates, resulting in the causal reduction of the latter to the former. In our experiments, psychologization is generally operationalized by asking subjects to discern the personality traits of the authors of a text after having informed them that 'psychologists are well aware of the psychological characteristics (for example, personality traits) that contribute to how individuals organize the content and form of the messages they issue' (cf. Mugny, Kaiser, and Papastamou, 1983, p. 10).

Now, whenever targets are led in this way to consider that the point of view of a minority is the product of its psychological characteristics, we repeatedly observe a substantial decrease in the amount of minority influence. This kind of resistance may even prevent the occurrence of the conversion effect typical of minority influence (cf. Papastamou, 1983, 1987, 1988). Let us look for an explanation of this in terms of our model.

6.1.1 Psychologization: the logic of indissociation

In the preceding chapter, we proposed a model defining the psychosocio-logical interconnection of two processes: the comparison process, which governs manifest influence, and the validation process, which governs latent, indirect, or delayed influence. We showed that *identification conflicts*, whenever highly salient, can explain how outward resistance based on the social definition of the source and its relationship with targets can be so strong that it inhibits the validation process.

With this conceptualization as a foundation, we shall attempt to understand the resistance effects of psychologization (Mugny and Pérez, 1989a). The sort of 'immunization' that psychologization is thought to often introduce will be explained (cf. Papastamou, 1983, 1987), starting from the idea that through it, a definition of the minority is made salient (one loaded with negative connotations, as well shall see), which in turn leads to a strong identification conflict. Consequently, the entire activity is centered on the social comparison, even governed by it. The dissociation of comparison and validation would thus be counteracted. It is as simple as that: psychologization might induce a sort of *indissociation*.

This analysis seems compatible with several effects found using the psychologization paradigm. First, studies comparing the impact of psycho-logization on the influence exerted by majority and minority sources have revealed that psychologization only elicits resistance when the source is a minority (Moscovici and Personnaz, 1986; Papastamou, 1986). This finding may indeed mean that only when the social costs of target-source identification are high, namely because of the borderline position of the source, does psychologization turn into resistance. Moreover, another experiment (Papastamou, 1985) has shown that psychologization can decrease the influence of a 'group' more than that of a minority leader. The 'group' source is thought to cause immunization since it makes the identification issue salient. It is known indeed that in an intergroup context, the dynamics of identification and comparison are more salient and have a greater hold on targets than they do in an interindividual context (Tajfel, 1978; Tajfel and Turner, 1979).

In addition, it appears that psychologization can even counteract the favouritism bias normally benefiting sources categorized as ingroup (Mugny *et al.*, 1983), without increasing outgroup minority discrimination and sometimes even decreasing it (cf. point 2.3.2). On this subject, remember the experiment presented in point 2.4.3. Using the paradigm on attitudes towards foreigners, subjects read a pro-foreigner text supposedly written either by a minority belonging to the same national ingroup or by a foreign minority. Subjects were (or were not) also asked to discern the psychological characteristics of the text's authors. In the conditions where the subjects did not have to ascertain these characteristics, the 'usual' ingroup favouritism bias was found for both source image and exerted influence (cf. Table 2.7), the minority having profited from its shared national identity. In the psychologization condition, no change was observed for the foreign source, although the influence of the psychologized native source decreased to the same level as that of the foreign source. Psychologization is thus thought to have induced a subdivision within the ingroup, whenever a subdivision did not already exist due to differing national identities. In minority-induced conflicts, psychologization may well be a substitute for intergroup discrimination. Moreover, this resistance effect persisted here, and was found again on a post-test two weeks later (Mugny *et al.*, 1983).

Thus, it may not be so much the minority's ideological position *per se* that counts, but rather the identification conflict in which it is involved. In the same study (Mugny *et al.*, 1983), we found accordingly that when subjects who were highly opposed ideologically to the minority position were placed in the same category as the minority (ingroup), they tended to differentiate themselves from it when psychologization was involved. Indeed, the xenophobic subjects reacted the most negatively to the psychologized, xenophilous minority with the same national identity as their own, even more than to the foreign minority. They thus resisted the minority's ideological position all the more when it was incompatible with their common national identity, obviously highly valued by xenophobes.

Applying the same line of reasoning, we can see why the resistance effects brought on by psychologization are observed above all when the minority expresses some degree of ideological commonality with the targets, for example by using a flexible rather than rigid style. In an experiment on pollution (Papastamou, Mugny, and Kaiser, 1980, experiment 1), we thus found that psychologization tended to reduce the amount of influence exerted by a flexible minority, bringing it down to that obtained by a rigid minority.

The same may be true of ideological distance: certain findings tend to indicate that it is often those subjects who are ideologically the closest to the minority that resist its influence the most when they are led to psychologize (cf. Papastamou *et al.*, 1980; Papastamou, 1988; Papastamou and Mugny, 1990). The fact is that the self-attribution of the characteristics assigned to the minority is more probable for these subjects due to their psychological proximity, in which case the identification conflict is all the more intense since the attributes become very negatively connoted following psychologization.

In all of the cases mentioned, what counts is not the actual conflict resulting from the ideological confrontation introduced by the dissidence of the counter-normative message, since this message remains constant, but rather the identity of the source in comparison to that of the targets, that is, the identification relationship that links them to each other. And it is indeed when the dynamics of an identification conflict are set in motion that the immunizing effects of psychologization appear, a conflict which in effect limits the targets to the exclusive striving for otherness, for differentiation from the source, all the more threatening to their social identity in that 'somehow, somewhere' it is psychologically like them.

6.1.2 Resistance and dimensionality of representation

What is the structure of the representations targets construct of psychologized minorities? The overall resistance induced by psychologization may in fact be due to a representation of the minority that is too *monolithic* (Ricateau, 1970–1) and governed by a one-dimensionality that does not enable targets to mentally construct the minority as an alternative. Indeed, in a very general manner, when the image of a minority is modified by psychologization, it tends to become negative, regardless of what dimension is considered. For example, the minority may be construed as more rigid, more sectarian, less objective, more deviant, more unbalanced, and so on (cf. Mugny, *et al.*, 1983; Papastamou and Mugny, 1985b, 1987). Such negatively connoted characteristics are a source of increased conflict, due precisely to the fact that in yielding to the minority position, targets may

self-attribute these characteristics, which are incompatible with a sat-
isfactory social identification.

Thus, the ambivalence we have seen otherwise to characterize the
representation of the minority when it is a source of conversion may be
masked by psychologization, the relational dimension taking precedence
over the cognitive aspects (Mugny and Papastamou, 1984). Social
disapproval prevails, and the independence and autonomy of the minority
standpoint are not acknowledged. The content of the psychologized position
of the minority is no longer actively considered, its specificity not being
recognized. Starting as virtually nomic, the minority is mentally constructed
as normatively anomic.

In all these respects, the image of the psychologized minority is in effect
a reflection of the social distance – the deviation – that separates the
minority from the other entities that support the dominant norm shared by
the subject. This norm and especially the groups that support it are what
serve as the sole anchor point for the social comparison that is necessarily
and exclusively negative for the minority: resistance is not based on the
normative (re-)definition of judgements, but is aimed solely at ensuring a
categorical subdivision that psychologically excludes the minority from the
field of possible identifications.

But all forms of resistance do not follow this same logic.

6.2 Beyond resistance: change

We must indeed get back to the more general problem that underlies our
conceptualization of minority influence, approaching it from two standpoints: the advantages minorities can draw from changes in norms,
discussed here by referring to the notion of *spirit of the times*, or 'Zeitgeist',
and the fundamental contribution of minorities to those changes in norms.

To make a long story short, *who* changes norms? The majority, the
ingroup, the power structures? Or the minority, the outgroup, the 'fringes'
of society, by the social constructivism they induce in targets? And *when* do
norms change? When resistance to change weakens, and a power structure
or the majority tolerates a change that does not fundamentally question its
own validity? Or precisely, as we contend, when resistance is activated?
Again, with experimental data for support, we are now in a position to
answer these questions.

6.2.1 Minorities and the spirit of the times: what causality?
Researchers have certainly not failed to raise one question that several
recent studies (cf. Clark, 1988; Maass and Clark, 1984; Paicheler, 1988)
have indeed investigated: what is the effect of the 'evolution of history'

upon minority influence? Minority influence is thought to be facilitated whenever the minority defends an alternative position that is nevertheless in accordance with the 'Zeitgeist', the spirit of the times, or stated in another manner, whenever it is part of the 'field of possibilities' or set of acceptable positions, even if not approved (bordering on the 'range of credibility', cf. de Montmollin, 1977), defined by the state of the normative system at the time the minority acts.

It has been shown accordingly that minority influence is exerted when a minority defends a forward position with respect to the current evolution of norms, but not when it advocates a backward position representing a 'regression' with respect to the way in which society is progressing. For example, Paicheler (1976, 1977, 1988) showed that a feminist minority could exert influence, whereas an anti-feminist minority, even a consistent one, tended to cause the bipolarization of the social field, making it the only one, or nearly the only one, to defend its position. Similarly, Maass *et al.* (1982) found that influence was granted by conservative subjects to a minority that took a pro-abortion stand, in accordance with the progression of norms, but not to a minority in favour of the death sentence, a norm that went against the spirit of the times. In the same line of thinking, Mucchi Faina (1987; Crespi and Mucchi Faina, 1988) defended the idea that minorities manage to be convincing when they call upon a 'superordinate' category membership, the landmark of a new collective identity suggesting the existence of a common normative principle that is shared by the minority and its targets and is a constituent of the current 'Zeitgeist'. In some of our own studies (Mugny, 1975b; Riba and Mugny, 1981), we found that in a context in which attitudes towards foreigners were not xenophobic and humanitarian values were appropriate, a consistent minority could be more influential if it defended xenophilous views than if it defended xenophobic ones. It is undeniable that the meanings associated with the alternative proposed by the minority – precisely because that alternative is specifically rooted in the spirit of the times – can, when they are favourable to that minority, facilitate its influence, particularly in the direct social mode. Our model of identification accounts perfectly for this.

By adopting this perspective, however, we run the risk of deducing, from these few effects, the causal relationship whereby it is *because* their positions 'flow along' with current trends that minorities are influential, when resistance to change is no longer operational. This would be a narrow view of things. We cannot limit ourselves to considering solely the causality wherein the spirit of the times favours minorities. In our mind, this would mean withdrawing from minorities their most essential social function: *introducing innovation* in a nearly inevitably conflictual and innovation-resistant context.

It can be misleading to consider only one truth: if the alternative positions of the minority are indeed located within the 'Zeitgeist', it can *only* be due to the past (and uncontrolled, or difficultly controlled by the researcher) accumulation of prior minority influence, that is to say, *to the completion of a collective conversion process*, of which the historical analysis of normative change ought to provide clear evidence. Moscovici (1985b) indeed contended that in this twentieth century, we have gone from an era of the majority to an era of the minority. Necessarily, then, our conceptualization of the causality must be reversed: in the long run, minority influence results in fundamental normative change, reflected by a new set of attitudes towards other ideologies than those at which the attempted influence was aimed. At the collective level, these are changes of a constructivist nature, ones that (re-)define the spirit of the times.

Our model accounts for the psychosocial aspects of such change. We have seen that the influence pattern with no direct or indirect influence is only one of the possible outcomes, and is difficult to maintain across time when targets are confronted with a consistent minority. In the face of innovation, individuals rarely remain indifferent. In one way or another, minority-initiated ideas seep into social representations and orient subjects towards new attitudes, following the typical influence pattern whereby direct target resistance to innovation unknowingly secretes indirect minority influence. Only with time, perhaps with the new spirit of the times, does minority influence come to the surface. As we have already stated regarding our model of dissociation, the diverse dynamics of direct and indirect influence overlap, are linked to, and succeed each other in accordance with the social and cognitive tensions introduced by the minority point of view.

In this chapter, we shall attempt to illustrate this hypothesis, fundamental to a theory of social change, and to 'operationalize' the spirit of the times. The 'Zeitgeist' will first be translated into an independent variable for manipulation. How can the spirit of the times be defined more empirically, that is, in more analytic terms? In any case, we cannot simply assert in a necessarily *post hoc* manner that a minority that exerted some influence must be pro-normative, and that it must not be if it did not. We shall propose several ways of introducing the spirit of the times as a conflict-regulating mechanism, essentially via resistance to change, postulated to increase as the minority position increases in its degree of innovativeness and the extent to which it contradicts the norm. The idea is to show once and for all that change is in some sense one of the prerogatives of minorities, outgroups, and those on the 'fringes' of society.

Then the 'Zeitgeist' will be defined as a dependent variable, and viewed as a consequence of the intervention of a minority. Once the factors assumed to be at the root of normative change have been determined, the next step will be to find the means of observing the effects of resistance, known to be indirect and delayed.

6.2.2 The paradoxical effects of resistance to change

The various forms of resistance to change constitute parameters enabling us to assess the regulatory power of a norm. It must be assumed that when the spirit of the times is favourable to minorities, resistance is less effective at counteracting innovative positions, and that if it is unfavourable to them, for instance when the minority position is first being revealed, then resistance on the contrary becomes vehement.

This issue is indeed important because we must acknowledge the fact that social groups and systems generally do everything in their power to oppose the spread of ideas and beliefs that contradict their own. At least since Schachter (1951), many kinds of resistance to change including ostracism, sanctions, censorship, dissuasion, inoculation, social disapproval, anathema, psychologization (discussed above), reactance, and *ad infinitum* have become part of the repertoire of social psychologists interested in social influence, attitudes, and attitude change. The obvious function of all these forms of resistance, which differ by culture and period in history, is to counteract innovation, granted with varying degrees of success ranging from a great deal at the beginning to less in the end. We shall approach them while keeping in mind an idea that is very simple but loaded with theoretical implications: what if change were the price paid for resistance to change?

The theses developed so far have led us to take an interest in the 'underwater part of the iceberg', which in our mind has escaped the attention of most researchers until now. Although it is certain that resistance to change often produces the desired effect – inhibition of influence resulting from the fact that resistance obviously involves difficult identification during the social comparison process – it is nevertheless possible that the effect of such resistance is limited to the social expression of influence (direct and immediate), and that *in the conditions stated in the preceding chapter*, resistance has the unintended effect of secretly engaging subjects in a validation activity which ends up increasing minority influence at the indirect level; in short, it may cause a genuinely paradoxical resistance effect. Take reactance for example, a kind of resistance thought to be based on the need for freedom (Brehm, 1966; Wicklund, 1974). Brehm and Mann (1975) found that the condition which gave rise to the greatest degree of reactance in public was also the one that induced the most influence in private, this time positive influence. This effect is paradoxical in that the change in attitude it causes is opposed to that intended by the resisting individuals.

As already noted in our discussion of the twofold dynamics of social cost, when a 'power structure' (in this case the Church) is said to make an anathematical declaration against those who go along with a minority point of view, the desired resistance effect is not necessarily obtained. This was only the case here when the subjects were identified *de facto* with the minority. When they were not, resistance was only expressed at the manifest level; at the indirect level, a paradoxical effect occurred (cf. preceding chapter). In order for resistance to have its full effect, targets must be bound by a conflictual social comparison where the only outlet is differentiation from the minority.

We might at least wonder about the effectiveness of resistance at the initial stage of the innovation process, since targets are highly unlikely to identify with the minority at that point, and resistance can only be fully operational when it explicitly and directly involves target identity, i.e. when the targets identify with the group towards which the resistance is directed. Yet minorities, as we have seen, are often categorized as outgroups. Moreover, it is by virtue of this outgroup categorization that they exert influence.

Stated in another manner, it is indeed the conflictual nature of the minority influence context that is responsible for its indirect and/or delayed influence, and it may be precisely in the most conflict-ridden situations that an authentic normative change is paradoxically observed.

6.2.3 Beyond denial, truth

These few ideas bring us now to the presentation of another experiment, again on abortion, in which we examined this hypothesis by varying the degree to which the minority position fell within the bounds of the spirit of the times. This was done in several ways, by stating that the innovative position was either majority-supported, credible, or ingroup (with the spirit of the times), or minority-supported, not credible, or outgroup (and thus, against the spirit of the times). The 'Zeitgeist' here was defined by representing the social field along three parameters: consensus, credibility, and identification. Being in the 'Zeitgeist' meant sharing some universal truth with others. Being out of the 'Zeitgeist' meant being the only one to support some singular truth.

The experiment (Pérez, Mugny, and Moscovici, 1986) included eight conditions. Before any experimental induction, resistance to the innovative content of the message (pro-abortion) was manipulated in half of the conditions by inducing a denial. To operationalize the counter-normative nature of the innovative position, subjects were asked to select which four out of five pro-abortion claims were the ones an alleged survey had shown to be generally considered by young people of both sexes (the subjects were young people) as invalid and unreasonable (for details on this manipulation, see point 4.4.5). In the remaining conditions, the subjects were asked to state which four claims were considered by young people to be valid and reasonable. In the former case, subjects were thus led to believe that the pro-abortion position was disapproved and went against the spirit of the times, and in the latter, that it indeed expressed the prevailing normative viewpoint of young people.

Then subjects in all conditions read the same extremely pro-abortion text. In four of the conditions (minority sources), the ideological position of the source was supposedly approved by only 12% of the previously questioned young people, whereas in the other four conditions (majority sources) the source position was supposedly supported by 88% of the questioned young people. With the normative content of the minority message held constant, then, we could determine the impact of representing the minority as a spokesman for either a universal viewpoint or a more explicitly deviant and rare viewpoint opposing current trends.

Finally, subjects were told in each case that the minority or majority was either of their same sex (ingroup sources) or of the opposite sex (outgroup sources). The idea here is also that expressing an opinion held by an ingroup majority would be more consistent with the spirit of the times than expressing an opinion supported by an outgroup minority.

Another important point: although the sources always defended an extremely favourable stand on abortion, the amount of influence exerted was measured for attitudes towards abortion (direct influence), con-traception (indirect influence), and finally, by means of a new questionnaire called the 'Zeitgeist' questionnaire which will be commented upon below. The measures were taken twice, first immediately after the text was read (immediate post-test), and then three weeks later (deferred post-test) in order to check for the delayed effects we predicted would occur by applying our model to the question of resistance. If indeed effective, the very induction of resistance would, at least in the immediate future, mask the changes resulting from the dynamics of validation, which they are still supposed to induce and which the deferred measures would reveal. Our model does allow for the fact that influence patterns are apt to evolve.

Two preliminary notes before going on to the delayed influence effects. First, consider the conditions involving denial! On the whole, the subjects went along with the manipulation of validity and invalidity, since on the average they selected more than three claims out of the required four. There was strong asymmetry, however, between the conditions with denial and those without denial: it appears to be much easier to judge pro-abortion claims as invalid and unreasonable ($m = 3.60$) than to acknowledge their

Table 6.1. *Delayed influence (a + sign indicates a positive change)*

	Abortion		Contraception	
	No denial	Denial	No denial	Denial
Majority				
Ingroup	−0.23	−0.15	+0.01	+0.05
Outgroup	−0.07	+0.01	−0.06	+0.15
Minority				
Ingroup	+0.19	−0.05	+0.20	+0.31
Outgroup	−0.08	−0.04	−0.24	+0.28

validity ($m = 3.12$). The exercise of denial, then, may be part of the 'Zeitgeist' in this context. Whatever the case may be, the position defended in the text was more conflictual and more strongly against the norm.

In addition, it should be noted that there was no systematic difference in the experimental variables for either abortion or contraception on the first post-test. One effect can nevertheless be highlighted by contrasting the non-denial ingroup majority condition to the rest of the conditions: more marked agreement with abortion and contraception was observed in this condition. For the other conditions, which in this respect did not differ from each other, we must indeed admit that the immediate influence of the source was thwarted whenever it was deemed to be on the fringes of the spirit of the times, because it was a minority, because of its outgroup identity, or because of its non-credibility, although these different kinds of resistance did not have a cumulative effect.

Now consider the delayed influence (cf. Table 6.1) found in the conditions involving the 'conflictualness' and 'normativeness' variables. The main effects observed in this experiment were delayed effects measured three weeks after the experimental phase. To summarize them, we shall group together the conditions with similar outcomes.

First, the ingroup majority, whether denied or not, did not obtain delayed influence, since targets even tended to 'move further away' from the source's position. This in itself is already a paradoxical effect, since the sources presented as being inspired the most by the spirit of the times had the least long-term effect.

The only majority condition to have obtained an indirect effect was the one in which the source was potentially the most conflictual, due both to its outgroup identity and to the denial it underwent. Yet this was the majority perceived as the farthest removed from the spirit of the times on two out of three parameters (outgroup identity and low credibility). For sure, approving is not changing!

We can see that the content of an innovative norm, known to be capable of inducing the social construction of positions, may have less chance of doing so when it is supported by a majority, and an ingroup one at that, since an exclusively ingroup context only involves a comparison process. When the content of an innovative norm is passed off as a truism, its implications may no longer be considered. In order for the content to be the object of validation and cognitive construction, it must obviously be perceived as coming explicitly from sources that are conflict-bearing, because they are minorities, outgroups, or have been denied in a context of intergroup tensions.

Now let us look a little closer at the minority conditions, while momentarily setting aside the non-denied outgroup minority, which is a special case. Delayed influence appeared in a systematic manner here. The non-denied ingroup minority, the least conflictual (since it fell within the spirit of the times on two parameters), 'already' obtained delayed influence on the abortion scale, influence which was maintained on the contraception scale. The denied minorities, whether ingroup or outgroup, only obtained influence 'starting from' (if we may say it that way) the contraception scale. Again we find that the more conflictual the minority, the more change there may be on measures that are indirectly related to its claims.

At this point in our analysis, we might note that all the involved minority sources exerted delayed influence at either the direct or indirect level, which was not the case for the majority sources, except the most conflictual one. Delayed influence also appeared at the indirect level for contraception when the validity of the innovative position had been previously denied, especially for sources with an outgroup identity, moreover. Thus, we can indeed say that delayed influence was typical here of minorities, outgroups (and also of women, since all the subjects were men!), and resistance to change, and that the combination of these factors in certain circumstances deferred the emergence of minority influence. The very fact, then, that it is located in the margins of the 'Zeitgeist' is what may cause an innovative point of view to trigger the constructivist dynamics of change, while the same point of view may simply be yielded to when it is situated within the limits of the spirit of the times.

. What meanings did the subjects attribute to these various conditions? Let us go on to the image of the source as expressed on the second post-test, which took place at the very time the attitudes whose dynamics we are studying were stated. This will clarify the reasons for the various influence patterns found. Three factors will be selected to do so, two pertaining to dimensions of particular importance to the progression of the comparison process, and the third, of importance to the validation process. The first two concern the approval and credibility (or disapproval) of the innovative position, and the flexibility (or rigidity) of the source, explicitly reflecting the spirit of the times and the degree of conflict inherent in a potential identification. The third pertains to the recognition of the alternative, here, its categorical reconstruction as feminist. The results are given in Table 6.2.

Let us begin by examining the strongest effects. First, the credibility and approval allotted to the source indeed depended upon the representation the targets made of its compatibility with the spirit of the times, which they granted more easily to a majority source than to a minority source. Only that which is shared by everyone is credible! Rigidity, on the other hand, which is an indicator of the intensity of the conflict subjects may have felt, and was assessed by the uncompromising style attributed to the source, varied above all as a function of the source's categorical identity. Indeed, an outgroup source was thought to be more rigid than an ingroup source. Finally, the minority sources were perceived as more feminist, like the outgroup sources, especially when their credibility had been denied. Since this factor is an indicator of whether or not the validation process took place, it is not surprising that the conditions involving the new categorization in terms of feminism were the ones exhibiting delayed influence.

Because these effects were cumulative and greater in certain conditions, let us look at them one by one. An initial striking result is that in a general manner, the majority sources were defined as more credible and more approved of than the minority sources. They were also perceived as feminist when they were ingroup. Finally, the non-denied ingroup majority was viewed as highly flexible. By allowing a comparison that was compatible with a positive identification, this majority source obtained immediate positive influence, but had no delayed effect. Note in contrast that the denied outgroup majority, the only one to have exerted any delayed influence, was the majority construed as the most rigid and the most feminist. Its insertion largely outside the 'Zeitgeist' caused it to be mentally reconstructed as a minority, and its influence pattern followed the well-known validation logic.

Let us now look at the results for the minorities. The minority sources, which we know had a delayed effect, exerted influence without being approved or considered as credible. The value of the alternative they proposed was nevertheless recognized since they were reconstructed as feminist. Two more conditions are worth pointing out. First, the non-denied ingroup minority most likely obtained delayed direct influence because it was the least conflictual minority, being perceived as particularly flexible. Finally, the non-denied outgroup minority is a special case. It was considered as the most rigid and the least credible minority, even less credible than when it had been denied. Curiously, although it was not

Table 6.2. *Delayed image of the source (a + sign indicates reference to the label)*

	'Credibility'		'Flexibility'		'Feminism'	
	No denial	Denial	No denial	Denial	No denial	Denial
Majority						
Ingroup	+0.28	+0.04	+0.29	+0.02	−0.07	−0.37
Outgroup	+0.16	+0.09	−0.01	−0.18	−0.06	+0.11
Minority						
Ingroup	−0.08	−0.12	+0.19	−0.07	+0.04	+0.09
Outgroup	−0.29	−0.07	−0.17	−0.07	+0.05	+0.21

intended to do so, this condition triggered a real denial activity, as if subjects found it particularly intolerable to attribute some degree of credibility to a minority source that was also an outgroup. This conflict accounts for the fact that delayed influence did not appear at the direct or indirect level. We shall see however that this condition did give rise to some impact after all.

Two essential things are to be retained from this experimental demonstration. First, delayed but direct influence indeed appears to have been due to the 'slackening' in the tension of the now less conflictual social comparison since it varied by source identity. The ingroup majority lost its initial influence, which is evidence of the fact that only simple yielding was involved. Moreover, the minority exerted direct delayed influence when as a non-denied ingroup its attributes somehow made the identification less dramatic. The dynamics of social comparison were indeed expressing themselves through immediate or delayed direct influence.

Regarding delayed indirect influence, it informs us about the process underlying the constructivism of positions, which does not result as much from the identity of the sources as from the exercise of explicit resistance, supposed to induce a validation activity. And the diverse influence patterns found do indeed, as we saw in the preceding chapter, result from the conjunction of the comparison and validation processes.

Next, the various effects observed confirm the fact that validation does not stem from a simple increase in 'cognitive concentration' upon the object (as most current research on conversion assumes), thought to 'spontaneously' ensure the recognition or approval of the very foundations of the minority message, but rather from a constructive activity carried out by subjects when faced with a message which for one reason or another is conflictual and initially rejected, and which leads them to completely reorganize the entire categorical field and the meanings associated with the various entities distinguished therein. Making a play on words, we must agree that in reality this activity does not stem from an approval at the social level and the search for minority view confirmation at the cognitive level (in the end, for...'validation'!), but rather from the cognitive negation ('invalidation'!) and social refutation of the assertions of minorities.

A socio-cognitive conflict that in one way or another initiates the cognitive activity of subjects is indeed the basis for conversion effects, and resistance to change is what makes this conflict salient. Thus, by accentuating the conflict inherent in the minority positions, this same resistance counteracts their open approval while making them salient, distinct, even cognitively attractive, and in the end, persuasive. The fact is that such resistance does not escape the logic we described as we linked the comparison process to the validation process: by forcing targets to keep their distance from the counter-normative positions of minorities, a source of resistance cannot prevent targets from engaging in a potential validation activity, precisely because any such validation is necessarily private and difficult to control.

In other words, we assume that the various forms of resistance can have conversion effects opposing their initial purpose since they make the minority conspicuous in the social field (which in itself is already a paradoxical effect!) and render salient the principles that underlie its positions and attributes, thus initiating the cognitive activity of targets by directing them towards the content of the prohibited objects in a situation that, by virtue of such resistance, has become 'aroused'. As additional proof, it would be convenient if minority influence went so far as to affect the very principles of the 'Zeitgeist', which we shall now demonstrate.

6.2.4 Changing the norms: a privilege of minorities
We have seen that even in conditions of strong conflict, minorities still have some social impact, and that this impact does not occur through the internalization of the specific content of a minority message, but rather through the adoption of the principle itself upon which that content is based and around which it is organized. In our case, this principle, tolerance, opposed the principle of majorities defining the 'Zeitgeist', founded on conservatism and the demand for morality in a society where the ideology of the Church was still an important source of regulation affecting behaviours, beliefs, and values. The question then became: Did the minority in the end only convince subjects on dimensions that were close to the ones it asserted, such as abortion or contraception, two issues linked to each other by the question of sexuality? Or could it lead to an even more fundamental change, manifested by the generalization of the tolerance principle to a wider range of behaviours and attitudes? In short, can a minority manage to cause change that affects the 'Zeitgeist'?

Table 6.3. *Delayed influence (a + sign indicates a positive change)*

	'Zeitgeist'	
	No denial	Denial
Majority		
Ingroup	−0.13	−0.28
Outgroup	−0.21	+0.10
Minority		
Ingroup	+0.07	+0.22
Outgroup	+0.19	−0.08

To answer this question, we asked the subjects of the experiment used for illustration in this chapter to answer a series of additional questions (cf. Appendix 7.3.3). They were to express to what degree they were in favour of either more progressive, open-minded, egalitarian, or tolerant attitudes, or on the contrary, more traditional, closed-minded, authoritarian, or uncompromising attitudes towards family life, schooling, and ethical norms, all daily living topics on which the minority had taken absolutely no stand. These measures were taken immediately after the minority text was read and then three weeks later. Any difference (between conditions) in changes in attitude towards a less authoritarian norm would be attributed to deep and private reflection based on the organizing principle of the innovative position inferred during the validation process. What were the effects?

The data in Table 6.3 show that a change in the spirit of the times did indeed take place within the time span of the experiment. But it did not occur for just any source. First, as we have already seen in the case of contraception, the greater impact occurred in the face of minority sources. The ability to change norms is indeed within the power of minorities.

Comparing these effects with the delayed influence effects measured on the abortion and contraception scales, we can see that six of the eight conditions provide support for the observed dynamics. Indeed, the three majority conditions without delayed influence were not accompanied by any change on the 'Zeitgeist' scale other than a tendency to exhibit more traditional attitudes. On the other hand, the denied outgroup majority, which we have seen was particularly conflictual, was to see its delayed influence take effect, unlike the other three majorities who gave rise to normative 'regression'.

As for the minorities, we can see that when the source was ingroup (and especially in the denial condition), the principle of tolerance was also carried over to the 'Zeitgeist' measures. Since the ingroup minority exerted no direct delayed influence, we must conclude that the observed pattern of change resulted from the dynamics of comparison and validation that we have previously seen.

Let us finish by looking at the non-denied outgroup minority. These subjects were shown to resist the experimental induction and to judge the minority as less credible and more rigid (cf. Table 6.2). This was also the only minority condition that had no delayed influence, neither direct nor indirect (cf. Table 6.1). It is true that this minority was particularly conflictual. Yet on the 'Zeitgeist' measure, its impact did finally emerge: the targets expressed attitudes in favour of the new norm proposed by the source, albeit an outgroup minority, despite the refusal to concede it some credibility. This is proof of the fact that the apparent effects observed on the spirit-of-the-times measure were not a manifestation of a simple extension, a simple 'generalization' of responses, but indeed a reflection of the dynamics resulting from the conflict induced by the minority, in fact reconstructed as a denied outgroup.

Whatever the case may be, minorities appear to have a social impact that a majority can only obtain in reality if it is outgroup, is stripped of its credibility and, in the end, is represented as a...minority. We must admit three things in this respect.

First, if indirect or delayed influence is granted to a minority, then it is by virtue of the conflict it has induced and the mental construction of that conflict. Second, the more intense the conflict, the more the place and time at which its influence emerges become socially remote. It thus becomes delayed, indirect, or only reflected in new attitude domains. This can explain the fact that normative changes are rarely attributed to minorities, but considered as 'going without saying', giving targets the illusion of continuity due to the very fact that they are the ones who initiated the change, and in a constructive manner. Finally and logically, it must be admitted once and for all that minority influence does not naturally take on the form of mere yielding or compliance. It is quite rare for minority influence to be directly 'profitable' to its innovators and to spread in its initial form (Mugny and Pérez, 1989b). One does not adopt the positions of minorities; one does not imitate them. One transforms them, reconstructs them. And what is internalized in the end is the mental reconstruction of the ideas they initiated and oriented.

6.3 Conclusion

Minority influence follows more winding paths than majority persuasion. The factors that ruin its credibility and make it conflictual do not, paradoxically, destroy its influence. They only defer it, making it all the more imperceptible and underground by transferring its effects from the specific positions defended by the minority to the principles that underlie those positions. Since they are principles, they are of a more general order, acting as new norms, and hence in the long run, are likely to be activated and affect other attitudes and other behaviours.

It is indeed a kind of constructivism, in all of its aspects, that is at the heart of a minority influence and accounts for the fact that in spite of the many manifestations of resistance to the change advocated by minorities, it nevertheless ends up taking effect sooner or later, and in the eyes of each of us, appears to occur 'just naturally'.

The explicit introduction of resistance and the assignment of innovative positions to sources which are to be differentiated since they are on the fringes of the spirit of the times, or outside the boundaries of the ingroup, merely cause influence patterns to be shifted in time. By limiting research to the direct and immediate measures of influence, as is most often done in studies on persuasion, social influence, and attitude change, only the foreground of the minority phenomenon can be observed, namely, the dynamics of comparison and the apparent effectiveness of resistance to change.

But appearances are misleading, and uncover only a part of things. The reality of the minority phenomenon is another story, history has told us so, and the laboratory cannot take the countercurrent of history. Besides – and we hope to have convinced the reader of this – it is possible to experimentally create a sort of artificial synthesis of the psychosocial aspects of the phenomenon of social change, even in the laboratory. To do so, however, we needed a theory upon which to base the staging of experimental situations, one that was in a position to provide evidence of what simple observation is incapable of revealing. It is up to the reader now to judge the facts, and the theory.

7 Appendices

We have not attempted here to provide a complete description of the experimental paradigms developed: most of these paradigms are described in detail in the original publications reporting the many applicable experiments. The purpose of these appendices is rather to give the unfamiliar reader a precise idea of the procedure generally followed in our experiments. To this end, the reader may wish to study the second section of the appendices (7.2), which thoroughly describes the typical procedure used in our attitudes-towards-foreigners paradigm. The first section (7.1) presents the material (questionnaire and minority text) used for the pollution paradigm, which is based on a very similar experimental procedure. The same remark holds true for the third section (7.3), which provides a detailed description of the material designed for the abortion/contraception paradigm, used only in Spain where this issue is currently being debated.

7.1 Pollution paradigm

In this paradigm, subjects begin (pre-test) by answering an opinion questionnaire, presented in its full form below. Approximately one week later, they read a text, also presented here in its unabridged form. Before filling in the opinion questionnaire a second time (post-test), they first state their impressions of the minority on an image questionnaire like the one described in Appendix 7.2.4. Influence is assessed by subtracting the mean of the 16 pre-test answers from the mean of the 16 post-test answers, in such a way that minority influence is reflected by a positive number. (The scale on some of the items is reversed for that reason.) The influence of a minority that is highly critical of industry and against blaming individuals is reflected by greater post-test agreement with the items accusing industry or taking the blame off individuals (this corresponds to the direct dimension, since the questionnaire items are nearly word-for-word copies of the claims in the text), and by greater disagreement with the items accusing individual categories or taking the blame of industry (indirect dimension). The scales generally have 7 points, unless stated otherwise. The agreement and disagreement scale is only shown on the first item, for your information.

164

7.1.1 Opinion questionnaire

1. Housewives are seriously at fault: without second thought, they use large quantities of highly polluting laundry and other detergents:

disagree 1 2 3 4 5 6 7 agree

2. The automobile industry is actively and effectively fighting against pollution. Just look at the enormous amounts of money invested in designing cleaner and cleaner engines.
3. Objectively, it is unrealistic to blame detergent manufacturers since their products are not dangerous if used as indicated.
4. As long as drivers are too undisciplined to turn off their engines at red lights or during extended waiting, for example, the pollution problem will never be solved.
5. Chain stores and chemical manufacturers purposely work together to denature natural products.
6. How can we accuse farmers when we know very well that in order to stay in business, they are forced against their will to use chemical fertilizers?
7. People who unfairly say that picnickers are responsible for the degradation of nature are only hiding the real problem, the real culprits.
8. By strategically setting up factories at sufficiently spaced locations throughout the countryside, industries demonstrate their ongoing concern for saving nature.
9. For petty reasons based on profit, the automobile industries refuse not only to participate in the fight against pollution, but contribute even more to the problem by continuing to increase automobile production.
10. We must acknowledge the commendable efforts of the chemical industries that spend substantial amounts of money on research for the development of effective products to increase production while still conserving the natural quality of agricultural produce.
11. Because of their lack of discipline, weekend tourists contribute heavily to the slow but irreversible deterioration of nature.
12. Through the extensive, ignorant, and self-centered use of chemical fertilizers, farmers are selling us agricultural produce of increasingly poor quality.
13. The detergent manufacturers should be blamed even more since they continue (and even promote) the sale of products they know are harmful.
14. It is simply lying to accuse drivers of being the main culprits of pollution.

15. We should refuse to accept accusations made of housewives, who in fact are but victims of flashy advertising that conceals the harmfulness of the products sold.
16. For reasons based on convenience and profit, big industries move in anywhere and damage nature by the fumes and industrial dusts they release.

7.1.2 *Example of a minority text*

Below is an example of a text used to induce influence. This is the rigid version. The flexible version can be obtained by replacing the three slogans (marked with asterisks) in the text by the three statements given below the text.

Not a single week ever goes by without someone talking about pollution on TV or in the papers. Not only is this a serious problem today, but it's getting worse every day. It has reached the point where we must act as quickly as possible, both by trying to handle existing pollution and by preventing it in the future. But we must first find out the main causes of pollution. Who is really responsible?

IN ITS FRANTIC COMPETITION FOR PROFIT, INDUSTRY IS MORE TO BLAME FOR POLLUTION THAN ANYONE ELSE.

We all know about the harmful effects of exhaust (a car puts out about 5,000 m³ of polluting fumes and 10 kg of dust every 1,000 km driven). Yet supported by outrageous advertising, the automobile industries use petty reasons based on profitability to force the sale of a product that poisons the air in our cities and even in the countryside. There's nothing a driver can do about it. The industry ought simply to give drivers cars with emission controls: but it refuses to do so because that costs money and would thus reduce the profit margin.

FACTORIES THAT DO NOT ABIDE BY THE STANDARDS SHOULD BE CLOSED DOWN!*

Housewives are often unfairly blamed for polluting our water by washing their laundry. Don't forget that the laundry detergents they use are manufactured by a chemical industry that cares little about toxicity: just so long as they wash whiter, faster, and are used up more quickly. Competition for profit continues to push industry to manufacture more and more products they are forced to sell by any available means: misleading advertising, reduced prices...whatever will trick housewives.

WE SHOULD IMMEDIATELY PROHIBIT INDUSTRIES FROM MANUFACTURING DETERGENTS!**

Some people have tried to blame picnickers and weekend tourists by launching no-littering, clean-up, and other types of campaigns. These are nothing more than ways of covering up for the real culprits. What harm is done by a few pieces of paper or tin cans thrown out by hikers or travellers in comparison to the tons of smoke, toxic fumes, and industrial dust spread miles around by factories and plants?

ALL POLLUTING INDUSTRIES SHOULD BE BANNED!***

More flexible slogans:

*THE AUTOMOBILE INDUSTRIES SHOULD BE REQUIRED TO EQUIP ALL VEHICLES
WITH EMISSION CONTROLS!

**THE MANUFACTURE OF DETERGENTS SHOULD BE REGULATED!

***POLLUTING INDUSTRIES SHOULD BE FINED!

7.1.3 McHolson Test

McHolson's black/white figure classification test

Your task is as follows:

(1) FIRST carefully examine the figures below by looking at the sets of six figures in a given
     column or row.
(2) THEN determine WHICH COLUMN (of 6 figures) YOU INTUITIVELY PREFER, and write
     down the number of that column in the space provided below (put the number of the
     COLUMN YOU CHOOSE next to the letter K...).
(3) NOW determine WHICH ROW (of 6 figures) YOU INTUITIVELY PREFER, and write
     down the number of that row in the space provided below (put the number of the ROW
     YOU CHOOSE next to the letter R...).

ANSWER HERE: (Write down the number of the COLUMN THEN THE
ROW THAT YOU PREFER). I prefer column K...and row R...

Do not write in this box. For classification by researcher only.
  (1) SCORE OBTAINED _____
  (2) CLASSIFICATION: Group _____ (X or Y)

7.2 Attitudes-towards-foreigners paradigm

So that the reader might get a feeling for how our experiments are conducted, a detailed description is given below of what subjects generally do. For simplicity's sake, this example is an experimental prototype since it would be too lengthy to present all possible versions of the material. The experiments using this paradigm are all based on similar logic, which this example summarizes perfectly. Specific differences between experiments can be found by referring to the original publications reporting the studies using this paradigm (see in particular Mugny *et al.*, 1983, 1984; Mugny and Pérez, 1985).

7.2.1 Pre-test question
In this paradigm, subjects first answer the following question which serves as a pre-test. The answer given allows us to immediately assess the general attitudes of target subjects towards foreigners.

In Switzerland today, there are nearly 900,000 foreigners for a Swiss-born population of 5,500,000. This means that 16% of the people in Switzerland are foreigners.

Given the critical economic situation in our country today (as in other countries), some argue that the crisis could be eliminated by reducing the number of foreigners authorized to work in our country.

In order to alleviate the current economic crisis (and the concomitant threat of unemployment), what in your opinion would be the desirable percentage of authorized foreign residents in Switzerland?

Answer by circling the number (one answer only) that corresponds best to what you personally feel would be the most desirable percentage in the current situation (for your information, remember that the percentage of foreigners in Switzerland today is approximately 16%):

I am personally in favour of limiting the number of foreigners to:

9% 10% 11% 12% 13% 14% 15% 16% 17% 18% 19% 20% 21% 22% 23%

7.2.2 Examples of minority texts
Subjects then read a leaflet-style text said to have been written by some minority and presented on a sheet of typewriter-size paper. Below are two contrasting examples (fictitious) used to illustrate the main variables manipulated in experiments on this paradigm. Reading them will give you a precise idea of the kind of message presented to subjects. The first example

represents the kind of text that would be written by a native-born minority defending a humanitarian argumentation via a flexible style ('it would be desirable') and supporting humanitarian claims. The second is the kind of text that would be written by a foreign minority defending a class-oriented argumentation via an uncompromising style ('it is imperative') and supporting radical sociopolitical claims. The first typifies a non-conflictual (or only very slightly conflictual) style, the second, an extremely conflictual style. The reader will easily see why.

Example of a hardly conflictual minority text

Please read the following text carefully. It was written by the members of a Swiss minority group fighting in favour of foreign workers. You will be asked to answer a few *questions about this text later*.

'In our opinion, as Swiss, the distinction between foreign worker and Swiss-born worker should not exist. Our humanitarian principles state that we are all equal since we are all human beings. And all human beings have the right to obtain respect for their dignity, regardless of their origin. This is a humanitarian principle that we as Swiss must recognize: workers, whether foreign or not, are not machines to be used at will, but full-fledged individuals, and they must be recognized and respected as such. Foreign workers must therefore be guaranteed the rights required by our humanitarian outlook on social justice. The humanitarian principle we are defending as Swiss citizens is indeed one of fundamental equality between Swiss and foreign workers.

It is thus in application of these humanitarian principles that we feel it would be desirable that the Swiss actively support the following demands:

On humanitarian grounds, it would be desirable if all foreigners could benefit from current social protection provisions, in particular, in the event of an accident or unemployment.

On humanitarian grounds, it would be desirable if all foreigners could be free to choose their job.

On humanitarian grounds, it would be desirable if all foreigners could have the right to freedom of speech and association.

In application of the humanitarian principles just stated, we feel that it would be desirable that the Swiss support these demands in favour of foreign workers.'

Example of a highly conflictual minority text

Please read the following text carefully. It was written by the members of a foreign minority group fighting in favour of foreign workers. You will be asked to answer a few *questions about this text later*.

'In our opinion, as foreigners, the distinction between foreign worker and Swiss-born worker should not exist. Our political principles state that we are all equal since we are all workers. And all workers have the right to obtain respect for their work, regardless of their origin. This is a political principle that the Swiss must recognize: workers, whether foreign or not, are not just members of a work force that employers can exploit at will. The Swiss must therefore guarantee us, as foreign workers, the rights required by our political outlook on social justice. The political principle we are defending as foreigners is indeed one of fundamental equality between Swiss and foreign workers.

It is thus in application of these political principles that we feel it is absolutely imperative that the Swiss actively support the following demands:

On political grounds, it is imperative that we, as foreigners, cannot be sent back to our country for economic reasons, even in the event of unemployment.

On political grounds, it is imperative that residency permit extensions be automatically granted to all foreigners.

On political grounds, it is imperative that we foreigners have the right to participate in political and union-related decision making in Switzerland.

In application of the political principles just stated, we feel that it is absolutely imperative that the Swiss support these demands in our favour, that is, favouring foreign workers.'

7.2.3 Explanation of the agreement/disagreement response scales

The following explanation of how to use the response scales is given to target subjects. In some experiments, they are also asked first to express to what extent they agree or disagree with the minority text they have just read.

Below you will find several questions about the text you have just read. For each question, there are 7 possible answers:

disagree   1   2   3   4   5   6   7   agree

The meaning of the numbers is as follows:

1. I totally disagree.
2. I disagree.
3. I more or less disagree.
4. I can't decide. I neither agree nor disagree.
5. I more or less agree.
6. I agree.
7. I totally agree.

Answer the questions in the order in which they occur. Be careful to only give one answer per question, the one that corresponds best to your opinion.

Answer the following question first:

To what extent do you agree (or disagree) personally with the text you have just read?

disagree 1 2 3 4 5 6 7 agree

7.2.4 Minority image questionnaire

Subjects are then asked to state their impressions of the minority source on a questionnaire similar to the one shown below. The items included in a given questionnaire vary by experiment and subject sample.

In your opinion, to what extent do the following characteristics apply to the authors of the text you have just read?

Answer by circling the number (only one) that corresponds best to your impression.

According to you, the authors of the text are:

self-confident	1	2	3	4	5	6	7	lacking self-confidence
authoritarian	1	2	3	4	5	6	7	not authoritarian
competent	1	2	3	4	5	6	7	incompetent
intolerant	1	2	3	4	5	6	7	tolerant
incoherent	1	2	3	4	5	6	7	coherent
dogmatic	1	2	3	4	5	6	7	not dogmatic
unselfish	1	2	3	4	5	6	7	selfish
flexible	1	2	3	4	5	6	7	rigid
trustworthy	1	2	3	4	5	6	7	not trustworthy
anti-foreigner	1	2	3	4	5	6	7	pro-foreigner
conservative	1	2	3	4	5	6	7	progressive
minority members	1	2	3	4	5	6	7	majority members
politically-oriented	1	2	3	4	5	6	7	apolitical
trustful	1	2	3	4	5	6	7	distrustful
brave	1	2	3	4	5	6	7	cowardly
aggressive	1	2	3	4	5	6	7	pacifist
moral	1	2	3	4	5	6	7	immoral
realistic	1	2	3	4	5	6	7	unrealistic
selfish	1	2	3	4	5	6	7	generous
proud of their country	1	2	3	4	5	6	7	not proud of their country
narrow-minded	1	2	3	4	5	6	7	open-minded
respectful of human values	1	2	3	4	5	6	7	disrespectful of human values

To what extent do you feel that each of the following reasons contributes to explaining the ideas (and the way those ideas are expressed) of the authors of the text you read?

Answer by circling the number (only one) that corresponds best to your impression.

I think the authors of the text express their ideas and express them in that manner:

- because they defend humanitarian ideals.
  No 1 2 3 4 5 6 7 Yes
  (the scale is only shown once)

- because they are seeking personal benefit.
- because their ideas represent their personality.
- because they are on the fringes of society.
- because they are expressing their party's position.
- simply because they are right, they are objective.
- because they are expressing one of the values of their national culture.
- because the current crisis forces them to do so.

The items included in the minority image questionnaire are input into a factorial analysis to determine the meanings associated to the minority. To present the results, a label that best summarizes each factor is used in the tables. A higher factorial score means that the factor in question is more applicable to the source.

7.2.5 Attitude questionnaire

In all of the experiments based on this paradigm, the minority influence measures are drawn from the following questionnaire. In general, the influence score represents the mean of the answers given to the eight questions. The 7-point scale that follows each question is only shown here on question one.

Please indicate the extent to which you agree or disagree with each of the proposals stated below. Circle the number (one only) that corresponds best to your opinion.

1. Foreigners should be free to choose and change their canton (and place) of residency.
                       disagree 1 2 3 4 5 6 7 agree
2. Foreigners should be able to benefit fully from social protection provisions, particularly in the event of an accident or unemployment.
3. Foreigners should be able to choose their own job.
4. Foreigners should have the same kind of legal protection as the Swiss (right to appeal if dismissed, for example).
5. All foreigners should have the right to freedom of speech and association.
6. It should not be possible to send foreigners back to their country for economic reasons (namely, in the event of unemployment).
7. Residency permit extensions should be granted automatically to all foreigners.
8. Foreigners should be able to participate in political and union-related decision making in our country.

7.3 Abortion/contraception paradigm

7.3.1 *Example of a minority text*

You will be presented here with a text that clearly defends a *pro-abortion, minority-supported position*. This is the minority text we told you about. Please read it carefully.

(text:)

In favour of the legalization of free abortion

One of the issues that must be examined more closely is abortion. Our minority group has been aware of this problem for quite some time, and has declared publicly that abortion must be totally legalized. In other words, it is imperative that abortion be given a legal status, as any real democracy dictates.

Having said that, simply legalizing abortion is not enough. Legalization only implies that everyone be granted the same right to have an abortion, but equal right obviously does not mean equal opportunity from an economic point of view. Abortions are costly, and members of all social classes will not have the same means to obtain an abortion if they have to pay for it themselves.

When our minority group demands legalized abortion, it also demands that abortion be free for everyone. More specifically, this means that it must be included in health insurance policies, just like any other risk. In other words, it is imperative that the costs of abortion be automatically covered by the national health programme. This is the only way that all classes, both rich and poor, can be given the same chance to resort to abortion. This is the only way to make abortion really democratic.

In summary, our minority group demands totally legalized abortion, and declares that it is absolutely imperative that abortion be completely free for everyone.

7.3.2 *Attitude questionnaire*

The five items preceded by an asterisk enter into the pre-test measure, the mean of which is used in certain cases to assess the subjects' initial positions. The scale is shown on the first item for illustration only.

1. Once abortion is legalized, a great deal of publicity is necessary before people will be able to resort to it.

   disagree 1 2 3 4 5 6 7 agree

2. Everyone has to be informed so that people who resort to abortion will not feel guilty.
3. All social classes, rich and poor, should have the same opportunity to obtain an abortion.
4. A woman should be allowed to have an abortion without her husband's consent.
5. *Minors should also be allowed to demand an abortion.
6. *Abortion should be legalized.
7. *Abortion should be free for everyone.

8. Working women who have had an abortion should be granted a paid leave of absence.
9. The freedom to have an abortion constitutes a fundamental human right.
10. The legalization of abortion should be accompanied by a massive campaign in favour of contraceptives.
11. *Whenever a woman becomes pregnant following rape, she should be allowed to have an abortion.
12. The use of contraceptives has nothing to do with morals.
13. The right to abortion is a necessary condition for the dignity of both men and women.
14. Information about contraception should be given in the schools.
15. Abortion should be included in the national health programme, just like any other risk.
16. A public information campaign in favour of contraceptives should be launched (on TV, etc.).
17. Abortion should be recommended to large families.
18. Contraceptive devices should be used by members of both sexes.
19. Once abortion is legalized, the government should launch a campaign stressing family planning.
20. Abortion should be proposed to low-income families.
21. Even if only one person wanted to have an abortion, it should be legalized.
22. Abortion is a possibility for the rich; it should be a right for the working class.
23. Contraceptives should be paid for by the national health system.
24. The right to have an abortion is as important as the right to strike.
25. *Legalizing abortion is a requirement for democracy.

In general, the answers to the 25 items in this questionnaire are input into a factorial analysis, which usually points to two main factors. The first encompasses all questions pertaining to abortion. The corresponding factorial scores are a direct influence index. The second factor includes all of the questions on contraception. Its corresponding scores are an *indirect* influence index. Note on this subject that, for a given experiment, the mean and standard deviation of the factorial scores for all subjects pooled are equal to 0 and 1, respectively. The items are set up in such a way that positive minority influence is reflected by a relatively higher score.

In the experiments in which two abortion and contraception measures are taken, one immediate and one delayed by a few weeks, the means of the answers given on the abortion items (18 questions) and on the contraception items (7 questions) are calculated. For each dimension (direct and indirect) delayed influence is assessed by subtracting the first post-test mean from the second post-test mean. A positive score in each case indicates a delayed change in the direction of the minority position. The same applies to the following questionnaire.

7.3.3 So-called 'Zeitgeist' questions

The eight attitudes used to study the generalization of the tolerance principle are listed below. The influence score is the mean of the eight responses (the scale being reversed for conservative attitudes). For each of the eight attitudes below, subjects answer the following question:

I am against 1 2 3 4 5 6 7 I am for:

1. A family with traditional customs.
2. A more liberal education in the schools.
3. Traditional moral standards.
4. Adolescent obedience of parents.
5. A more liberal and egalitarian family.
6. A stricter educational system.
7. More tolerant moral standards.
8. Independence of young people with respect to their parents' beliefs.

7.3.4 Manipulation of interdependent or independent judgements

In the judgement *interdependence* conditions, the procedure used was the one suggested in the intergroup research conducted by Mummendey and Schreiber (1983). Subjects allot a total of 100 points (of tolerance or morality) to the 'pro-abortion minority' and the 'anti-abortion majority'. The points given to one group are thus necessarily taken away from those allotted to the other group. For each argument, the questions are worded as follows (the example given here pertains to morality):

Out of 100 points 'of MORALITY', how many do you allot to the minority IN FAVOUR of this idea (an argument is stated first!), and how many do you allot to the majority AGAINST this idea?

I allot...points of morality to the minority 'for'.
I allot...points of morality to the majority 'against'.
Total 100 points

Check the sum to make sure it is equal to 100!

In the judgement independence conditions, subjects allot as many points as they wish out of a possible 100 to the minority, and then again as many as they wish out of an additional 100 to the majority (the example given here pertains to tolerance):

Out of 100 points 'of TOLERANCE', how many do you allot to the minority that is IN FAVOUR of this idea (an argument is stated first!)?

I allot...points of tolerance to the minority 'for'.

Out of another 100 points 'of TOLERANCE', how many do you allot to the majority that is AGAINST this idea?

I allot...points of tolerance to the majority 'against'.

References

Abrams, D., Hogg, M. A. 1990. Social identification, self-categorization and social influence. *European Review of Social Psychology*.

Abrams, D., Wetherell, M., Cochrane, S., Hogg, M. and Turner, J. C. 1990. Knowing what to think by knowing who you are: self-categorization and the nature of norm formation, conformity and group polarization. *British Journal of Social Psychology*, 29.

Aebischer, V., Hewstone, M. and Henderson, M. 1984. Minority influence and musical preference: innovation by conversion not coercion. *European Journal of Social Psychology*, 14, 23–33.

Allen, V. L. 1965. Situational factors in conformity. In L. Berkowitz (Ed.), *Advances in experimental social psychology* (Vol. 2). New York: Academic Press.

Asch, S. E. 1951. Effects of group pressure upon the modification and distortion of judgment. In H. Guetzkow (Ed.), *Groups, leadership and men*. Pittsburgh: Carnegie Press.

1956. Studies on independence and conformity: a minority of one against an unanymous majority. *Psychological Monographs*, 70, no. 416.

Austin, W. G. and Worchel, S. 1979. *The social psychology of intergroup relations*. Monterey, California: Brooks, Cole.

Balandier, G. 1985. *Anthropo-logiques*. Paris: Librairie Générale Française.

Bassili, J. N. and Provencal, A. 1988. Perceiving minorities: A factor–analytic approach. *Journal of Personality and Social Bulletin*, 14, 5–15.

Beauvois, J.-L. 1984. *La psychologie quotidienne*. Paris: Presses Universitaires de France.

Beauvois, J.-L., Joule, R. V. and Monteil, J. M. 1987. 1989. *Perspectives cognitives et conduites sociales* (Vol. 1), Cousset: Delval (Vol. 2).

Billig, M. 1985. Prejudice, categorization and particularization: from a perceptual to a rhetorical approach. *European Journal of Social Psychology*, 15, 75–103.

Bolzman, C., Mugny, G. and Roux, P. 1987. Comparaisons entre groupes de statut social différent: attributions sociocentriques ou logique d'une représentation sociale? *Social Science Information*, 26, 129–54.

Brandstaetter, V., Ellemers, N. *et al.* 1989. 'The cheese effect': a contribution to a model of majority and minority influence. Report, E.A.E.S.P. Summer School, Tilburg.

Breakwell, G. M. 1983. *Threatened identities*. New York: Wiley.

Brehm, J. W. 1966. *A theory of psychological reactance*. New York: Academic Press.

Brehm, J. W. and Mann, M. 1975. Effects of importance of freedom and attraction to group members on influence produced by group pressure. *Journal of Personality and Social Psychology*, 31, 816–24.

Brewer, M. B. 1979. In-group bias in the minimal intergroup situation: a cognitive-motivational analysis. *Psychological Bulletin*, 86, 307–24.

Brewer, M. B. and Kramer, R. M. 1985. The psychology of intergroup attitudes and behavior. *Annual Review of Psychology*, 36, 219–43.

Brewer, M. B. and Miller, N. 1984. Beyond the contact hypothesis: theoretical perspectives on desegregation. In N. Miller and M. B. Brewer (Eds.), *Groups in contact: the psychology of desegregation*. San Diego: Academic Press.

Brown, H. 1985. *People, groups and society*. Philadelphia: Open University Press.

Brown, R. J. 1984a. Intergroup processes. *The British Journal of Social Psychology*, 23, whole issue.

1984b. The role of similarity in intergroup relations. In H. Tajfel (Ed.), *The social dimension*, (vol. 2). London: Cambridge University Press.

Chaiken, S. 1987. The heuristic model of persuasion. In M. P. Zanna, J. M. Olson and C. P. Herman (Eds.), *Social influence: the Ontario Symposium*. Vol. 5. Hillsdale, N.J.: Erlbaum.

Chaiken, S. and Stangor, C. 1987. Attitudes and attitude change. *Annual Review of Psychology*, 38, 575–630.

Cialdini, R. B. 1987. Compliance principles of compliance professionals: psychologist of necessity. In M. P. Zanna, J. M. Olson and C. P. Herman (Eds.), *Social influence: The Ontario Symposium*. Vol. 5. Hillsdale, N.J.: Erlbaum.

Clark, R. D. 1988. On predicting minority influence. *European Journal of Social Psychology*, 18, 515–26.

Clark, R. D. and Maass, A. 1988. Social categorization in minority influence: the case of homosexuality. *European Journal of Social Psychology*, 18, 347–64.

Collier, R. M. 1944. The effect of propaganda upon attitude following a critical examination of the propaganda itself. *Journal of Social Psychology*, 20, 3–17.

Cook, T. D. and Flay, B. R. 1978. The persistence of experimentally induced attitude change. In L. Berkowitz (Ed.), *Advances in experimental social psychology* (Vol. 11). New York: Academic Press.

Crespi, F. and Mucchi Faina, A. (Eds.) 1988. *Le strategie delle minoranze attive*. Napoli: Liguori.

Crutchfield, R. S. 1955. Conformity and character. *American Psychologist*, 10, 191–8.

Deconchy, J. P. 1971. *L'orthodoxie religieuse, essai de logique psycho-sociale*. Paris: Editions Ouvrières.

1980. *Orthodoxie religieuse et sciences humaines*. La Haye: Mouton.

1985. The paradox of 'orthodox minorities': when orthodoxy infallibly fails. In S. Moscovici, G. Mugny and E. Van Avermaet (Eds.), *Perspectives on minority influence*. Cambridge: Cambridge University Press.

De Paolis, P. and Mugny, G. 1985. Régulations relationnelles et sociocognitives du conflit et marquage social. In G. Mugny (Ed.), *Psychologie sociale du développement cognitif*. Berne: Peter Lang.

Deschamps, J. C. 1977. *L'attribution et la catégorisation sociale*. Berne: Peter Lang.

Deschamps, J. C. and Clémence, A. 1987. *L'explication quotidienne*. Cousset: Delval.

Deschamps, J. C. and Doise, W. 1978. Crossed category membership in intergroup relations. In Tajfel H. (Ed.), *Differentiation between social groups: studies in the social psychology of intergroup relations*. London: Academic Press.

Di Giacomo, J. P. 1980. Intergroup alliances and rejections within a protest movement. *European Journal of Social Psychology*, 10, 329–44.

Doise, W. 1972. Recontres et représentations intergroupes. *Archives de Psychologie*, 41, 303–20.

1978. *Groups and individuals*. Cambridge: Cambridge University Press.

1982. *L'explication en psychologie sociale*. Paris: Presses Universitaires de France.

1986. *Levels of explanation in social psychology*. Cambridge: Cambridge University Press.

1987. Identité, conversion et influence sociale. In S. Moscovici and G. Mugny (Eds.), *Psychologie de la conversion*. Cousset: Delval.

Doise, W., Gachoud, J. P. and Mugny, G. 1986. Influence directe et indirecte entre groupes dans des choix esthétiques. *Cahiers de Psychologie Cognitive*. 6, 283–301.

Doise, W. and Moscovici, S. 1969–70. Approche et évitement du déviant dans des groupes de cohésion différente. *Bulletin de Psychologie*, 23, 522–5.

Doms, M. 1983. The minority influence effect: an alternative approach. In W. Doise and S. Moscovici (Eds.), *Current issues in European social psychology*. (Vol. 1). Cambridge: Cambridge University Press.

1987. Support social et innovation. In S. Moscovici and G. Mugny (Eds.), *Psychologie de la conversion*. Cousset: Delval.

Eagly, A. H. 1987. Social influence research: new approaches to enduring issues. In M. P. Zanna, J. M. Olson and C. P. Herman (Eds.), *Social influence: the Ontario Symposium*. (Vol. 5). Hillsdale, N.J.: Erlbaum.

Eiser, J. R. 1984. (Ed.) *Attitudinal Judgment*. New York: Springer-Verlag.

Eiser, J. R. and Stroebe, W. 1972. *Categorization and social judgment*. London: Academic Press.

Festinger, L. 1954. A theory of social comparison processes. *Human Relations*. 7, 117–40.

1957. *A theory of cognitive dissonance*. Evanston, Ill.: Row and Peterson.

Grisez, J. 1975. *Méthodes de la psychologie sociale*. Paris: Presses Universitaires de France.

Guillaumin, C. 1972. *L'idéologie raciste: Genèse et langage actuel*. Paris, La Haye: Mouton.

Heider, F. 1958. *The psychology of interpersonal relations*. New York: John Wiley and Sons.

Hewstone, M. and Brown, R. 1986. (Eds.) *Contact and conflict in intergroup encounters*. New York: Blackwell.

Hollander, E. P. 1964. *Leaders, groups and influence*. New York: Oxford University Press.

Ibáñez, T. 1987. Pouvoir, conversion et changement social. In S. Moscovici and G. Mugny (Eds.), *Psychologie de la conversion*. Cousset: Delval.

Janis, I. L. 1972. *Victims of groupthink*. Boston: Houghton-Mifflin.

Jaspars, J. 1986. Forum and focus: a personal view of European Social Psychology. *European Journal of Social Psychology*, 16, 3–15.

Joule, R. V. 1987. Tobacco deprivation: The foot-in-the-door technique versus the low-ball technique. *European Journal of Social Psychology*, 17, 361–5.

Joule, R. V. and Beauvois, J. L. 1987. *Petit traité de manipulation à l'usage des honnêtes gens*. Grenoble: Presses Universitaires de Grenoble.

Joule, R. V., Mugny, G. and Pérez, J. A. 1988. When a compliance without pressure strategy fails due to a minority dissenter: a case of 'behavioural conversion'. *European Journal of Social Psychology*, 18, 531–5.

Kaiser, C. 1989. Consistance diacronique et contextes normatifs dans l'influence minoritaire. Doctoral dissertation. University of Geneva.

Kaiser, C. and Mugny, G. 1987. Consistance et significations du conflit. In S. Moscovici and G. Mugny (Eds.), *Psychologie de la conversion*. Cousset: Delval.

Kelman, H. C. 1958. Compliance, identification and internalization, three processes of attitude change. *Journal of Conflict Resolution*, 2, 51–60.

Kiesler, C. A. and Pallak, M. S. 1975. Minority influence: the effect of majority reactionaries and defectors, and minority and majority compromisers, upon majority opinion and attraction. *European Journal of Social Psychology*, 5, 237–56.

Kimball, R. K. and Hollander, E. P. 1974. Independence in the presence of an experienced but deviate group member. *Journal of Social Psychology*, 93, 281–92.

Latané, B. and Wolf, S. 1981. The social impact of majorities and minorities. *Psychological Review*, 88, 438–53.

Lemaine, G. 1974. Social differentiation and social originality. *European Journal of Social Psychology*, 4, 17–52.

  1975. Dissimilation and differential assimilation in social influence (situations of 'normalization'). *European Journal of Social Psychology*, 5, 93–120.

Lemaine, G., Lasch, E. and Ricateau, P. 1971–2. L'influence sociale et les systèmes d'action: les effets d'attraction et de répulsion dans une expérience de normalisation avec 'l'allocinétique'. *Bulletin de Psychologie*, 25, 482–93.

Levine, J. M. and Moreland, R. L. 1985. Innovation and socialisation in small groups. In S. Moscovici, G. Mugny and E. Van Avermaet (Eds.), *Perspectives on minority influence*. Cambridge: Cambridge University Press.

Levine, J. M. and Russo, E. M. 1987. Majority and minority influence. In C. Hendrick (Ed.), *Group processes*. Newbury Park: Sage.

Levine, J. M., Sroka, K. R. and Snyder, H. N. 1977. Group support and reaction to stable and shifting agreement/disagreement. *Sociometry*, 40, 214–24.

Levine, R. A. and Campbell, D. T. 1972. *Ethnocentrism: theories of conflict, ethnic attitudes and group behavior*. London: Wiley.

Leyens, J-P. 1983. *Sommes-nous tous des psychologues?* Bruxelles: Mardaga.

Maass, A. 1987. Minorités et processus de conversion. In S. Moscovici and G. Mugny (Eds.), *Psychologie de la conversion*. Cousset: Delval.

Maass, A. and Clark, R. D. 1983. Internalization versus compliance: differential processes underlying minority influence and conformity. *European Journal of Social Psychology*, 13, 197–215.

  1984. The hidden impact of minorities: Fourteen years of minority influence research. *Psychological Bulletin*, 95, 428–50.

  1986. Conversion theory and simultaneous majority/minority influence: can reactance offer an alternative explanation? *European Journal of Social Psychology*, 16, 305–9.

Maass, A., Clark, R. D. and Haberkorn, G. 1982. The effects of differential ascribed category membership and norms on minority influence. *European Journal of Social Psychology*, 12, 89–104.

Maass, A., West, S. G. and Cialdini, R. B. 1987. Minority influence and conversion. In C. Hendrick (Ed.), *Group processes*. Newbury Park: Sage.

Mackie, D. M. 1987. Systematic and nonsystematic processing of majority and minority persuasive communications. *Journal of Personality and Social Psychology*, 53, 41–52.

Markus, H. and Zajonc, R. B. 1985. The cognitive perspective in social psychology. In G. Lindzey and E. Aronson (Eds.), *Handbook of social psychology* (Vol. 1). New York: Random House.

Marques, J. M., Yzerbyt, V. Y. and Leyens, J.-P. 1988. The 'Black Sheep Effect': extremity of judgments towards ingroup members as a function of group identification. *European Journal of Social Psychology*, 18, 1–16.

Martin, R. 1987a. Influence minoritaire et relations entre groupes. In S. Moscovici and Mugny (Eds.), *Psychologie de la conversion*. Cousset: Delval.

1987b. *Minority influence and social categorization*. Open University.

1988a. Ingroup and outgroup minorities: Differential impact upon public and private responses. *European Journal of Social Psychology*, 18, 39–52.

1988b. Minority and social categorization: a replication. *European Journal of Social Psychology*, 18, 369–73.

1988c. Minority influence and trivial social categorization. *European Journal of Social Psychology*, 18, 465–70.

McGuire, W. J. 1964. Inducing resistance to persuasion. In L. Berkowitz (Ed.), *Advances in experimental social psychology* (Vol. 1). New York: Academic Press.

1985. Attitudes and attitude change. In G. Lindzey and E. Aronson (Eds.), *The handbook of social psychology* (Vol. 2). New York: Random House.

1986. The vicissitudes of attitudes and similar representational constructs in twentieth-century psychology, *European Journal of Social Psychology*, 16, 89–130.

Monteil, J.-M. 1985. *Dynamique sociale et systèmes de formation*. Paris: Editions Universitaires.

Montmollin, G. de. 1977. *L'influence sociale: phénomènes, facteurs et théories*. Paris: Presses Universitaires de France.

Moscovici, S. 1976. *Social influence and social change*. London: Academic Press.

1980. Toward a theory of conversion behavior. In L. Berkowitz (Ed.), *Advances in experimental social psychology* (Vol. 13). New York: Academic Press.

1981. On social representations. In J. P. Forgas (Ed.), *Social cognition*. London: Academic Press.

1985a. Innovation and minority influence. In S. Moscovici, G. Mugny and E. Van Avermaet (Eds.), *Perspectives on minority influence*. Cambridge: Cambridge University Press.

1985b. Social influence and conformity. In G. Lindzey and E. Aronson (Eds.) *The handbook of social psychology* (Vol. 2). New York: Random House.

1987. Le déni. In S. Moscovici and G. Mugny (Eds.), *Psychologie de la conversion*. Cousset: Delval.

Moscovici, S. and Lage, E. 1978. Studies in social influence IV: minority influence in a context of original judgments. *European Journal of Social Psychology*, 8, 349–65.

Moscovici, S. and Mugny, G. 1983. Minority influence. In P. Paulus (Ed.), *Basic group processes*. New York: Springer-Verlag.

Moscovici, S. and Nemeth, C. 1974. Social influence II: minority influence. In C. Nemeth (Ed.), *Social psychology: classic and contemporary integration*. Chicago: Rand McNally College Publishing Company.

Moscovici, S. and Personnaz, B. 1980. Studies in social influence V: minority influence and conversion behavior in a perceptual task. *Journal of Experimental Social Psychology*, 16, 270–82.

  1986. Studies on latent influence using spectrometer method I: psychologization effect upon conversion by a minority and a majority. *European Journal of Social Psychology*, 16, 345–60.

Moscovici, S., Mugny, G. and Pérez, J. A. 1984–5. Les effets pervers du déni (par la majorité) des opinions d'une minorité. *Bulletin de Psychologie*, pp. 365–80.

Moscovici, S., Mugny, G. and Van Avermaet, E. (Eds.) 1985. *Perspectives on minority influence*. Cambridge, Paris: Cambridge University Press, Editions de la Maison des Sciences de l'Homme.

Moscovici, S., Mugny, G. and Papastamou, S. 1981. 'Sleeper effect' et/ou effet minoritaire? Etude théorique et expérimentale de l'influence sociale à retardement. *Cahiers de Psychologie Cognitive*, 1, 199–221.

Mucchi Faina, A. 1987. Mouvement social et conversion. In S. Moscovici and G. Mugny (Eds.). *Psychologie de la conversion*. Cousset: Delval.

Mugny, G. 1975a. Negotiations, image of the other and the process of minority influence. *European Journal of Social Psychology*, 5, 209–28.

  1975b. Bedeutung der Konsistenz bei der Beeinflussung durch eine konkordante oder diskordante minderheitliche Kommunikation bei sozialen Beurteilungsobjekten. *Zeitschrift für Sozialpsychologie*, 6, 324–32.

  1981. Identification sociale et influence sociale. *Cahiers de Psychologie Cognitive*, 1, 124–6.

  1982. *The power of minorities*. London: Academic Press.

  1983. Jugements sociaux de sujets modérés et extrêmes dans des contextes d'originalité et de déviance. *Revue Suisse de Psychologie*, 42, 47–55.

  1984. Compliance, conversion and the Asch paradigm. *European Journal of Social Psychology*, 14, 353–68.

  1984b. The influence of minorities: ten years later. In H. Tajfel (Ed.), *The social dimension*. (Vol. 2). Cambridge: Cambridge University Press.

  1985a. Direct and indirect influence in the Asch paradigm: effects of 'valid' or 'denied' information. *European Journal of Social Psychology*, 15, 457–61.

  1985b. (Ed.) *Psychologie sociale du développement cognitif*. Berne: Peter Lang.

Mugny, G. and Carugati, F. 1989. *The social representations of intelligence*. Cambridge: Cambridge University Press.

Mugny, G. and Doise, W. 1979. Niveaux d'analyse dans l'étude expérimentale des processus d'influence sociale. *Social Science Information*, 18, 819–76.

  1983. *La construcción social de la inteligencia*. Méjico: Trillas.

Mugny, G., Gachoud, J. P., Doms, M. and Pérez, J. A. 1988. Influences majoritaire directe et minoritaire indirecte: une confirmation avec un paradigme de choix esthétiques. *Revue Suisse de Psychologie*, 47, 13–23.

Mugny, G., Ibáñez, T., Elejabarrieta, F., Iñiguez, L. and Pérez, J. A. 1986. Conflicto, identificaciòn y poder en la influencia minoritaria. *Revista de Psicología Social*, 1, 39–56.

Mugny, G., Kaiser, C. and Papastamou, S. 1983. Influence minoritaire, identification et relations entre groupes: Etude expérimentale autour d'une votation. *Cahiers de Psychologie Sociale*, 19, 1–30.

Mugny, G., Kaiser, C., Papastamou, S. and Pérez, J. A. 1984. Intergroup relations, identification and social influence. *British Journal of Social Psychology*, 23, 317–22.

Mugny, G. and Papastamou, S. 1980a. When rigidity does not fail: individualization and psychologization as resistances to the diffusion of minority innovations. *European Journal of Social Psychology*, 10, 43–61.

1980b. 'Réactance psychologique' et ordre social. *Cuadernos de Psicología*, 2, 103–14.

1982. Minority influence and psycho-social identity. *European Journal of Social Psychology*, 12, 379–94.

1982–3. Rigidité et influence minoritaires: le discours comme régulateur d'appartenance. *Bulletin de Psychologie*, 36, 723–34.

1984. Les styles de comportement et leur représentation sociale. In S. Moscovici (Ed.), *Psychologie sociale*. Paris: Presses Universitaires de France.

Mugny, G. and Pérez, J. A. 1985. Influence sociale, conflit et identification: étude expérimentale autour d'une persuasion 'manquée' lors d'une votation. *Cahiers de Psychologie Sociale*, 6, 1–13.

1987. Le constructivisme social en psychologie sociale: le cas de l'influence des minorités. In J. L. Beauvois, R. V. Joule and J. M. Monteil (Eds.), *Perspectives cognitives et conduites sociales*. Cousset: Delval.

1988a. Minority influence and constructivism in social psychology. Newsletter British Psychological Society, Social Psychology Section, 19, 56–77.

1988b. Conflicto intergrupal, validación e influencia minoritaria inmediata y diferida. *Revista de Psicología Social*, 3, 23–36.

1989a. La psychologisation: l'indissociation de la comparaison et de la validation. In J. L. Beauvois, R. V. Joule and J. M. Monteil (Eds.), *Perspectives cognitives et conduites sociales*. (Vol. 2.) Cousset: Delval.

1989b. L'effet de cryptomnésie sociale. *Bulletin Suisse des Psychologues*, 7, 3–5.

Mugny, G., Pérez, J. A., Kaiser, C. and Papastamou, S. 1984. Influence minoritaire et relations entre groupes: l'importance du contenu du message et des styles de comportement. *Revue Suisse de Psychologie*, 43, 331–51.

Mugny, G., Pierrehumbert, B. and Zubel, R. 1972–3. Le style d'interaction comme facteur de l'influence sociale. *Bulletin de Psychologie*, 26, 789–93.

Mugny, G., Rilliet, D. and Papastamou, S. 1981. Influence minoritaire et identification sociale dans des contextes d'originalité et de déviance. *Revue Suisse de Psychologie*, 40, 314–32.

Mugny, G., Sanchez–Mazas, M., Roux, P. and Pérez, J. A. 1991. Independence and interdependence of intergroup judgments: xenophobia and minority influence. *European Journal of Social Psychology*.

Mummendey, A. and Schreiber, H-J. 1983. Better or just different? Positive social identity by discrimination against, or by differentiation from outgroups. *European Journal of Social Psychology*, 13, 389–97.

1984. 'Different' just means 'better': some obvious and some hidden pathways to in-group favouritism. *British Journal of Social Psychology*, 23, 363–8.

Mummendey, A. and Simon, B. 1989. Better or different III: the impact of importance of comparison dimension and relative in-group size upon intergroup discrimination. *British Journal of Social Psychology*, 28, 1–16.

Nail, P. R. 1986. Toward an integration of some models and theories of social response. *Psychological Bulletin*, 100, 190–206.

Nemeth, C. J. 1986. Differential contributions of majority and minority influence. *Psychological Review*, 93, 23–32.

1987. Au-delà de la conversion: formes de pensée et prise de décision. *Psychologie de la conversion*. Cousset: Delval.

Nemeth, C. and Brilmayer, A. 1987. Negotiation versus influence. *European Journal of Social Psychology*, 17, 45–56.

Nemeth, C. and Chiles, C. 1988. Modelling courage: the role of dissent in fostering independence. *European Journal of Social Psychology*, 18, 275–80.

Nemeth, C. and Endicott, J. 1976. The midpoint as an anchor: another look at discrepancy of position and attitude change. *Sociometry*, 39, 11–18.

Nemeth, C. and Kwan, J. 1985. Originality of word associations as a function of majority vs. minority influence. *Social Psychology Quarterly*, 48, 277–82.

1987. Minority influence, divergent thinking, and detection of correct solutions. *Journal of Applied Social Psychology*, 9, 788–99.

Nemeth, C., Mayseless, O., Sherman, J., Brown, Y. 1990. Exposure to dissent and recall of information. *Journal of Personality and Social Psychology*, 58, 429–37.

Nemeth, C. and Wachtler, J. 1973. Consistency and modification of judgment. *European Journal of Social Psychology*, 9, 65–79.

1974. Creating the perceptions of consistency and confidence: a necessary condition for minority influence. *Sociometry*, 37, 529–40.

1983. Creative problem solving as a result of majority vs minority influence. *European Journal of Social Psychology*, 13, 45–55.

Nemeth, C., Swedlund, M. and Kanki, B. 1974. Patterning of the minority's responses and their influence on the majority. *European Journal of Social Psychology*, 4, 53–64.

Nisbett, R. E. and Ross, L. 1980. *Human inference: Strategies and shortcomings of social judgment*. Englewood Cliffs, N.J.: Prentice-Hall.

Pagès, R. 1987. L'intelligence entre le conflit et l'aménité: à propos du conflit socio-cognitif. In J. L. Beauvois, R. V. Joule and J. M. Monteil (Eds.), *Perspectives cognitives et conduites sociales*. Cousset: Delval.

Paicheler, G. 1976. Norms and attitude change I: polarization and styles of behaviour. *European Journal of Social Psychology*, 6, 405–27.

1977. Norms and attitude change II: the phenomenon of bipolarization. *European Journal of Social Psychology*, 7, 4–14.

1988. *The psychology of social influence*. Cambridge: Cambridge University Press.

Papastamou, S. 1983. Strategies of minority and majority influences. In W. Doise and S. Moscovici (Eds), *Current issues in European social psychology* (Vol. 1). Cambridge: Cambridge University Press – L.E.P.S.

1985. Effets de la psychologisation sur l'influence d'un groupe et d'un 'leader' minoritaires. *L'Année Psychologique*, 85, 361–81.

1986. Psychologization and processes of minority and majority influence. *European Journal of Social Psychology*, 16, 165–180.

1987. Psychologisation et résistance à la conversion. In S. Moscovici and G. Mugny (Eds.), *Psychologie de la conversion*. Cousset: Delval.

1988. *La psychologisation: l'us et l'abus de l'explication psychologique dans l'appréhension des phénomènes de la persuasion*. Paris: Ecole des Hautes Etudes en Sciences Sociales, Thèse d'Etat.

Papastamou, S. and Mugny, G. 1985a. Rigidity and minority influence: the influence of the social in social influence. In S. Moscovici, G. Mugny and E. Van Avermaet (Eds.), *Perspectives on minority influence*. Cambridge: Cambridge University Press.

1985b. Effets de la psychologisation sur l'influence minoritaire dans des contextes d'originalité et de déviance. *Cahiers de Psychologie Cognitive*, 5, 43–63.

1987. Psychologisation, conflit, et influence minoritaire. *Anuario de Psicología*, 36/37, 127–42.

1990. Synchronic consistency and psychologization in minority influence. *European Journal of Social Psychology*.

Papastamou, S., Mugny, G. and Kaiser, C. 1980. Echec à l'influence minoritaire: la psychologisation. *Recherches de Psychologie Sociale*, 2, 41–56.

Paulus, P. B. 1983. *Basic group processes*. New York: Springer–Verlag.

Peabody, D. 1968. Group judgments in the Phillipines: evaluative and descriptive aspects. *Journal of Personality and Social Psychology*, 10, 290–300.

1985. *National Characteristics*. Cambridge, Paris: Cambridge University Press, Editions de la Maison des Sciences de l'Homme.

Pérez, J. A. 1985. Influencia minoritaria y procesos intergrupales: el conflicto frente a la discriminación. Universidad Complutense, Madrid, doctoral dissertation.

Pérez, J. A. and Mugny, G. 1985a. Categorización e influencia minoritaria. *Anuario de Psicología*, 32, 100–16.

1985b. Influencia minoritaria sobre las opiniones frente al aborto y los anticonceptivos. *Estudios de Psicología*, 23/24, 29–54.

1986a. Efectos paradójicos de la categorización en la influencia minoritaria. *Boletín de Psicología*, 12, 65–89.

1986b. Induction expérimentale d'une influence minoritaire indirecte. *Cahiers de Psychologie Sociale*, 32, 15–24.

1987. Paradoxical effects of categorization in minority influence: when being an out-group is an advantage. *European Journal of Social Psychology*, 17, 157–69.

1989. Discrimination et conversion dans l'influence minoritaire. In J. L. Beauvois, R. V. Joule and J. M. Monteil (Eds.), *Perspectives cognitives et conduites sociales* (Vol. 2). Cousset: Delval.

In press. El intragrupo y el exogrupo como filtros sociocognitivos en la influence minoritaria: el efecto de la 'paralisis intragrupal'. *Revista de Psicologia Social*.

Pérez, J. A., Mugny, G. and Moscovici, S. 1986. Les effets paradoxaux du déni dans l'influence sociale. *Cahiers de Psychologie Sociale*, 32, 1–14.

Pérez, J. A., Mugny, G. and Roux, P. 1989. Evitement de la confrontation idéologique: quelques déterminants psychosociaux des stratégies persuasives. *Revue Internationale de Psychologie Sociale*, 2, 153–63.

Processos socio cognitivos de la influencia minoritaria. Revista de Psicología Social, (in press).

Personnaz, B. 1981. Study on social influence using the spectrometer method: dynamics of the phenomena of conversion and covertness in perceptual responses. *European Journal of Social Psychology*, 11, 431–8.

Personnaz, B. and Guillon, M. 1985. Conflict and conversion. In S. Moscovici, G. Mugny and E. Van Avermaet (Eds.), *Perspectives on minority influence*. Cambridge: Cambridge University Press.

Personnaz, B. and Personnaz, M. 1987. Un paradigme pour l'étude de la conversion.

In S. Moscovici and G. Mugny (Eds.), *Psychologie de la conversion*. Cousset: Delval.

Petty, R. E. and Cacioppo, J. T. 1986. *Communication and persuasion*. New York: Springer-Verlag.

Pratkanis, A. R., Greenwald, A. G., Leippe, M. R. and Baumgardner, M. H. 1988. In search of a reliable persuasion effect: III. The sleeper effect is dead. Long live the sleeper effect. *Journal of Personality and Social Psychology*, 54, 203–18.

Reicher, S. D. 1984. Social influence in the crowds: attitudinal behavioral effects of de-individuation in conditions of high and low group salience. *British Journal of Social Psychology*, 23, 341–50.

Riba, D. and Mugny, G. 1981. Consistencia y rigidez: reinterpretaciòn. *Cuadernos de Psicologìa*, 2, 37–56.

Ricateau, P. 1970–1. Processus d'influence sociale et niveaux d'analyse. *Bulletin de Psychologie*, 24, 418–47.

Rijsman, J. B. 1984. Group characteristics and individual behavior. In P. J. D. Drenth, H. Thierry, P. J. Willems and C. J. de Wolff (Eds.), *Handbook of work and organizational psychology*, New York: Wiley.

Roux, P. 1988. L'insolite au service des groupes minoritaires. Manuscript, University of Lausanne.

1989. Les effets d'une rhétorique inattendue sur l'influence minoritaire. 3rd Workshop on minority influence, Perugia.

Roux, P., Mugny, G. and Pérez, J. A. 1989. Conflit, degré de résistance, et influence minoritaire. *Bulletin de Psychologie*, 42, 788–95.

Schachter, S. 1951. Deviation, rejection, and communication. *Journal of Abnormal and Social Psychology*, 46, 190–207.

Sherif, M. 1936. *The psychology of social norms*. New York: Harper.

Sorrentino, R. M. and Hancok, D. 1987. Information and affective value: a case for the study of individual differences and social influence. In M. P. Zanna, J. M. Olson and C. P. Herman (Eds.), *Social influence: the Ontario Symposium*. (Vol. 5). Hillsdale, N.J.: Erlbaum.

Stephan, W. G. 1985. Intergroup relations. In G. Lindzey and E. Aronson (Eds.), *The handbook of social psychology*. (Vol. 2). New York: Random House.

Tajfel, H. 1972. La catégorisation sociale. In S. Moscovici (Ed.), *Introduction à la psychologie sociale* (Vol. 1). Paris: Larousse.

1981. *Human groups and sociale categories*. Cambridge: Cambridge University Press.

1982. *Social identity and intergroup relations*. Cambridge: Cambridge University Press.

Tajfel, H. 1978. (Ed.) *Differentiation between social groups: studies in the social psychology of intergroup relations*. London: Academic Press.

Tajfel, H. and Turner, J. C. 1979. An integrative theory of intergroup conflict. In W. G. Austin and S. Worchel (Eds.), *The Social Psychology of Intergroup Relations*. Monterey, CA. Brooks, Cole.

Tajfel, H., Billig, M., Bundy, R. P. and Flament C. 1971. Social categorization and intergroup behaviour. *European Journal of Social Psychology*, 1, 149–78.

Tesser, A. 1978. Self-generated attitude change. In L. Berkowitz (Ed.), *Advances in Experimental Social Psychology* (Vol. 11). New York: Academic Press.

Touraine, A. 1973. Production de la société. Paris: Editions du Seuil.

Turner, J. C. 1978. Social categorization and social discrimination in the minimal group paradigm. In H. Tajfel (Ed.), *Differentiation between social groups: studies in the social psychology of intergroup relations*. London: Academic Press.

  1981. Towards a cognitive redefinition of the social group. *Cahiers de Psychologie Cognitive*, 1, 93–118.

Turner, J. C. and Giles, H. 1981. *Intergroup behavior*. Oxford: Blackwell.

Turner, J. C. with Hogg, M., Oakes, P. J., Reicher, S. D. and Wetherell, M. S. 1987. *Rediscovering the social group. A self-categorization theory*. Oxford: Basil Blackwell.

Turner, J. C. and Oakes, P. 1989. Self-categorization theory and social influence. In P. B. Paulus (Ed.), *The psychology of group influence*. 2nd edn. Hillsdale, N.J.: Erlbaum.

Tversky, A. and Kahneman, D. 1973. Availability: a heuristic for judging frequency and probability. *Cognitive Psychology*, 5, 207–32.

van Knippenberg, A. 1978. Status differences, comparative relevance, and intergroup differentiation. In H. Tajfel (Ed.), *Differentiation between social groups*. New York: Academic Press.

van Knippenberg, A. and Ellemers, N. 1990. Social identity and intergroup differentiation processes. *European Review of Social Psychology*.

Weber, R. and Crocker, J. 1983. Cognitive processes in the revision of stereotypic beliefs. *Journal of Personality and Social Psychology*, 45, 961–7.

Wegner, D. M., Schneider, D. J., Carter, S. R. and White, T. L. 1987. Paradoxical effects of thought suppression. *Journal of Personality and Social Psychology*, 53, 5–13.

Wicklund, R. A. 1974. *Freedom and reactance*. Potomac, Md.: Lawrence Erlbaum Ass. Publishers.

Wilder, D. A. 1981. Perceiving persons as a group: Categorization and intergroup relations. In D. Hamilton (Ed.), *Cognitive Processes in stereotyping and intergroup behavior*. Hillsdale, N.J.: Erlbaum.

Wolf, S. 1979. Behavioral style and group cohesiveness as sources of minority influence. *European Journal of Social Psychology*, 9, 381–95.

  1987. Majority and minority influence: a social impact analysis. In M. P. Zanna, J. M. Olson and C. P. Herman (Eds.), *Social influence: the Ontario Symposium*. (Vol. 5). Hillsdale, N.J.: Erlbaum.

Worchel, S. 1987. Processes and effects of achieving group independence. Workshop on the Psychology of the Social Group, Manuscript, London.

Wyer, R. S. and Hartwick, J. 1980. The role of information retrieval and conditional inference processes in belief formation and change. In L. Berkowitz (Ed.), *Advances in Experimental Social Psychology* (Vol. 13). New York: Academic Press.

Zanna, M. P., Olson, J. M., and Herman, C. P. 1987. (Eds.), *Social influence: the Ontario Symposium*. (Vol. 5). Hillsdale, N.J.: Erlbaum.

Zavalloni, M. 1971. Cognitive processes and social identity through focused introspection. *European Journal of Social Psychology*, 1, 235–60.

Zavalloni, M. and Louis-Guérin, C. 1984. *Identité sociale et conscience. Introduction à l'égoécologie*. Les Presses de l'Université de Montréal, Privat.

Index